CHRISTIE'S
Review of the Season 1990

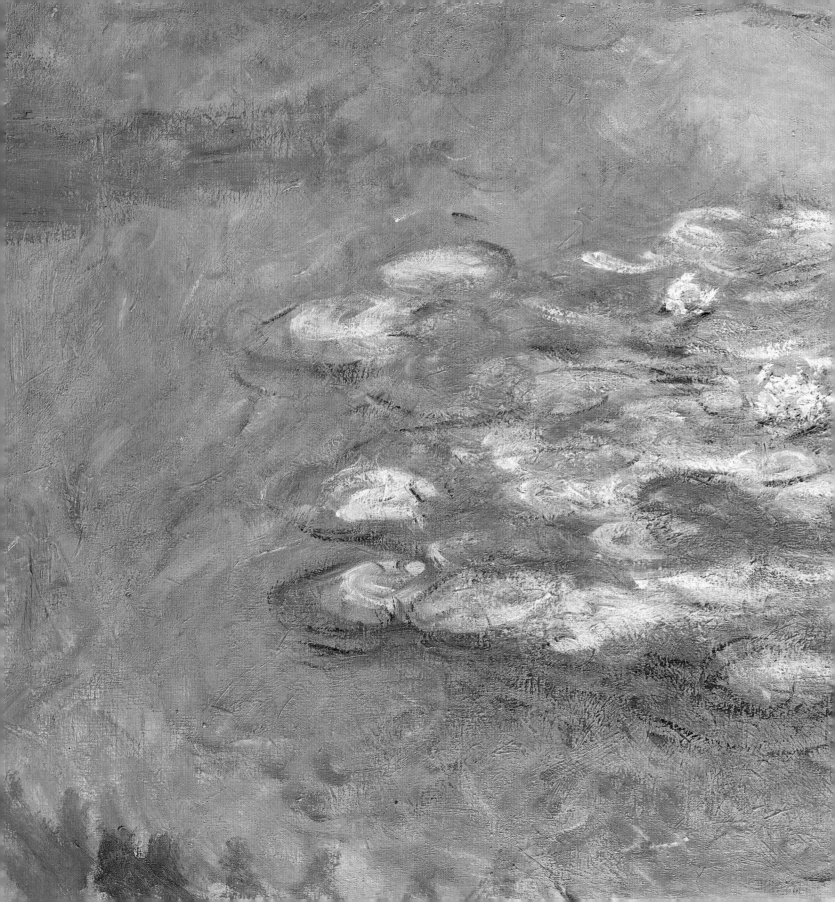

CHRISTIE'S
Review of the Season 1990

EDITED BY MARK WREY
AND ANNE MONTEFIORE

A CIP catalogue record for this book is available
from the British Library

ISBN 0-903432-38-2

Printed and bound in the Netherlands by Dukkerij
Onkenhout b.v., Hilversum

Endpapers:
Panels from the Badminton Cabinet, Florentine
pietra dura cabinet made for the 3rd Duke of
Beaufort (see p.234)

Half-title page:
Ming blue and white 'palace' bowl
Chenghua six-character mark and of the period
5¾ in. (14.7 cm.) diameter
Sold 20 March 1990 in Hong Kong for
HK$10,450,000 (£815,133)

Title-page:
Claude Monet
French 1840–1926
Nymphéas (detail)
Signed and dated 1907
Oil on canvas 39½ × 39½ in.
(100.3 × 100.3 cm.)
Sold 14 November 1989 in New York for
$11,550,000 (£7,237,230)

Opposite:
Christie's auction of the DVLC Classic Collection
registrations, by direction of the Secretary of State
for Transport, on 14 December 1989. The sale
totalled £1,540,000 ($2,490,000), including the
highest price for the plate 1A at £176,000
($284,064).

**All prices include the buyer's premium where
applicable. The currency equivalents given
throughout the book are based on the rate of
exchange ruling at the time of sale.**

CONTENTS

FOREWORD

Lord Carrington

Even those of you who read this *Review* regularly and who follow the art market must have found last year remarkable. How much more so would James Christie have found it? He would not, of course, have been surprised that the firm that he founded has survived and is the longest established firm of fine art auctioneers in Great Britain, but he would have raised an eyebrow to learn that in a country as yet undiscovered by the British, in a city of two million people named after a statesman yet to be born, Melbourne, Christie's have a thriving business.

No doubt, having read about China, he would be gratified to know that, in partnership with one of those enterprising merchants who were so much responsible for the success of the British Empire, Christie's has a profitable and expanding venture there. At the same time, he would be puzzled to hear that we are soon to have a sale of China stamps and postal history – unknown in England in the middle of the eighteenth century. He must, however, have had a much closer association with Europe and would find it both encouraging and perhaps in a way rather puzzling that Christie's European company is headed by one of the most distinguished and knowledgeable French Ambassadors of his generation.

What, I imagine, would really astound him is the progress of Christie's in what he would have thought of as the American colonies, where, for the first time, last year's profits and turnover overtook those in London. Even allowing for inflation, and perhaps the more relevant fact that James Christie died eighty-seven years before van Gogh was born, the astonishing price paid for *Dr Gachet*, sold in New York in less than three minutes by the President of the New York company for the sum of $82.5 million (£43.1 million), the highest figure paid for a work of art, would have confirmed him in the belief that the firm he founded has proved to be successful.

It is interesting to note that the sum of money paid for *Dr Gachet* was the same sum as our annual sales world-wide fifteen years ago. What will happen during the next ten years is impossible to predict but the last decade has been remarkable in the history of the art market and Christie's has played a central role. There have been days when my colleagues in America, Europe, Australia and the Far East have been holding sales virtually non-stop. The sales total for this season has exceeded $2 billion – ten times the figure of a decade ago and one hundred times that of twenty years ago. This is very impressive, but what really lies behind these facts is a remarkable principle as relevant today as it was when James Christie founded the firm – the confidence in our standard of service and the integrity that has underwritten our business for over two centuries.

The Badminton Cabinet being auctioned at Christie's London for the record auction price of £8,580,000 ($15,178,020)

It is perhaps of some interest to pick out a few of the highlights. The magnificent Badminton Cabinet, commissioned from the Grand Ducal Workshops in Florence by the 3rd Duke of Beaufort when he was only nineteen years old, was a highlight of the London season. For me, it was an object that had to be seen, since the photographs did not do justice to its skill or its magnificent workmanship. At £8.58 million ($15.2 million) it brought the highest price for any item in the field of the applied arts.

To some extent it has overshadowed some extremely good items of European furniture but in the United States two Philadelphia furniture makers were, in their way, just as successful: Thomas Tufft's Chinese-taste pier table became the most expensive table ever sold, fetching $4.62 million (£2.8 million); and the beautifully carved tea table by Thomas Affleck was also sold at the high price of $2.21 million (£1.3 million).

While Impressionist and modern art were inclined to catch the public eye and continued to achieve high prices for outstanding pictures, it was very encouraging to note the high prices paid in the more traditional collecting areas, notably, Lucas Cranach's diptych of the Electors of Saxony, which became the rarest and most expensive German Old Master we have ever sold, while the Agra Diamond, pink and with an appropriately colourful history, became the most expensive pink diamond in the world at £4.07 million ($6.95 million).

So I could continue: the Sicilian table fountain by Giuseppe d'Angelo; the wine coolers, ewer and basin from the Raby plate; the Chesterfield wine coolers, to which we made a handsome contribution to help save them for the nation at the Victoria and Albert Museum and the National Museums of Scotland.

Over the past year thousands of people have passed through the doors of Park Avenue and Christie's East, King Street and South Kensington, and our other salerooms around the world, and have either sold or bought something that they wanted. None of this could have happened – the volume, the variety, the quality of the business, some of which is reflected in the pages of this book – without an expert, dedicated and hard-working staff, and I express my thanks to every member throughout the world for what they have done to make this such a successful season and such an enjoyable company in which to work.

Van Gogh's *Portrait du Dr Gachet* being auctioned at Christie's New York for the record auction price of $82,500,000 (£43,107,142)

Carrington

NEGOTIATED SALES

Christopher Ponter, LL.B.

Of the many private sales and offers in lieu of tax handled by Christie's over the past year, the successful outcome of three major transactions is particularly satisfying to record.

The late Mrs Eva Borthwick Norton inherited a very fine collection of family portraits and Dutch and Flemish paintings from her husband's family home at Southwick estate in Hampshire. In her will she directed her executors to offer paintings of national or artistic interest to the Inland Revenue in lieu of tax, on condition that, if accepted, such paintings be allocated to the Royal Scottish Academy or permanently displayed there. After complex negotiations with the official bodies on both sides of the border, an agreement was reached whereby four major paintings were accepted at an overall gross valuation of £9.5 million ($15.77 million). These comprised a magnificent pair of full-length portraits of Robert Thistlethwayte and his wife Selina by Thomas Gainsborough; a large portrait of Pierre Pecquius (1562–1625) by Sir Peter Paul Rubens; and an enchanting landscape of Wageninen by Hercules Seghers. Together with other paintings of national importance due to pass to the Royal Scottish Academy, this group will comprise the most important bequest to Scotland in recent years.

One of the most complete assemblages of High Victorian art is contained in Brodsworth Hall, near Doncaster, Yorkshire, a house whose future was in question following the death of Mrs Grant-Dalton in 1988. However, Brodsworth Hall, and some seventeen acres of grounds, including the Victorian stable block, was the subject of a generous gift to English Heritage by Mrs Pam Williams, and negotiations opened to secure the major part of the original furnishings, including a very fine portrait of Mrs Sabine Thellusson and her young son Charles by Sir Thomas Lawrence, 1804, and a group of remarkable horse paintings by James Ward. After complex negotiations, an overall net price of £3,365,000 ($5,585,900) was agreed with the National Heritage Memorial Fund, which had been called in to provide the purchase monies to preserve this unique survival of mid-Victorian furnishings.

The Westerkerk, with the Keizersgracht by Jan van der Heyden is generally acknowledged as one of the greatest of Dutch townscape paintings of the seventeenth century. This painting was commissioned by the governing body of the church, itself a monument to the civic pride of Amsterdam, and hung there until 1864, when it disappeared from public view. Subsequently acquired by a member of the Rothschild family, the painting formed part of the estate of the late Mrs James de Rothschild, and was offered in lieu of the huge tax liabilities of that estate. Although Christie's advised that, in their opinion, this painting was

THOMAS GAINSBOROUGH
British 1727–88
Portrait of Robert Thistlethwayte
Oil on canvas
91 × 60 in.
(231 × 152.3 cm.)
Now in the Royal Scottish Academy, Edinburgh

worth considerably more on the international market, the executors of the estate agreed to accept the offer of £4 million ($6.4 million) put forward by the expert advisers to the Museums and Galleries Commission. In so doing, the executors were appreciative of the Minister's decision to allocate the painting to the National Gallery, London, in accordance with the express wish of Mrs de Rothschild. There it will hang as a pendant to Hobbema's supreme landscape *The Avenue at Middelharnis*, and together with Cuyp's *River Landscape with Horseman and Peasants* will provide a display of three high points of Dutch seventeenth-century landscape art.

Another highly satisfactory transfer was the offer of the painting by Jean Baptiste Camille Corot of *Richmond près Londres* (*c*.1862) from the estate of the late Sir Antony Hornby, a lifelong supporter of the arts and chairman of the National Art Collections Fund from 1970 to 1975. A gross value of £550,000 ($891,000) was agreed for this painting, which has yet to be allocated to a UK public collection.

Unquestionably, the virtual Treasury freeze on the level of purchase grants to public collections in recent years has led to great difficulties in securing direct sales through private treaty, but the patience and goodwill of private owners has resulted in a number of interesting and varied transactions.

During the past fifty years, the archive of some 200 unpublished poems, unseen plays and short stories of the great literary giant G.K. Chesterton (1874–1936) was carefully tended by his loyal secretary Dorothy Collins. Following her death in September 1988, her executors instructed Christie's to negotiate the transfer of this archive to the British Library. With the aid of the Shaw Fund (the sale included some correspondence with G.B. Shaw) this large and fascinating collection, together with a few personal items – his famous cloak and enormous felt hat among them – have been secured for the nation.

Included in the *English Romanesque Art Exhibition* of 1984 at the Victoria and Albert Museum were two Portland stone reliefs of St. Peter and St. Paul from the Augustinian Priory at Ivychurch, Wiltshire. Stylistically of the 1160s, they represent the maturity of the Romanesque style of sculpture, and have now been sold by private treaty to the Victoria and Albert Museum.

From a private collection, we have negotiated the sale to the Tate Gallery of a William Blake drawing *A Vision: The Inspiration of the Poet, c.1820.* Different in character from the usual visionary heads by Blake, this drawing depicts an angel standing by a seated writing figure in a chamber set into the end of a vast bare room. A current gross value of £30,000 ($48,000) was agreed for this negotiated private sale.

For many years, the owners of a gold arm band had not realized its significance until it was recognized by the British Museum to be a rare example of a Viking gold arm-ring, now known as the Shotton Hall arm-ring. On the basis of an agreed gross value of £15,000 ($25,500), it has now joined the permanent collection of the British Museum.

A rearrangement of the family trust holdings at Anthony House near Plymouth gave rise to a tax charge, and Christie's advised on the selection and valuation of a family portrait to satisfy that tax. As a result, a striking portrait of Sir Alexander Carew attributed to Marcus Gheerhaerts has now joined the permanent collection of the National Trust at Anthony House.

JAN VAN DER HEYDEN
Dutch 1637–1712
The Westerkerk, with the Keizersgracht
Oil on panel
36 × 45¾ in.
(91.5 × 116.2 cm.)
Now in the National Gallery, London

HERITAGE EXEMPTIONS

Nicholas Parnell

Since the introduction of death duties in 1894, successive governments have endeavoured to protect the 'national heritage' from dispersal for reasons of tax.

Almost from the start, exemption has been available for objects of national, scientific, historic or artistic interest. In other words, objects or collections worthy of display in a public collection, whether national, local authority or university.

Instead of paying death duties, or Inheritance Tax, beneficiaries or trustees have the option to claim exemption and defer paying the tax until the objects are sold. Since 1950 the claimant has had to provide undertakings to preserve and keep the objects in the UK. A further undertaking to provide public access was introduced in 1976. A breach of one of these undertakings triggers the postponed tax charge.

The 1975 and 1976 Finance Acts were particularly significant because they extended the definition of national heritage property to include land of outstanding scenic, historic or scientific interest, buildings of outstanding historic or achitectural interest, land which is essential for the protection of the character and amenities of an outstanding building, objects which are historically associated with an outstanding building and income-producing assets transferred into a maintenance fund settlement with the specific objective of supporting these 'new' categories of heritage property.

Owners can therefore benefit from substantial capital tax exemption and help preserve the heritage property as a unit, but in return they must undertake to maintain, repair and preserve the character of the land and the outstanding building, to keep objects historically associated with the building, and to provide public access.

The degree of recommended public access to the interior of an outstanding house can vary, depending on the circumstances, but in general it is about twenty-eight days every year during the spring and summer months.

For many years Christie's has assisted owners and their advisers in identifying chattels which are worthy of exemption. In recent years we have also advised on the practical procedures and tax implications attached to applications for conditional exemption and maintenance fund designation in respect of houses and land. Two recent successes are Whittington Court in Gloucestershire and Cottesbrooke Hall in Northamptonshire.

On the death of Miss Stephanie Evans-Lawrence her entire Gloucestershire estate passed unexpectedly to a friend living quietly with her retired husband in Surrey. The new owners, Mr and Mrs Robert Charleston, decided to move to Whittington Court, a fine

The south front of Cottesbrooke Hall

Robert Mitchell's bridge and the view looking north towards Cottesbrooke – a perfect example of scenic and essential amenity land

The south front of Whittington Court

Whittington village, a rare example of a village considered essential for the protection of the character and amenities of an outstanding house

Cotswold manor house constructed of stone principally in the early part of the seventeenth century, with a nucleus reputedly dating back to the 1550s.

With a remarkable display of determination and enthusiasm they have set about renovating the house together with its estate, which includes a Tudor barn and stables, land with both scenic and amenity qualities, a historic moat, the sites of a Roman villa and medieval village and the modern-day village of Whittington.

The death of the Honourable Lady Macdonald-Buchanan gave rise to a sizeable Inheritance Tax liability, part of which was satisfied by the surrender of one of Constable's greatest works *Stratford Mill on the Stour*, negotiated through Christie's. The deceased's family, with considerable regard for the public interest, decided they were prepared to share the architectural delights of Cottesbrooke Hall, a little-known example of an elegant classical house, with balancing pavilions. Principally constructed in the early eighteenth century of local stone and brick under a balustraded roof, the main elevations are divided into bays by large stone pilasters. The most spectacular internal feature is the staircase hall covered with an eye-catching Rococo decoration of papier mâché, almost unique in a private home.

In both cases substantial liabilities to Inheritance Tax were mitigated by means of claims for exemption and the creation of maintenance funds which secured these houses, their grounds and contents as coherent heritage units for several generations to come.

In 1991 Whittington Court, near Cheltenham, will be open to the public from Saturday 30 March to Sunday 14 April inclusive, and from Saturday 10 August to Monday 26 August inclusive. Cottesbrooke Hall, near Northampton, will be open to the public in the summer but dates have not yet been finalized.

CHRISTIE'S AND GLASGOW'S YEAR
AS THE EUROPEAN CITY OF CULTURE

Liz Taylor

HARRY BENSON
The Beatles'
Pillowfight
1964
In a Paris hotel, the
Beatles had just heard
that their song 'I
Want to Hold your
Hand' had reached
No. 1 in the
American charts, and
that they would be
travelling to the USA
on tour.
From the exhibition
Harry Benson's People
at Christie's Glasgow
16 July–3 August
1990

Glasgow's 'annus mirabilis' 1990 was celebrated in many different ways and Christie's Scotland contributed to the Year of Culture with a number of notable exhibitions. Several of these had an unique connection with the city and for the first time Christie's mounted displays in Glasgow which were not connected to any particular sale but were purely for public interest and pleasure.

The series started in April with a brilliantly colourful show of Wemyss ware entitled *Fife Flowers, Fruits and Farmyards*. Wemyss ware was originally a product of a Fife-based pottery with works in Kirkcaldy, but there was a Glasgow connection to justify the exhibition. There would never have been any Wemyss ware pottery at all without the liberality of the Glasgow Bank Co. In 1817 the bank lent the original capital for starting up the Fife enterprise and it continued to back the pottery through years of unprofitability. This forbearance lasted until 1885, when the loan was finally paid back by Robert Heron, whose grandfather had taken over the pottery, debts and all, in 1827.

After that the fortunes of Wemyss rose. Heron's application and far sightedness, plus the genius of a Bohemian artist called Karel Nekola, made the pottery a fashionable and successful purveyor of brightly painted domestic wares. In the late nineteenth century it was a *sine qua non* for all aristocratic households to have Wemyss pieces in the bedrooms. The wares were sold in Thomas Goode's exclusive London china shop, where orders flooded in for special items to mark the christenings and birthdays of children of noble families. After World War I, however, Wemyss went into decline. Modern plumbing removed the need for washstand sets, gas and electric lighting did away with candlesticks, and the Wemyss Pottery closed in 1930.

But fate took another turn within a decade when a few far-sighted collectors started seeking out examples of the pottery's prettiest pieces. Little by little its popularity grew again and, as a consequence, prices also rose so that Wemyss pieces are now among the most highly sought-after items of pottery. The grinning cats, shamrock-adorned pigs, and commemorative cups painted so attractively with garlands of roses, all of which could be bought for shillings fifty years ago, now fetch thousands of pounds at auction.

The reason Wemyss ware is so popular is easy to see. It is pretty, cheerful and bright. The roses which bloom on some of the pieces speak nostalgically of blissful summer days and even the pigs seem to smile benignly. Christie's exhibition, which contained sixty-six carefully chosen pieces, delighted the crowds of people who flocked to see it. All had reason to be grateful to a long-dead Glasgow banker.

Another Glasgow man, one who is very much alive, is 'The Raging Scot', photographer Harry Benson. He was the moving spirit – or perhaps it would be fairer to say the discerning eye – behind Christie's second exhibition, *Harry Benson's People*. His exhibition of photographs of some of the world's most famous people and most significant events of recent times ran during the second half of July at Christie's Bath Street rooms and showed how a Glasgow lad's talent had taken him to the top echelons of society.

Harry's story is the archetypal Scottish fairy-tale of success from obscure beginnings. He started his career as a 'snapper' at weddings after being disappointed in his first ambition to become a professional footballer. From taking wedding pictures, he moved on to newspapers in Glasgow before going to London with the *Daily Express*. After that, Harry went from strength to strength, proving there is still some truth in Dr Johnson's adage that a Scotsman's highway to success is the road to London. He did not stop there, however, but travelled to Paris, where, in 1964, he took a photograph of the Beatles having a pillow fight. This now famous picture was taken when they heard that 'I Want to Hold your Hand' had reached No. 1 in the USA, news which meant they would be going there on tour. Benson's talent is for the 'one-off' picture that sums up everything in a click of the shutter.

His next stop was America, where he photographed an array of presidents – Kennedy, Nixon, Carter and Reagan. Harry has the journalistic knack of being in the right place at the right time. He was there with his camera on the night Robert Kennedy was assassinated. More happily, he was also there in Antigua in the mid-1970s, sunning himself on the beach

A selection of Wemyss ware from the exhibition *Fife Flowers, Fruits and Farmyards*, held during April 1990 at Christie's Glasgow in celebration of Glasgow's year as the European City of Culture 1990

A Caledonian salt-glazed figure, *c.*1860, of the Glasgow character Wee Willie White, a well-known blind street musician in Glasgow during the first half of the 19th century; and a Bell's earthenware ashet, *c.*1860

Two items from *Glimpses of Glasgow's Pottery Tradition – 1800 to 1900*, an exhibition of Delftware pottery made in Glasgow during the 19th century, displayed at Christie's Glasgow during August 1990

– again with loaded camera – when the obsessively reclusive Greta Garbo swam bleakly past. He was a 'papparazzi' before the term was invented; a feared photographer, he finds photo-opportunities wherever he goes and is as sharp as a razor when it comes to exploiting them.

Christie's third exhibition, held in August 1990, highlighted a little-known area of the city's history. It was called *Glimpses of Glasgow's Pottery Tradition – 1800 to 1900*, and the title alone must have surprised the many Glaswegians who did not know their city was once the centre of an important pottery industry.

'Delftware' pottery was made in Glasgow during the eighteenth century, but when thousands of workers flooded into the city during the early years of the Industrial Revolution, the trade could not cope with the demand for cheap crockery and other potteries sprang up.

One of the earliest was the Caledonian Pottery in Townhead, which opened in 1801 and became famous for its salt-glazed and Bristol-glazed stonewares. It did not close until 1925. Another old firm was the Clyde Pottery, which opened at Greenock in 1816 and supplied the nearby shipping trade.

Perhaps the best known was Bell's Pottery, founded by two brothers John and Matthew Bell in 1842 and lasting until 1910. Not only did they supply the local market but they also had a large export trade and made stoneware, decorated earthenware, parian ware, terracotta and porcelain. Another pottery which came into existence about the same time was the Barrowfield Pottery based in Glebe Street, Port Dundas, which did a roaring trade with America.

The Victorian taste for elaborate garden ornaments, which are once more becoming fashionable, was catered for by the Viewpark Pottery of Kilmarnock, which became famous for stoneware garden ornaments. Terracotta pots were also produced by the Wellington Pottery, while some of the 'pawkiest' pieces came from the Cumnock Pottery, which made 'motto ware', brown vessels with a cream slip scratched through with cheerful Scottish sayings. These too are now favourites with collectors, who look for them in car boot sales and local jumbles.

The astonishing line-up of Glasgow potteries represented in Christie's exhibition provided enthusiasts with a great deal of information and new quarries to hunt down. It also gave another sidelight on the industrial history of the second City of the Empire – which in 1990 enjoyed recognition as the 'Cultural Capital of Europe'.

PICTURES

CHRISTIAEN LUYCKS
Dutch *fl.*1623–53
Still Life with Silver Jug and Pie
Signed
Oil on copper
31½ × 78¾ in. (80.5 × 200 cm.)
Sold 28 November 1989 in Amsterdam for
D.fl.1,610,000 (£511,923)
Record auction price for a work by the artist

A DIPTYCH BY LUCAS CRANACH

Charles Beddington

The sale of Lucas Cranach the Elder's diptych was the sensation of the season in the field of Old Master pictures. After inspiring widespread admiration in exhibitions organized by Christie's in Paris, Zürich, Munich and Tokyo as well as in London, it far exceeded both its estimate and the previous record price for a painting by the artist, setting a new record for a German work of art. German Renaissance pictures of the highest quality very rarely appear on the open market, the two examples to have changed hands in the last ten years, Albrecht Altdorfer's *Christ taking Leave of his Mother* and the *Deposition* by the Master of the St. Bartholomew Altarpiece, both having been the subjects of private treaty sales by Christie's to the nation (in 1980 and 1981 respectively).

Cranach's diptych is exceptional both in the artist's *œuvre* and in what it reveals of the cultural ambient in which it was created. As his career developed, Cranach became one of the most commercially orientated of painters, the quality of his work decreasing sharply as the volume of his studio's output multiplied. From about 1515 he ran a large and well-organized workshop on which he increasingly relied to give form to his ideas, and it is only in the work of his early periods in Vienna and Wittenberg that Cranach's abilities as a technician match his visual imagination to make him one of the greatest German painters in the golden age of German art. The date of 1509 on this diptych confirms it as a work of the artist's first years at the Saxon court at Wittenberg and as one of the earliest works by the artist still in private hands. Wittenberg, on the Elbe, was a small university town which was to achieve an international significance a decade later as the home of Martin Luther; Cranach had arrived there in 1505 and at this stage evidently still felt the need to impress his employers by finding new aesthetic solutions to artistic challenges.

The year 1509 was a particularly auspicious moment in the life of the young prince Johann Friedrich. His mother's death while giving birth to him, her first child, in 1503, had made Johann Friedrich the sole heir not only of his father but also to the Electorship of his uncle Frederick the Wise, who had undertaken not to have children of his own. Johann Friedrich had been publicly presented by his father and uncle in Wittenberg in 1508 and his education, under the notable humanist Spalatin, had commenced in January 1509. This diptych was evidently commissioned by the Elector Johann to express his faith in his son as *unica spes patriae*, and in it father and son are shown paired as equals in a way normally reserved for married couples. Moreover, the portrait of Johann Friedrich is the earliest known painted portrait of a child prince in German art. Cranach imbues this new iconography with life by providing numerous subtle contrasts between the characterizations of the two sitters.

The diptych had not been on the market since 1808, when it was purchased by a direct ancestor of the 1990 vendor at the Margrave of Baden-Durlach's sale at the Marksgräfler Hof in Basel. It had been in store there since 1688, and the care with which it was evidently treated during more than three centuries in Basel contributed considerably to the exceptional condition in which it has survived, complete with the original frames.

The sale of the diptych by Cranach in Christie's Great Rooms on 6 July 1990

LUCAS CRANACH I
German 1472–1553
*Portrait of Kurfürst
Herzog Johann von
Sachsen* and *Portrait of
his son Johann
Friedrich, later Kürfurst
von Sachsen*
The second inscribed
and dated 1509
On panel
Painted surfaces
16¼ × 12¼ in.
(41.3 × 31 cm.) and
16½ × 12¼ in.
(42 × 31.2 cm.)
The diptych sold
6 July 1990 in London
for £4,840,000
($8,581,320)
Record auction price
for any German
work of art
From Schloss
Wildenstein,
Basel-Land,
Switzerland

MATTIA PRETI, IL CAVALIERE CALABRESE
Italian 1613–99
The Liberation of St. Peter
Oil on canvas
57¼ × 77¾ in. (145.5 × 197.5 cm.)
Sold 8 December 1989 in London for £825,000
($1,3000,000)
From St. Catharine's Episcopal Church, Blairgowrie,
Perthshire

Opposite:
PAOLO CALIARI, called VERONESE
Italian 1528–88
Cupid Disarmed by Venus
Oil on canvas
62½ × 54½ in. (158.3 × 139 cm.)
Sold 10 January 1990 in New York for $2,970,000
(£1,789,156)
Record auction price for a work by the artist

CORRADO GIAQUINTO
Italian 1703–66
The Adoration of the Magi
Oil on canvas
18⅞ × 21½ in. (48 × 54.5 cm.)
Sold 15 June 1990 in Monaco for F.fr.2,886,000 (£296,000)
Record auction price for a work by the artist

FRANCESCO DE MURA
Italian 1696–1782
Juno Punishing Argus
Oil on canvas
39⅜ × 61¼ in. (100 × 155 cm.)
One of a pair sold 8 March 1990 in Rome for L.402,500,000
(£194,444)

MICHELE MARIESCHI
Italian 1710–44
The Grand Canal, Venice, with the Rialto Bridge
Oil on canvas
23¼ × 34¼ in. (59 × 87 cm.)
One of a pair sold 8 December 1989 in London for £902,000
($1,443,200)
From the celebrated collection formed by Sir Otto Beit, 1st Bt., and
formerly at Tewin Water, Welwyn, Hertfordshire

LUCA CARLEVARIJS
Italian 1663–1730
The French Ambassador's Arrival at the Doge's Palace, Venice
Signed with initials
Oil on canvas
35⅜ × 62¼ in. (90 × 158 cm.)
Sold 15 June 1990 in Monaco for F.fr.5,500,000 (£569,230)
Record auction price for a work by the artist

GIOVANNI ANTONIO CANAL, IL CANALETTO
Italian 1697–1768
The Thames at Westminster
Oil on canvas
16¼ × 28¼ in. (41.3 × 71.8 cm.)
Sold 17 November 1989 in London for
£1,320,000 ($2,112,000)
From the Paul Mellon Collection

Previously sold in London in 1976 for £110,000, this picture set a new record auction price for the artist on its sale in 1989, underlining the enormous demand shown for Canaletto's pictures in recent sales and in particular those of his English period, 1746–55. The picture may well have been painted in 1750: Westminster Bridge was finally opened, after three years of structural repairs due to subsidence, on 18 November of that year.

GIOVANNI ANTONIO CANAL, IL CANALETTO
Italian 1697–1768
The Piazza del Campidoglio and the Cordonata, Rome
Oil on canvas
20½ × 24¼ in. (52 × 61.5 cm.)
Sold 8 December 1989 in London for
£1,100,000 ($1,760,000)
Previously sold at Christie's in 1884 for
74 gns. and in 1973 for 170,000 gns.

A label on the stretcher of this picture records that it was commissioned by Thomas Hollis, an eccentric recluse who devoted much of his time to the dissemination of his radical democratic political beliefs and was an important benefactor of Harvard University. The picture records his visit to Rome on the Grand Tour, and he is depicted in the foreground along with his lifelong companion Thomas Brand, his servant and tour guide Francesco Giovannini, and his dog 'Malta'.

DAVID TENIERS II
Flemish 1610–90
A Kermesse in a Village
Signed
Oil on canvas
19¼ × 38½ in. (49.5 × 97.6 cm.)
Sold 28 November 1989 in Amsterdam for D.fl.805,000 (£255,961)

FRANCESCO GUARDI
Italian 1712–93
The Villa Loredan at Paese
Oil on canvas
18⅞ × 30½ in.
(48 × 77.5 cm.)
Sold 8 December
1989 in London for
£3,080,000
($4,928,000)

Previously sold at Christie's in 1800, as one of a pair, for 7 gns. and in 1883, with three other pictures, for 700 gns.

Although it had not been on the market for nearly fifty years, this is one of the most widely published of Guardi's paintings. Exceptional in the artist's work for the precision of the brushwork and the subtlety of the light effects, the picture is also of particular importance as one of the few works by Guardi of which the early history is known. It was almost certainly commissioned by John Strange (1732–99), British Resident at Venice 1773–88, who owned a number of pictures by Guardi and also acted as his dealer. Strange rented the Villa Loredan, near Treviso, as a summer residence, and judging from the number of drawings and paintings which Guardi executed in the area, he probably invited the artist to stay with him there. The costumes of the foreground figures suggest that the painting was done in the late 1770s or early 1780s.

PIETER BRUEGHEL II
Flemish *c.*1564–1637/8
The Outdoor Wedding Dance
Signed and dated 161(0?)
Oil on panel
15¼ × 22⅝ in. (38.7 × 57.7 cm.)
Sold 6 July 1990 in London for £528,000 ($936,144)

SIR PETER PAUL RUBENS
Flemish 1577–1640
*A Forest at Dawn with
a Deer Hunt*
Oil on panel
24¼ × 35½ in.
(61.8 × 90 cm.)
Sold 8 December
1989 in London for
£3,300,000
($5,280,000)
Record auction price
for a work by the
artist

Rubens seems to have first executed pure landscapes *c.*1615 but he turned to the genre with new vigour in the mid-1630s around the time that he purchased his country estate of Het Steen, immortalized in the famous picture in the London National Gallery. The work illustrated here is generally dated to the last decade of the artist's life. Rubens's landscapes of this type are unique in seventeenth-century art for their direct response to nature, and they look forward two hundred years to the work of the great landscape painters of the Romantic era. This picture is probably to be identified with the *Wood with a Huntinge, with the Sun riseinge, uppon bord* recorded in Rubens's house at the time of his death in 1640. Later it seems to have been owned by Sir Joshua Reynolds before entering the collection of William, 1st Marquis of Lansdowne, at whose sale at Lansdowne House in 1806 it was purchased by Sir Watkin Williams Wynn for 305 guineas.

The painting was sold by order of the Trustees of the Williams-Wynn Settlement. It is now in the Metropolitan Museum of Art, New York.

PIERRE–HUBERT
SUBLEYRAS
French 1699–1749
*Portrait of a Young
Hungarian Prince*
Oil on canvas
47 × 35½ in.
(119.5 × 90 cm.)
Sold 9 April 1990 in
London for £374,000
($609,620)
Record auction price
for a work by the
artist

One of the most
interesting French
painters of his
generation,
Subleyras, like many
of his forebears
during the
seventeenth century,
spent most of his life
in Rome. A major
exhibition of his
work held in Paris
and Rome in 1987
established his
importance and also
revealed how few of
his paintings, other
than sketches, remain
in private hands.
This picture, which
was a new discovery,
would seem to have
been painted during
the artist's later years
and may represent
Prince Paul Anton II
von Esterhazy, the
son of Haydn's great
patron.

JEAN–AUGUSTE–
DOMINIQUE INGRES
French 1780–1867
Jupiter and Thetis
Oil on canvas
32¼ × 25¾ in.
(82 × 65 cm.)
Sold 2 December
1989 in Monaco for
F.fr.14,430,000
(£1,515,756)
Record auction price
for a work by the
artist

A previously
unrecorded version
of the large picture
painted by Ingres in
Rome in 1811 and
now in the Musée
Granet,
Aix-en-Provence.

JUAN BAUTISTA DE ESPINOSA
Spanish *fl.* early 17th century
Still Life with Silver-Gilt Salvers
Signed and dated 1624
Oil on canvas
39 × 47⅛ in. (99 × 119.5 cm.)
Sold 9 April 1990 in London for £605,000
($986,150)
From the Hilmar Reksten Collection
Previously sold at Christie's in 1920 for 26
gns., in 1934 for 34 gns. and in 1968 for
3,800 gns.

This picture has been extensively published as one of the earliest signed and dated – as well as one of the most opulent – examples of Spanish still-life painting. Recognized as one of the masterpieces of the genre, it was included in the major exhibition at Fort Worth and Toledo, Ohio in 1985. A number of silver-gilt objects virtually identical to those depicted were sold at Christie's, New York, in 1988, having been recovered from the galleon *Nuestra Señora de Atocha* sunk off the Florida Keys in 1522.

GEORG FLEGEL
German 1566–1638
Still Life with Irises, Tulips and other Flowers in a Pewter Jug
Signed with monogram
Oil on canvas
24½ × 17¾ in. (62.2 × 45 cm.)
Sold 10 January 1990 in New York for $1,980,000 (£1,192,771)
Record auction price for a work by the artist

Flegel was born at Olmutz in Moravia (now Czechoslovakia) but spent most of his life in Frankfurt. In recent years he has been recognized as one of the most important German still-life painters as well as one of the earliest of the European specialists in the genre. This particularly fine example set a considerable new auction record for his work.

HENDRICK AVERCAMP
Dutch 1585–34
Skaters, Kolf Players and other Townsfolk on the Ice at Campen
Signed twice with monogram
Oil on panel
17½ × 28½ in.
(44.5 × 72.5 cm.)
Sold 6 July 1990 in London for £770,000
($1,365,210)
Record auction price for a work by the artist

Hendrick Avercamp's winter landscapes represent a high point of Dutch landscape painting in the seventeenth century but good examples rarely appear on the market. This example, unusually signed twice, had been in the famous collection at Althorp from the time of Robert, 2nd Earl of Sunderland (1641–1702), until it was sold by the 8th Earl Spencer some years ago. It depicts accurately the town wall and Broederpoort at Campen, Avercamp's home town, exactly as in a drawing by the artist in the Royal Library at Windsor.

POMPEO GIROLAMO
BATONI
Italian 1708–87
*Portrait of John Crewe,
later 1st Baron Crewe*
Signed and dated
'Roma 1760', and
inscribed by a later
hand 'John Crewe
Esq, of Crewe'
Oil on canvas
54 × 39 in.
(137.2 × 99.1 cm.)
Sold 17 November
1989 in London for
£319,000 ($513,590)

MARCUS GHEERAERTS
THE YOUNGER
British 1561–1635
Portrait of Anne Hale
Signed, inscribed and
dated 1629
44½ × 32¾ in.
(113 × 83.2 cm.)
Sold 20 April 1990 in
London for £99,000
($168,300)

Opposite:
WILLIAM DOBSON
British 1611–46
*Portrait of King
Charles I*
Oil on canvas
25⅜ × 20 in.
(54.5 × 50.8 cm.)
Sold 17 November
1989 in London for
£165,000 ($265,650)

In 1642, in the early
stages of the Civil
War, King Charles I
moved his court
to Oxford, and by
1643 Dobson was
established in the city
as Court Painter. He
set up his studio in
the High Street, near
St. Mary's Church,
and the king sat to
him on several
occasions. This
portrait of the king,
on the coarse canvas
so much favoured by
Dobson, is one of the
works painted at this
time, and is a recent
discovery of major
importance.

JOHANN ZOFFANY, RA
British 1733–1810
Portrait of the Colmore Family
Oil on canvas
39½ × 50 in. (100.3 × 127 cm.)
Sold 12 July 1990 in London for £2,090,000 ($3,762,000)
From the property of the late Marquess of Cholmondeley

JOHANN ZOFFANY, RA
British 1733–1810
Portrait of the Willoughby de Broke Family
Oil on canvas
39½ × 49½ in.
(100.5 × 125.5 cm.)
Sold 17 November
1989 in London for
£3,080,000 ($4,958,800)
Record auction price
for a work by the artist

Zoffany's hearth-side scene, which shows John 4th Lord Willoughby de Broke with his wife and children, is one of the most delightful images of domestic life in Georgian England. Lady Broke's parlour reflects aristocratic taste of the 1760s. An 'Italian' landscape picture hangs above a marble mantelpiece, which is carved in the 'antique' manner. A mahogany tripod tea-table has been set out on the 'Turkey' carpet beside the fire and a tray of colourful Chinese porcelain is laid on the damask tablecloth.

This picture can be dated to the mid-1760s, when Lord Willoughby de Broke was a Lord of the Bedchamber to King George III. It was probably as a result of this royal connection that he chose Zoffany to paint a group portrait of his family, as the artist had just painted the queen and her two eldest sons in 1764. Like these royal commissions, the Willoughby de Broke portrait reveals the artist at the height of his powers. The painting was sold by Christie's from the property of the Dowager Lady Willoughby de Broke.

JOHN CONSTABLE, RA
British 1776–1837
Judge's Walk, Hampstead
Inscribed on the reverse
Paper laid down on canvas
11¾ × 13¾ in. (30 × 35 cm.)
Sold 17 November 1989 in London for £242,000 ($389,620)

JOHN FREDERICK HERRING, SR.
British 1795–1865
The Leamington Hunt (Mr Harry Bradley's Hounds)
Signed and dated 1841
Oil on canvas
30 × 50 in. (76.2 × 126.9 cm.)
Sold 17 November 1989 in London for £660,000 ($1,062,600)
From the property of Mr and Mrs David M. Malcolm

FROM VENICE TO PERTH VIA 'THE BRIDGE OF LIFE': SOME MAJOR VICTORIAN PICTURES REDISCOVERED

John Christian

The explosion of interest in Victorian art witnessed in the last quarter-century has brought many masterpieces out of the attics, but fresh and exciting material still continues to appear. Luke Fildes' *Venetian Life*, exhibited at the Royal Academy in 1884, could hardly be described as lost since it had been lent to Keele University prior to its recent sale. It was not, however, 'on the map' in the sense of comparable works by the artist in public collections. Fildes was something of a split personality. Although best known for his social-realist pictures, including *Applicants for Admission to a Casual Ward* (1874; Royal Holloway College), which so impressed van Gogh, he was intensely ambitious and ready to satisfy the popular taste for sentimental genre. In the 1880s, with a growing family to support and a large new house in fashionable Holland Park, he joined the ranks of contemporary artists who sought such subjects in Venice. *Venetian Life* was the first major result. It was bought by the contractor Sir John Aird and generally regarded as 'the picture of the [RA] exhibition', but it did not escape criticism. Even the *Art Journal* thought it 'superficial', and William Morris dismissed it as 'useless cleverness' which 'I say emphatically...is not art'.

  The Awakening of Adonis by J.W. Waterhouse is a more intellectual picture which was last recorded when sold at Christie's in 1956. The fact that it fetched 34 guineas, in contrast to the £308,000 it realized in November 1989, speaks for itself. Waterhouse's mature style represents a synthesis of contemporary classicism, Burne-Jones influence, and a technique derived ultimately from Bastien-Lepage. In our picture, appropriately in view of the subject, the classical element prevails, although not at the expense of the artist's essential romanticism.

  Walter Crane's *The Bridge of Life* also inhabits that nebulous area where classical and Pre-Raphaelite traditions meet. But if the Waterhouse is an idyll which aims to beguile, Crane's elaborate allegory speaks with a moral fervour born of his deep commitment to Socialism and the Arts and Crafts. It failed to find a buyer at the Grosvenor Gallery in 1884 or at Crane's one-man exhibition held at the Fine Art Society in 1891 and subsequently toured in the United States and Canada. Only when the show went off on a further lap round Europe was it bought by Ernst Seeger of Berlin. Indeed Seeger acquired several of Crane's late paintings, while others also found homes in Germany. No doubt Crane was right in suggesting that 'the symbolic and figurative character' of these pictures was 'more in sympathy with the Teutonic mind'. Whatever the case, the fact that so many went abroad has meant that this vital aspect of his work was almost unrepresented in England, and the reappearance of a major example was welcome.

GEORGE EARL
British fl.1856–95
Perth Station Coming South
Signed and dated
1895
Oil on canvas
48¾ × 84 in.
(122.9 × 213.4 cm.)
Sold 22 June 1990 in
London for £308,000
($526,064)
Record auction price
for a work by the
artist

In stark contrast to Crane's essay in didactic symbolism are the two paintings by George Earl, *Going North King's Cross Station* and *Perth Station Coming South*. Earl is generally known as a conventional sporting artist, specializing in portraits of dogs, but he had ambitions to transcend this limited genre and, like Landseer before him, to make animals the basis of elaborate compositions of much wider reference. With their wealth of period detail and social comment, *Going North* and *Coming South* are not only fascinating in a sporting context but document the crucial significance of railways in the Victorian age. They were totally unknown to scholarship until a Christie's expert discovered them hanging in the Vine pub in Lime Street, Liverpool. Earl had exhibited pictures with these titles at the Royal Academy in 1876 and 1877, and ours, which are dated 1893 and 1895, are later, updated versions, probably commissioned by Sir Andrew Barclay Walker, head of a Liverpool brewing firm and founder of the Walker Art Gallery, or his son. In the catalogue we described the early versions as lost, but it later emerged that *Going North* had been for many years in the possession of the Wigan Heritage Service. *Coming South* too may well turn up one day, proving once again that in the world of Victorian pictures 'lost' is a relative term.

SIR SAMUEL LUKE FILDES, RA
British 1844–1927
Venetian Life
Signed and dated
1884
Oil on canvas
84½ × 62 in.
(214 × 158 cm.)
Sold 24 November
1989 in London for
£101,200 ($176,000)

Opposite above:
WALTER CRANE, RWS
British 1845–1915
The Bridge of Life
Signed and dated
1884
Oil on canvas
38 × 60 in.
(96.5 × 152.4 cm.)
Sold 30 March 1990
in London for
£242,000 ($411,400)
Record auction price
for a work by the
artist

Opposite below:
JOHN WILLIAM
WATERHOUSE, RA
British 1849–1917
*The Awakening of
Adonis*
Signed and dated
1899
Oil on canvas
37¾ × 74 in.
(95.9 × 188 cm.)
Sold 24 November
1989 in London for
£308,000 ($492,800)
Record auction price
for a work by the
artist

JEAN LÉON GÉRÔME
French 1824–1904
Hunting Scene in the Forest of Meudon (The Hunt of the Baron Salomon de Rothschild)
Signed and inscribed
Oil on canvas
21¼ × 32¼ in.
(54 × 81.9 cm.)
Sold 1 March 1990 in New York for $638,000 (£384,337)

ANDREAS SCHELFHOUT
Dutch 1787–1870
Skaters in a Frozen River Landscape
Signed and dated 1839
Oil on canvas
23¼ × 30¼ in.
(59.5 × 77 cm.)
Sold 2 May 1990 in Amsterdam for D.fl.483,000
(£164,846)

Opposite:
ULPIANO CHECA Y SANZ
Spanish 1860–1916
L'Arc de Triomphe, Paris
Signed
Oil on canvas
19½ × 39½ in.
(51 × 101 cm.)
Sold 15 February 1990 in London for £385,000
($654,400)
Record auction price for a work by the artist

RAFFAELLO SORBI
Italian 1844–1931
Osteria all'aperto
Signed and dated
1892
Oil on canvas
18¾ × 31½ in.
(48 × 80 cm.)
Sold 14 December
1989 in Rome for
L.299,000,000
(£145,075)

JEAN LÉON GÉRÔME
French 1824–1904
L'Entrée du taureau or *Plaza de Toros*
Signed
Oil on panel
18 × 30 in. (45.7 × 72.6 cm.)
Sold 24 November 1989 in London for
£330,000 ($528,000)

Gérôme's conception of this composition
developed during visits to Spain in 1872 and
1883. More important, his friendly rivalry
with Edouard Manet, who had painted a
series of bullfighting scenes in the mid-1860s,
stimulated Gérôme to paint with all the
precision and accuracy of the Academic
Realist style, as if to show Manet what he
should have done by correcting his 'errors' in
perspective and foreshortening.

Gérôme, here at the height of his powers,
called on all his skills of drawing,
composition and imagination in this scene.
Most extraordinary is the drawing of the
figures of the toreadors; they are all in relaxed
poses, but there is nonetheless a springy
alertness in their legs, and their eyes all focus
on the bull. The perspective places us as
viewers on the floor of the arena so that we
can look through the loosely grouped
toreadors. The grouping itself is splendid, and
our attention is led by the red flags, through
the groups, to the hesitant bull. The crowd,
detailed yet softly painted, shows Gérôme's
command over optical effects; and the overall
brilliance of the sunlight is part of the tension
that holds everything together and reminds us
that – despite the glorious colours of the
costumes – this is a drama of death.

L'Entrée du taureau is not only a masterpiece
of Gérôme's fullest maturity, it is also a
masterpiece of nineteenth-century European
Realism which had been lost for over forty
years.

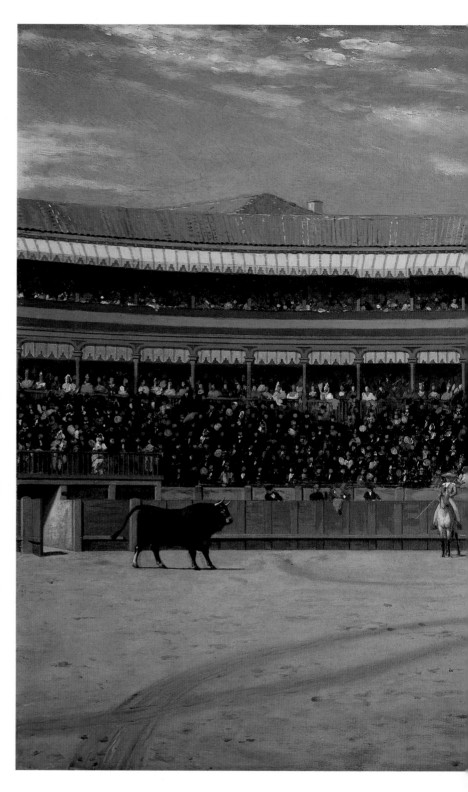

NIKOLAI ASTRUP
Norwegian 1880–1928
An Interior with a Still Life; the Parlour at Sandalstrand
Signed and dated 1911
Oil on canvas
32¼ × 39¼ in. (81.9 × 100.4 cm.)
Sold 29 March in London for £374,000 ($635,800)
Record auction price for a work by the artist

JOHAN LAURENTZ JENSEN
Danish 1800–56
Hydrangea in an Urn and a Basket of Lemons, Oranges and Figs on a Stone Ledge
Signed and dated Sorrento 1834
Oil on canvas
29¼ × 34½ in. (74.4 × 87.6 cm.)
Sold 29 March 1990 in London for £242,000 ($411,400)
Record auction price for a work by the artist

ANDERS LEONARD ZORN
Swedish 1860–1920
Les Baigneuses
Signed and dated Dalarö 1889
Oil on canvas
38¾ × 27 in.
(98.5 × 68.5 cm.)
Sold 29 March 1990 in
London for £1,760,000
($2,992,000)
Record auction price for a
work by the artist and for
any Swedish picture

Les Baigneuses, considered one
of Zorn's most important
depictions of nudes set in a
landscape, was painted *en
plein air* between June and
mid-July 1889 on the island
of Dalarö in the Stockholm
archipelago. It was purchased
that same year directly from
the artist by the leading
French collector of
Impressionist paintings Jean
Baptiste Fauvre, in whose
collection it remained until
his death in 1914, when it
was purchased by Galerie
Durand-Ruel.

GIUSEPPE DE NITTIS
Italian 1846–84
I Pioppi
Signed and dated 70
Oil on panel
16 × 12¾ in.
(40.7 × 32.4 cm.)
Sold 1 March 1990 in
New York for
$440,000 (£265,060)
From the property of
Alida White, New
York

Opposite:
JEAN FRANÇOIS MILLET
French 1814–75
*Les Moissoneurs
endormis*
Signed
Oil on canvas
18 × 15 in.
(45.7 × 38.1 cm.)
Sold 22 May 1990 in
New York for
$770,000 (£455,621)

GUSTAVE MOREAU
French 1826–98
The Apparition
Signed
Oil on canvas
12¾ × 8⅞ in.
(32.5 × 22.5 cm.)
Sold 1 December
1989 in London for
£605,000 ($968,000)
From a sale devoted
solely to Symbolist
works of art

WILLIAM DEGOUVE DE NUNCQUES
Belgian 1867–1935
La Nuit à Bruges
Signed and dated 1897
Oil on canvas
23⅝ × 35½ in. (60 × 90 cm.)
Sold 1 December 1989 in London for £462,000 ($739,200)
From a sale devoted solely to Symbolist works of art

WILLIAM CLARK OF
GREENOCK
British 1803–83
*The Hydrabad at the
Tail of the Bank with
Roseneath Peninsular
beyond*
Signed and dated 1865
Oil on canvas
31 × 55 in.
(79 × 140 cm.)
Sold 5 October 1989
in London at South
Kensington for
£29,700 ($47,520)

EDWARD WILLIAM
COOKE, RA
British 1811–80
*Bragozzi – the Fishing
Craft of Venice*
Signed and dated
1851
Oil on canvas
35¾ × 50 in.
(91 × 127 cm.)
Sold 5 October 1989
in London at South
Kensington for
£85,800 ($137,280)

CHARLES EDWARD
CONDER
English 1868–1909
A Pastoral
Oil on canvas
8¾ × 14 in.
(22.2 × 35.5 cm.)
Sold 11 April 1990 in
Melbourne for
Aus$154,000
(£70,255)

WALTER WITHERS
British 1854–1914
Beach Scene, Port Phillip Bay
Signed
*c.*1910
Oil on canvas
7 × 19½ in. (17.5 × 49.5 cm.)
Sold 11 April 1990 in Melbourne for Aus$77,000 (£35,128)

SIR HANS HEYSEN
Australian 1877–1968
The Picnic
Signed and dated
1905 and 1917
Oil on canvas
48⅛ × 36¼ in.
(122.2 × 92 cm.)
Sold 30 November
1989 in London at
South Kensington for
£143,000 ($223,509)

C. J. MARTIN
fl. mid-19th century
View of Rio de Janeiro
Signed and dated
1850
Oil on canvas
26¾ × 41¼ in.
(67.9 × 104.8 cm.)
Sold 24 May 1990 in
London at South
Kensington for
£60,500 ($101,040)

JOHN GLOVER
British 1767–1849
*The River Derwent
and Hobart Town,
Tasmania*
1831–2
Oil on canvas
20 × 28 in.
(50.8 × 71.1 cm.)
Sold 24 May 1990 in
London at South
Kensington for
£143,000 ($235,760)

SIR ARTHUR STREETON
Australian 1867–1943
Hawkesbury River
1896
Signed
Oil on board
39 × 42¾ in.
(98.9 × 108.2 cm.)
Sold 11 April 1990 in
Melbourne for
Aus$770,000
(£351,277)

FITZ HUGH LANE
American 1804–65
The Annisquam River Looking toward Ipswich Bay
Signed and dated 1848
Oil on canvas
18½ × 27 in.
(47 × 68 cm.)
Sold 1 December 1989 in New York for $825,000 (£525,478)
Record auction price for a work by the artist

ALBERT BIERSTADT
American 1830–1902
Passing Storm in Yosemite
Signed and dated 65
Oil on canvas
22 × 30 in.
(56 × 76.3 cm.)
Sold 23 May 1990 in New York for $715,000 (£423,076)

THOMAS HART BENTON
American 1889–1975
Homeward Bound
Signed and dated '44
Oil on canvas
29½ × 47½ in.
(75 × 120 cm.)
Sold 1 December
1989 in New York
for $1,540,000
(£980,892)
Record auction price
for a work by the
artist

THOMAS
COPPERTHWAITE EAKINS
American 1844–1916
*John Biglin in a Single
Scull*
Signed and dated
1873
Watercolour on paper
16⅞ × 24 in.
(42.9 × 61 cm.)
Sold 23 May 1990 in
New York for
$3,520,000
(£2,082,840)
Record auction price
for a work by the
artist and for any
nineteenth-century
American
watercolour

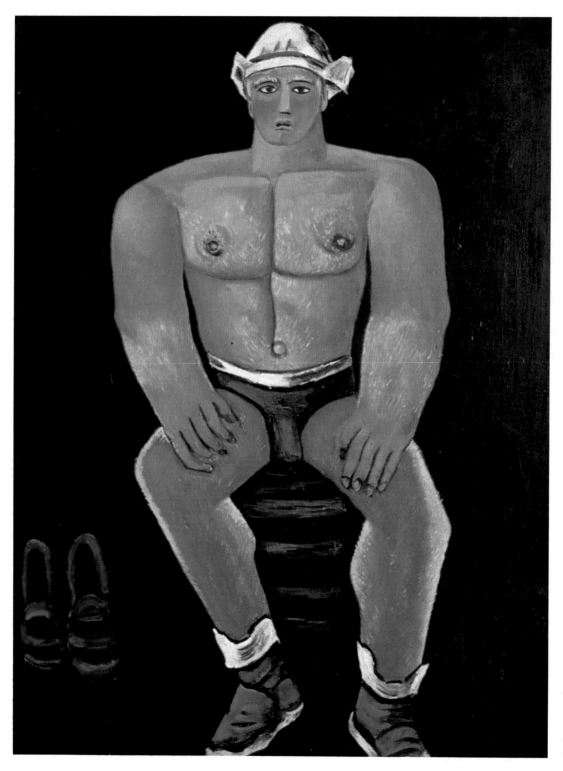

MARSDEN HARTLEY
American 1877–1943
*The Flaming American
Swim Champ*
Signed and dated
1939/40
Oil on masonite
40 × 30 in.
(131.6 × 76.2 cm.)
Sold 23 May 1990 in
New York for
$550,000 (£325,443)
Record auction price
for a work by the
artist

Opposite:
GEORGIA O'KEEFFE
American 1887–1986
Red Poppy, No. VI
Signed and dated
1928
Oil on canvas
35½ × 29¾ in.
(100 × 50.5 cm.)
Sold 23 May 1990 in
New York for
$1,100,000 (£650,887)

FREDERICK CHILDE
HASSAM
American 1859–1935
*The Fourth of July,
1916*
Signed and dated
1916
Oil on canvas
36 × 26 in.
(91.4 × 66 cm.)
Sold 1 December
1989 in New York
for $3,190,000
(£2,031,847)
Record auction price
for a work by the
artist

Opposite:
ERNEST LAWSON
American 1873–1939
The Flatiron Building
Signed
Oil on canvas laid
down on board
30 × 25 in.
(76.2 × 63.5 cm.)
Sold 1 December
1989 in New York
for $528,000
(£336,306)
Record auction price
for a work by the
artist

MODERN PICTURES
AND SCULPTURE

MARC CHAGALL
Russian 1887–1985
La Ferme, le village
Signed
Oil on canvas
24 × 29 in. (61 × 73.7 cm.)
Sold 25 June 1990 in London for
£1,540,000 ($2,633,400)

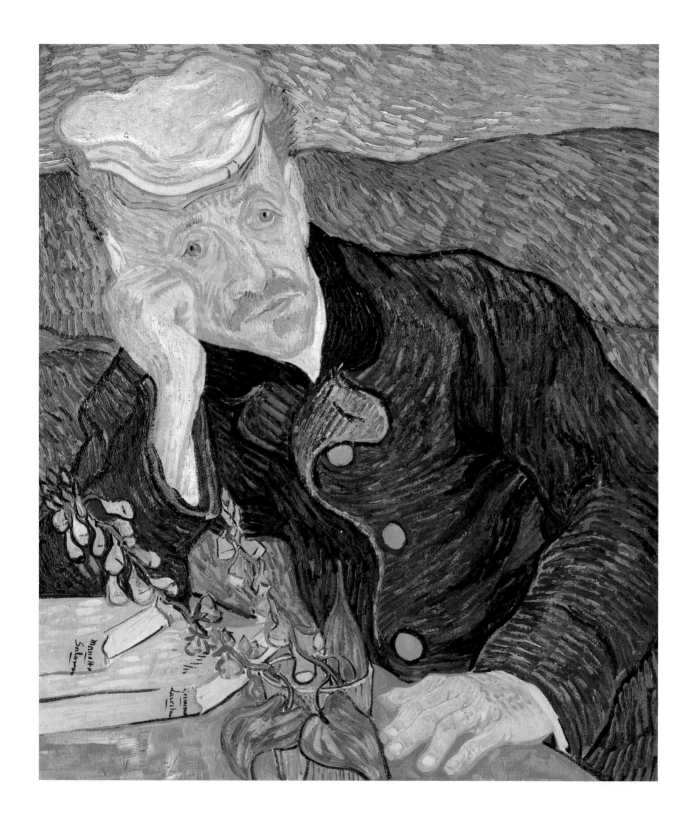

'GACHET IS VERY, YES VERY LIKE YOU AND ME'
PORTRAIT DU DR GACHET

Matthew Armstrong

VINCENT VAN GOGH
Dutch 1853–90
Portrait du Dr Gachet
Painted in
Auvers-sur-Oise,
3–5 June 1890
Oil on canvas
26 × 22½ in.
(66 × 57 cm.)
Sold 15 May 1990 in
New York for
$82,500,000
(£43,107,142)
From the collection
of the late
Mr Siegfried Kramarsky
Record auction price
for any work of art

Anyone can see that Vincent van Gogh's *Portrait du Dr Gachet* is a great painting, but to ask 'what makes it so?' is to pose a question that might confound the Sphinx herself. None the less, since the image is both van Gogh's finest portrait and arguably one of the greatest portraits since the Renaissance, it is incumbent on us to speculate on van Gogh's intentions when the evanescent quality we call genius blossomed within him as he undertook to capture the mind and spirit of his last dear friend.

In the spring of 1890, Vincent left the asylum at Saint-Rémy where he had been confined for almost a year. There he had suffered miserably at the hands of doctors who understood nothing of him or his art, and he was more than happy to follow his brother Theo's suggestion to put himself in the care of the respected physician Paul-Ferdinand Gachet, who had been recommended to Theo by Vincent's friend, the painter Pissarro. Gachet, twenty-five year's van Gogh's senior, maintained a practice in Paris as well as in the more therapeutic environment of Auvers-sur-Oise, where Vincent sought him out. Gachet knew a thing or two about cracking up: he had written his thesis on melancholia at Montpellier University and, having lost his wife some years previously, was himself of a rather sombre disposition. He also knew enough about modern methods of psychiatry to distrust them and argued for the use of more natural, homoeopathic remedies. (He went so far as to imply to the artist's brother that Vincent's crisis had little to do with madness but much to do with the solitude and loneliness under which he laboured.) An outspoken and unusual man, known for his unyielding opinions on a vast number of controversial topics (modern medicine, French politics and naturalism among others), Dr Gachet was also a tireless proselytizer for subjects as diverse as phrenology, modern anthropology and free love. In his youth he had known not only the writers Victor Hugo and Champfleury, but several of van Gogh's idols, including the painters Courbet, Corot, Monticelli and Daumier. Moreover, Gachet had as a young man exhibited at the Salon des Indépendants and subsequently became a collector of modern painting and a vigorous supporter of the French avant-garde, most notably the work of the Impressionists Pissarro, Renoir, Sisley, Cézanne and Guillaumin. No doubt it was this fortuitous combination of familiarity with melancholic neurosis, advanced modern literature and avant-garde painting that made Gachet and van Gogh so especially well disposed towards each other. To van Gogh, Gachet was not merely an informed and sympathetic man of the world, but a kind of *doppelgänger*:

> I have found a true friend in Dr Gachet, something like another brother, so much do we resemble each other physically and also mentally. He is himself a very nervous man and rather odd in his behaviour; he has extended much friendliness to the artists of the new school, and he has helped them as much as was in his power...
> He lost his wife some years ago, which greatly contributed to his becoming a broken man. I believe I may say we have been friends from the very first.

Furthermore, van Gogh was overjoyed to learn that Gachet understood and appreciated his paintings: 'He understands them exactly, *exactly*, I tell you, as they are.'

Vincent wrote that upon seeing the *Self-Portrait* of 1889 Gachet was 'absolutely fanatical' about it and implored van Gogh to 'do one for him...exactly like it'. Vincent endeavoured to do just this and shortly thereafter wrote that the image of his new friend 'has the same sentiment as the self-portrait I did when I left for this place', and was done in 'nearly the same way'.

What was it that Gachet so well appreciated and that van Gogh struggled to inject into the portrait of his caretaker? We know that both men shared an admiration for clarity and simplicity in painting and that this primary element is usually seen as the hallmark of van Gogh's portraits, which are, at the outset anyway, exceptionally straightforward and unambiguous. But after years of painting simple, rural working people, Vincent now had the opportunity to paint the image of a far more complex gentleman who sincerely and sympathetically understood the painter and his advanced aesthetic predilections and artistic intentions. John Rewald has convincingly suggested that it was precisely this unique combination of Gachet's psyche, intellect and knowledge of art that enabled van Gogh to make what is his most exhaustive investigation of transpersonal psychology. (The definitive description of Gachet at the time van Gogh knew him can be found in John Rewald's *Post-Impressionism: From van Gogh to Gauguin*, New York, The Museum of Modern Art, 3rd edn., 1978.)

Firstly, although to some extent all portraits may be self-portraits, *Portrait du Dr Gachet* comes closer than most to functioning as such a dual portrait. On a superficial level – a notion about which the painter, his brother and the doctor all shared a good laugh – Vincent and Gachet looked remarkably similar. With only slight modification, any description of Gachet could apply to the painter as well: glittering woebegone blue eyes, a pensive furrowed brow, an aquiline nose, a narrow downward-tending mouth and protruding chin, and what van Gogh described as 'the face of an overheated brick, scorched by the sun, with reddish hair'.

As with many of Vincent's paintings – most powerfully seen in the great 1889 *Self-Portrait* of which Gachet was so enamoured – everything both solid and insubstantial is here invested with ecstatic, supernatural energy. Gachet is engulfed in mesmerizing, vivifying lines of force which animate not only the woof and weave of his coat, his hair, his hands, and his eyes but appear to emanate out from the contours of his body and enliven the earth behind him. Nevertheless, the facture is laid down with somewhat less frenzy and with thinner impasto than is usual in van Gogh's mature work, and the artist's tendency to spike his brushwork with tempestuous, barely controlled force seems to have been abated somewhat by the resigned and baleful calm of the doctor's face. The overall effect suggests

VINCENT VAN GOGH
Dutch 1853–90
Self-Portrait
Painted in
Saint-Rémy,
September 1889
Oil on canvas
25⅝ × 21¼ in.
(65 × 54 cm.)
By kind permission
of the Musée
d'Orsay, the gift of
Paul and Marguerite
Gachet

that a momentary sobriety and quietude has been established, a harmonized counterpoint between the wistful man before the easel and the agitated man behind it.

More important affinities existed between the two men, however, and van Gogh took great lengths to include them in the image. The attributes prominently displayed on the red garden table before Gachet clearly refer to both men: the foxglove sprigs inside the tumbler represent digitalis, Gachet's standard homoeopathic prescription for heart disease, and the two bound yellow volumes *Germinie Lacerteux* and *Manette Salomon*, novels by the Goncourt Brothers, were, while by no means unknown to the highly literate Gachet, especially dear to van Gogh's heart. Paradigmatic of French *modernité*, the works of the Goncourt brothers have been described as having heightened 'the theme of consolation despite the inevitable griefs of modern life', griefs which certainly weighed on the minds of both Gachet and his patient.

Most compelling of all is the mysterious information van Gogh revealed concerning this work in an unsent letter to his erstwhile friend Paul Gauguin. Van Gogh likened his portrait of Gachet to Gauguin's *Christ in the Garden of Gethsemane: Self-Portrait* – an amalgamation of the image of Christ and a Gauguin self-portrait – and lamented that, like Gauguin's painting, the image of Gachet, wearing 'the heart-broken expression of our time', was destined to be misunderstood. Such a notion is bewildering unless one surmises that, like Gauguin's lonely, *Angst*-ridden *Christ*, van Gogh's *Portrait du Dr Gachet* is both a straightforward image and a cipher for something else.

The most important qualities one should strive to extract from one's sitters, van Gogh insisted, were not merely physical aspects nor even psychological distinctions, but the particular sensibilities with which the sitter's psyche would convey what it meant to be living in the modern world:

> I painted a portrait of Dr Gachet with an expression of melancholy, which would seem like a grimace to many who saw the canvas. And yet it is necessary to paint of the extent to which, in comparison with the calmness of the old portraits, there is an expression in our modern heads, and a passion – like a waiting for things as well as a growth. Sad and yet gentle but clear and intelligent – this is how one ought to paint many portraits. At times this might make a certain impression on people. There are modern heads which people will go on looking at for a long time to come, and which perhaps they will mourn over after a hundred years.

Inspired by his sense of his accomplishment with the Gachet portrait, van Gogh explained a new philosophy of portraiture to his sister in a letter written within the same month:
What impassions me most – much, much more than all the rest of my metier – is the portrait, the modern portrait.... *I should like* – mind you, far be it from me to say that I shall be able to do it, although this is what I am aiming at – *I should like* to paint portraits which would appear after a century to the people living then as apparitions. By which I mean that I do not endeavour to achieve this by a photographic resemblance, but by means of our impassioned expressions.

Sadly, van Gogh's *Portrait du Dr Gachet* was to be both the first and last portrait to achieve this. Shortly afterwards, and with seeming inevitability, there was a falling out between the two men, ostensibly over some trifle – the framing of a *Nude* by Guillaumin – but more probably due to van Gogh's increasingly manic disposition. Such an alliance was bound to end in disaster; Vincent had already paid dearly for his experience in Arles with Gauguin with what precious little was left of his mind, and as he became more anguished in his paranoia and melancholy, he began to vehemently distrust his closeness to Gachet, and grew wary of anyone whom he felt understood what he had come to see as his own desperately sick mind. In early July he wrote to Theo:

> I think we must not count on Dr Gachet *at all*. First of all, he is a sicker man than I am, I think, or shall we say just as much. So that is that. Now when one blind man leads another blind man, don't they both fall into the ditch?'

Van Gogh, who had dashed frenetically up the summits of ecstasy then fell shrieking into the pits of despair, a man whose mind was too fragile for Paris and probably too fragile for Auvers-sur-Oise, went completely to pieces. The weight of oblivion descended on him, and six weeks after the completion of his greatest portrait he was dead by his own hand.

But whether he knew it or not, van Gogh achieved more than he had dreamed possible. One hundred years later *Portrait du Dr Gachet* appears to us as more than a humble portrait, more than a mystical double portrait, more than 'an apparition', and more than simply a tragic evocation of late nineteenth-century man. The final, mercurial, elusive element in this painting has less to do with van Gogh's intentions as a painter than it does with his heart.

Christian theology – and van Gogh's training as a lay preacher would have made him acutely aware of this – makes a strong distinction between sympathy and compassion. In the former, one beholds another with pity, while nevertheless retaining a sense of unique separation and thus superiority. Compassion, on the other hand, is to see oneself within the face of another's suffering and thereby forge a link with all those who toil on this earth. The late portraits by Rembrandt, arguably van Gogh's only rival in this regard, also exhibit – though more quietly – an attempt to reveal the sufferings of humanity at large within the craggy particulars of the working poor, the simple but wise, the adamantly devout, the meek and the lame. Compassion as a prism through which one paints a portrait is as rare a quality as compassion itself but is finally the virtue on which the salience of van Gogh's *Dr Gachet* is founded. The success of van Gogh's portrait can be judged by the degree to which we find ourselves transported past the small, fragile orbit of the benevolent doctor and the feverish, troubled painter to the larger circle wherein we recognize that the eyes which confront us are the deep, turbulent eyes of Everyman.

Van Gogh's art is a gift to humanity, and though his paintings may be bought and sold *ad infinitum,* the ennobling experience of having recognized what he has bequeathed cannot be possessed by the greatest gold. The compelling, silent mystery that passed between the painter and the doctor will be with us forever.

(Quotations from van Gogh's correspondence have been taken from *The Complete Letters of Vincent van Gogh*, Greenwich, Connecticut, New York Graphic Society, 1958.)

PAUL GAUGUIN
French 1848–1903
Christ in the Garden of Gethsemane: Self-Portrait
1889
Oil on canvas
29 × 36 in.
(73.7 × 91 cm.)
Collection of the Norton Gallery of Art, West Palm Beach, Florida

ADOLPHE MONTICELLI
French 1824–86
Bouquet de fleurs
Signed
*c.*1870
Oil on panel
20½ × 15 in.
(52 × 38 cm.)
Sold 3 April 1990 in
London for £253,000
($419,980)
Record auction price
for a work by the
artist

Opposite:
EDGAR DEGAS
French 1834–1917
Degas en gilet vert
1855–6
Oil on canvas
16⅛ × 12¾ in.
(41 × 32.5 cm.)
Sold 2 April 1990 in
London for
£1,870,000
($3,104,200)

ALFRED SISLEY
French 1839–99
Vaches au pâturage, Louveciennes
Signed
1874
Oil on canvas
23⅝ × 28¾ in. (60 × 73 cm.)
Sold 2 April 1990 in London for £1,540,000 ($2,556,400)

CLAUDE MONET
French 1840–1926
Fin d'après-midi, Vétheuil
Signed and dated 80, the stretcher inscribed 'Vue de Vétheuil Boussod'
Oil on canvas
29¾ × 39 in. (73 × 100 cm.)
Sold 27 November 1989 in London for £4,620,000 ($7,253,400)

EDOUARD MANET
French 1832–83
La Rue Mosnier aux drapeaux
Signed and dated 1878
Oil on canvas
25¾ × 31¾ in. (65.5 × 81 cm.)
Sold 14 November 1989 in New York for $26,400,000 (£16,603,773)
From the collection of Mr and Mrs Paul Mellon
Record auction price for a work by the artist

PAUL CÉZANNE
French 1839–1906
Pommes et serviette
1879–80
Oil on canvas
19⅜ × 23¾ in. (49.2 × 60.3 cm.)
Sold 27 November 1989 in London for
£11,000,000 ($17,270,000)
Record auction price for a work by the artist

EDOUARD MANET
French 1832–83
Le Banc (Le Jardin de Versailles)
Signed
Painted at Versailles, 1881
Oil on canvas
23⅝ × 32 in. (65.1 × 81.3 cm.)
Sold 15 May 1990 in New York for $16,500,000 (£9,821,428)
From the property of Mrs John Barry Ryan

CAMILLE PISSARRO
French 1830–1903
La Servante assise dans le Jardin d'Eragny
Signed and dated 84
Oil on canvas
23⅝ × 29½ in. (60 × 75 cm.)
Sold 25 June 1990 in London for £1,650,000 ($2,821,500)

HENRI DE
TOULOUSE–LAUTREC
French 1864–1901
Fille à la fourrure,
Mlle Jeanne Fontaine
Signed, dedicated and
dated 'HT-Lautrec 91
à mon ami M Guibert'
Peintre à l'essence
on board
26⅝ × 20¾ in.
(67.5 × 52.8 cm.)
Sold 15 May 1990 in
New York for
$12,980,000
(£7,726,190)
From the collection
of the late Robert
Lehman
Record auction price
for a work by the
artist

Opposite:
PIERRE–AUGUSTE RENOIR
French 1841–1919
La Liseuse
Signed
1877
Oil on canvas
25⅝ × 21¼ in.
(65 × 54 cm.)
Sold 14 November
1989 in New York
for $14,300,000
(£8,960,380)

PIERRE AUGUSTE RENOIR
French 1841–1919
Baigneuses
Signed
1892
Oil on canvas
18⅛ × 15 in.
(46 × 38 cm.)
Sold 25 June 1990 in
London for
£3,960,000
($6,771,600)
From the collection
of the late Jack
Cotton Esq.

Opposite:
CLAUDE MONET
French 1840–1926
Nymphéas
Signed and dated
1907
Oil on canvas
39½ × 39½ in.
(100.3 × 100.3 cm.)
Sold 14 November
1989 in New York
for $11,550,000
(£7,237,230)

CLAUDE MONET
French 1840–1926
Le Parlement, soleil couchant
Signed and dated 1902
Oil on canvas
51⅞ × 36¼ in. (81 × 92 cm.)
Sold 14 November 1989 in New York for $9,900,000 (£6,226,415)
From the Mr and Mrs George N. Richard Collection

GUSTAVE CAILLEBOTTE
French 1840–94
Pêcheurs sur la Seine
Signed and dated 1888
Oil on canvas
25⅝ × 31⅞ in. (65.5 × 81.2 cm.)
Sold 27 November 1989 in London for £1,320,000 ($2,072,400)
Record auction price for a work by the artist

VINCENT VAN GOGH
Dutch 1853–90
Le Vieil If
Painted in Arles,
October 1888
Oil on canvas
36¼ × 25⅝ in.
(92 × 72.4 cm.)
Sold 14 November
1989 in New York
for $20,350,000
(£12,798,742)
From the collection
of Mr and Mrs Paul
Mellon

Opposite:
VINCENT VAN GOGH
Dutch 1853–1890
Autoportrait
Signed and inscribed
'Vincent à l'ami
Laval'
Painted in Arles,
1888
Oil on canvas
18½ × 15⅜ in.
(46 × 39 cm.)
Sold 15 May 1990 in
New York for
$26,400,000
(£15,714,285)
From the collection
of the late Robert
Lehman

PABLO PICASSO
Spanish 1881–1973
Les Tuileries
Signed
Painted in Paris,
May/June 1901
Oil on board
20¼ × 26¼ in. (52 × 66.7 cm.)
Sold 25 June 1990 in London for £13,750,000 ($23,512,5000)

PABLO PICASSO
Spanish 1881–1973
La Maternité
Signed
Painted in Paris, 1901
Oil on board
39½ × 29 in.
(100 × 73 cm.)
Sold 27 November
1989 in London for
£7,150,000
($11,225,500)

EDOUARD VUILLARD
French 1868–1940
La Table de toilette (dans les fleurs)
Signed
1895
Oil on canvas
25⅝ × 44⅞ in. (65 × 114 cm.)
Sold November 14 1989 in New York for $7,700,000 (£4,824,820)
Record auction price for a work by the artist

TSUGUJI FOUJITA
Japanese 1886–1968
Jeune Fille dans le parc
Signed and dated 'Foujita Paris 1957'
Oil on canvas
20 × 25¾ in. (50.8 × 65.4 cm.)
Sold 16 May 1990 in New York for $6,050,000 (£3,601,190)
Record auction price for a work by the artist

MAURICE DE VLAMINCK
French 1876–1958
La Seine à Chatou
Signed
1906
Oil on canvas
29⅛ × 36½ in. (74 × 92.7 cm.)
Sold 14 November 1989 in New York for $7,150,000 (£4,480,190)

PAUL SIGNAC
French 1863–1935
La Salute
Signed and dated 1908
Oil on canvas
28¾ × 36 in. (73 × 91.5 cm.)
Sold on 25 June 1990 in London for £1,540,000 ($2,633,400)

MARC CHAGALL
Russian 1887–1985
Au dessus de la ville
Signed and dated 1915
Oil on thinned board laid down on canvas
19¼ × 27¾ in. (48.5 × 70.5 cm.)
Sold 15 May 1990 in New York for $9,900,000 (£5,892,857)

PABLO PICASSO
Spanish 1881–1973
Paysage de Cannes au crépuscule
Signed and dated 30.3.60
Oil on canvas
51⅛ × 76¾ in. (130 × 195 cm.)
Sold 2 April 1990 in London for £2,420,000 ($4,017,200)

EDVARD MUNCH
Norwegian 1863–1944
Strandmystik (Mystische in der Sommernacht)
Signed
Painted at Aasgardstrand, 1892
Oil on canvas
39½ × 55 in. (100 × 140 cm.)
Sold 2 April 1990 in London for £1,100,000 ($1,826,000)

ERNST LUDWIG KIRCHNER
German 1880–1938
Zwei Akte auf blauem Sofa
Signed
1910–20
Oil on canvas
19¾ × 27¾ in. (50.2 × 70.5 cm.)
Sold 13 November 1989 in New York for $1,540,000 (£980,892)
From the collection of Billy Wilder
Record auction price for a work by the artist

AMEDEO MODIGLIANI
Italian 1884–1920
Jeanne Hébuterne con
grande cappello
Signed
*c.*1918
Oil on canvas
21⅝ × 15 in.
(55 × 38 cm.)
Sold 15 May 1990 in
New York for
$8,250,000
(£4,910,714)
From the collection
of the late Robert
Lehman

RAOUL DUFY
French 1877–1953
La Grande Baigneuse
1914
Oil on canvas
96½ × 71⅝ in.
(245 × 182 cm.)
Sold 2 April 1990 in
London for £825,000
($1,369,500)

Above:
FERNAND LÉGER
French 1881–1955
Les Acrobates (Les Perroquets)
Signed and dated 33
Oil on canvas
51¼ × 63 in. (130 × 160 cm.)
Sold 27 November 1989 in London for £4,180,000
($6,562,600)

Opposite:
FERNAND LÉGER
French 1881–1955
Contrastes de formes
Signed and dated 13 on the reverse
Oil on canvas
31⅞ × 25⅝ in. (81 × 65 cm.)
Sold 27 November 1989 in London for £9,350,000
($14,679,500)
Record auction price for a work by the artist

GEORGES BRAQUE
French 1882–1963
L'Arlequin
Signed on the reverse
Executed at Sorges,
September 1912
Charcoal with collage
on Ingres laid paper
24½ × 18⅞ in.
(62 × 48 cm.)
Sold 27 November
1989 in London for
£2,860,000
($4,490,200)
Record auction price
for a collage by the
artist

Opposite:
PABLO PICASSO
Spanish 1881–1973
*Guitare et compotier
rose*
Signed and dated 24
Oil on canvas
39⅜ × 31⅞ in.
(100 × 81 cm.)
Sold 27 November
1989 in London for
£3,960,000
($6,217,200)

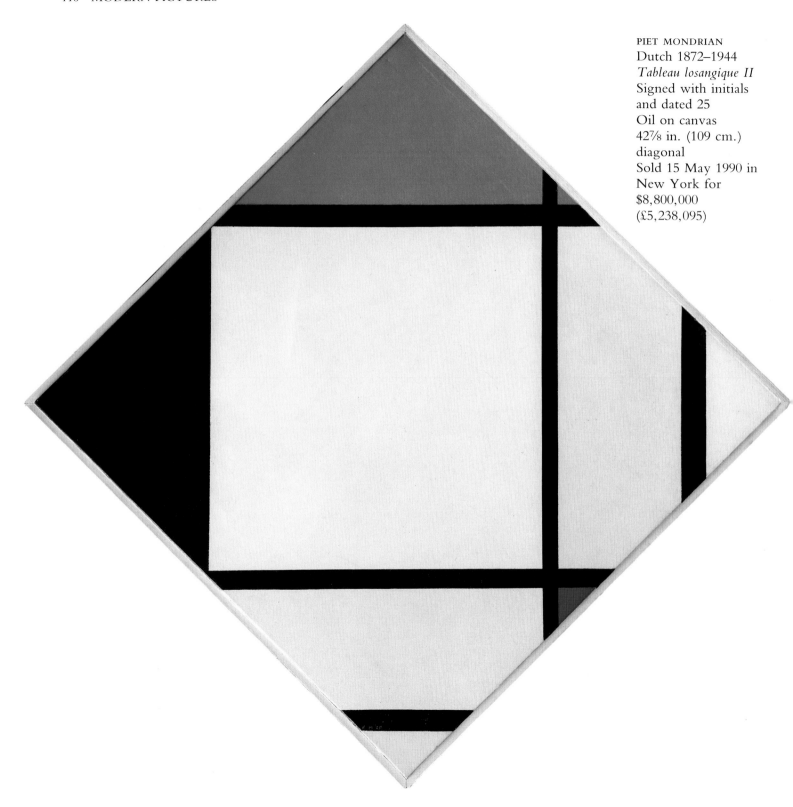

PIET MONDRIAN
Dutch 1872–1944
Tableau losangique II
Signed with initials
and dated 25
Oil on canvas
42⅞ in. (109 cm.)
diagonal
Sold 15 May 1990 in
New York for
$8,800,000
(£5,238,095)

RENÉ MAGRITTE
Belgian 1898–1967
*La Condition
humaine II*
Signed
1935
Oil on canvas
39½ × 28¾ in.
(100 × 73 cm.)
Sold 27 November
1989 in London for
£1,430,000
($2,245,100)
Record auction price
for a work by the
artist

Above:
CONSTANTIN BRANCUSI
Romanian 1876–1957
La Muse endormie III
c.1917
Marble
7¼ in. (18.5 cm.) high; 11⅝ in. (29.5 cm.) long
Sold 14 November 1989 in New York for $8,250,000
(£5,188,679)
From the collection of the late Mary A.H. Rumsey

Opposite:
BALTHUS (Balthasar Klossowski de Rola)
French b.1908
La Toilette
1957
Oil on canvas
64 × 51½ in. (162 × 130.8 cm.)
Sold 13 November 1989 in New York for $2,090,000
(£1,331,210)
From the collection of Billy Wilder
Record auction price for a work by the artist

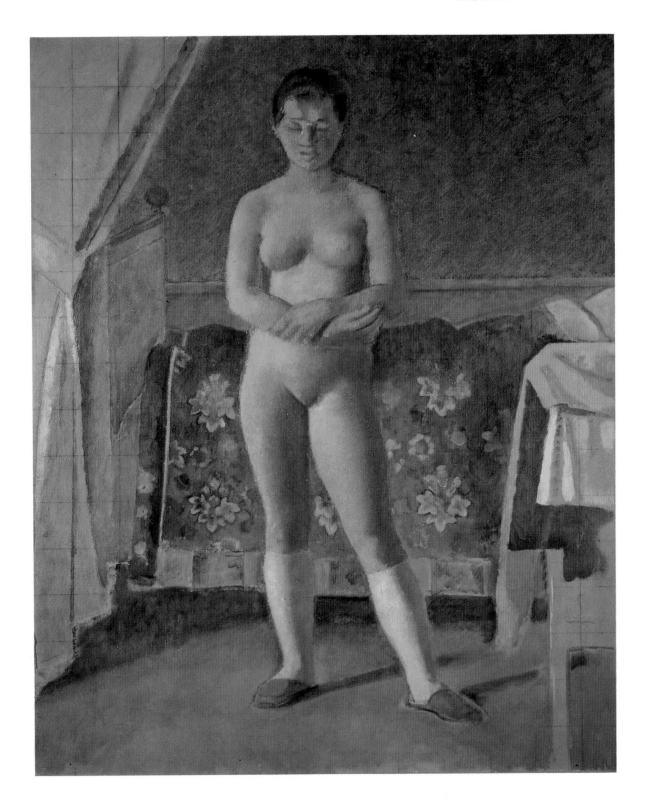

JOAN MIRÓ
Spanish 1893–1983
Peinture-objet
Signed
Executed 28 April
1936 and reworked
on the reverse in
1953
Oil on panel with
wood, wire 'whistle
brush' and
clothes-peg
18 × 11½ in.
(45.7 × 29 cm.)
Sold 29 November
1989 in London for
£473,000 ($804,100)

Opposite:
GIORGIO DE CHIRICO
Italian 1888–1978
*Arbres dans la chambre
(Equinoxe)*
Signed and dated
1926
Oil and pencil on
canvas
36¼ × 29 in.
(92 × 73.5 cm.)
Sold 29 November
1989 in London for
£528,000 ($897,600)

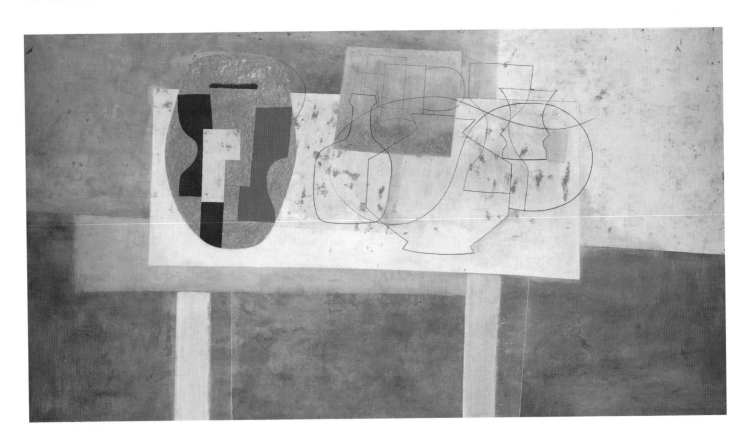

BEN NICHOLSON
British 1894–1982
Aug 56 – La Boutique fantastique
Signed and dated 56 on the reverse
Thinned oil and pencil on board
48 × 84 in. (122 × 213.5 cm.)
Sold 25 June 1990 in London for £1,210,000 ($2,069,100)
Record auction price for a work by the artist

HENRY MOORE
British 1898–1986
Working model for UNESCO *Reclining Figure*
Cast in 1957
Bronze with gold-brown and green patina over a copper *repoussé* base
57 in. (144.8 cm.) high (including base); 96 in. (243.9 cm.) wide;
52¼ in. (132.7 cm.) deep
Sold 15 May 1990 in New York for $4,070,000 (£2,422,619)
Record auction price for a work by the artist

GIORGIO MORANDI
Italian 1890–1964
Natura morta
Signed and dated 1938
Oil on canvas
16 × 21 in. (40.6 × 53.3 cm.)
Sold 16 May 1990 in New York for $1,485,000 (£883,928)
Record auction price for a work by the artist

MAX LIEBERMANN
German 1847–1935
Altmännerhaus
Signed, dated and inscribed 'M. Liebermann 82, Amsterdam'
Oil on canvas
21 × 28⅛ in. (53.5 × 71.5 cm.)
Sold 25 June 1990 in London for £484,000 ($827,640)
Record auction price for a work by the artist

PABLO PICASSO
Spanish 1881–1973
Famille de l'arlequin
Signed and dated
1905
Gouache, India ink
and collage on board
23⅞ × 17⅞ in.
(60.6 × 45.2 cm.)
Sold 14 November
1989 in New York
for $15,400,000
(£9,649,640)

Opposite:
MARC CHAGALL
Russian 1887–1985
Soldats
Signed and dated
1912
Gouache on board
15 × 12¾ in.
(38 × 32.5 cm.)
Sold 2 April 1990 in
London for
£1,430,000
($2,373,800)
Record auction price
for a gouache by the
artist

HENRI MATISSE
French 1869–1954
Lydia
Signed and dated
20 XI 35
Charcoal on paper
26½ × 18⅞ in.
(67.3 × 47.9 cm.)
Sold 15 November
1989 in New York
for $990,000
(£626,175)

PAUL KLEE
Swiss 1879–1940
Schneehühner
Signed, dated and numbered 1922/5
Pastel, gouache and pen and ink on paper
12½ × 18⅜ in. (32 × 46.5 cm.)
Sold 15 November 1989 in New York for $1,210,000 (£765,325)

TSUGUJI FOUJITA
Japanese 1886–1968
Colin-Maillard
Signed
Watercolour, pen and
black ink and gold
leaf on paper
17¼ × 13¼ in.
(43.7 × 33.7 cm.)
Sold 28 November
1989 in London for
£396,000 ($673,200)

Opposite:
PABLO PICASSO
Spanish 1881–1973
Le Faune aux pipes
Signed and dated
12.5.1957 and
dedicated 'Cannes
A.M. Pour David
Duncan'
Coloured wax
crayons on paper in
frame decorated by
Picasso with coloured
crayons
13½ × 11½ in.
(34.2 × 29.2 cm.)
with frame
Sold 3 April 1990 in
London for £41,800
($68,845)
Sold from the
collection of David
Douglas Duncan on
behalf of
AmeriCares, the
American
humanitarian
organization working
in support of
Romanian babies
suffering from AIDS

GIORGIO MORANDI
Italian 1890–1964
Self-portrait
1924
Oil on canvas
18½ × 16¼ in.
(47 × 41 cm.)
Sold 6 December
1989 in Rome for
L.1,092,500
(£530,855)

Opposite:
JEAN BRUSSELMANS
Belgian 1884–1953
*Retour du travail –
Terugkeer na het Werk*
Signed and dated
1929
Oil on canvas
45½ × 39½ in.
(115.6 × 110.2 cm.)
Sold 19 October 1989
in London for
£132,000 ($213,840)
Record auction price
for a work by the
artist

ALEKSANDRA ALEKSANDROVNA EKSTER (EXTER)
Russian 1884–1949
Paris Bridges
Initialled and dated 12
Oil on canvas
37⅜ × 60⅜ in. (95 × 153.5 cm.)
Sold 5 October 1989 in London for £330,000 ($531,300)

Opposite:
IURII PAVLOVICH ANNENKOV
1889–1974
Portrait of Aleksandr Nikolaevich Tikhonov
Signed and dated 1922
Oil, collage, glass, bell-push and 'enduit' on canvas
26⅜ × 22⅞ in. (67 × 58 cm.)
Sold 5 October 1989 in London for £110,000 ($177,100)

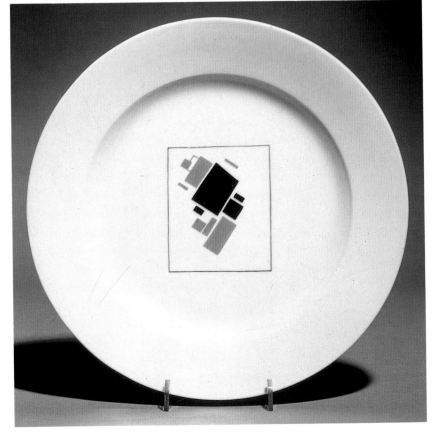

MIKHAIL FEDOROVICH LARIONOV and ALEKSEI KRUCHENYKH
Pomada
Moscow, 1913
Album incorporating collage, lithographs and hand-printed text
Sold 5 October 1989 in London for £13,750 ($22,138)
Record auction price for this album

Porcelain Soviet Suprematist plate
After a design by K. Malevich
By the Imperial Porcelain Factory (period of
Nicholas II), with later black overglaze State
Porcelain Factory mark (dated 1923 and
inscribed in Russian 'after the drawing of
Malevich')
9¾ in. (24.8 cm.) diameter
Sold 5 October 1989 in London for £44,000
($70,840)
Record auction price for a Soviet Suprematist
plate

VLADIMIR VASIL'EVICH LEBEDEV
Russian 1891–1967
Homage to Anna Akhmatova
*c.*1921
Collage of leather, wood and paper mounted
on canvas
30¼ × 13¾ in. (77 × 35 cm.)
Sold 5 October 1989 in London for £55,000
($88,550)

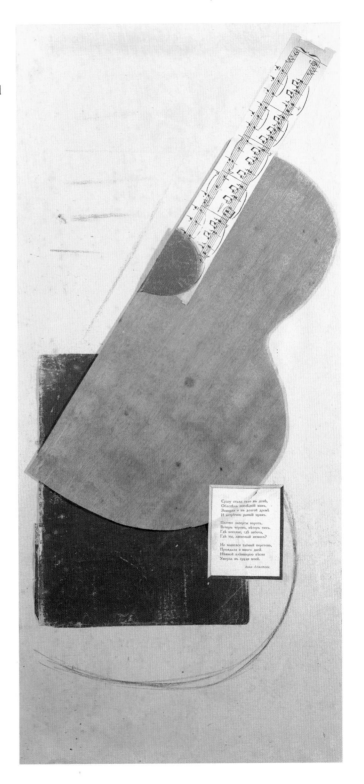

CONTEMPORARY ART SALES

Martha Baer

In 1982, the last year in which I commented on Christie's Contemporary Art sales for the *Review*, we had completed a season that had broken all market records. In 1981–2 the then record sale made $3.9 million (£2.2 million), and established record prices for more than a dozen artists.

The 1989–90 season produced sales totalling approximately $154.8 million (£96.7 million), up nearly seventy per cent from the previous year. Thirty-seven contemporary artist's records were broken at Christie's major evening sales in New York this season, and some twenty-four works sold for over $1 million on those two nights.

Underpinning this enormous growth were several developments: the rapid expansion of the number of people with considerable disposable wealth, the renewal of interest by established collectors in art which is being executed today, and the expansion of the contemporary art market-place to include Europe as well as New York.

Many young artists are reaching levels which only a few enjoyed in previous decades, in terms of prices, celebrity, and museum and collector interest. At the same time the works of established artists such as Stella and Diebenkorn, and earlier masters such as Pollock, Rothko, de Kooning and Johns, are breaking their previous records with each sale. The activity in the galleries is mirrored in the activities of the auction room and has a snowball effect.

Over the last eight years American enthusiasm for contemporary art has grown to encompass European contemporary works. This American support, added to the interest of collectors sharing the artists' nationalities, has strengthened the market in artists such as Clemente, Cucchi and Paladino in Italy, and Baselitz, Beuys and Kiefer in Germany.

As contemporary art has gained in status and international acceptance, collectors have begun a critical re-evaluation of earlier groups and schools. Thus we have seen renewed interest in Minimalism and Conceptual Art, movements which are in obvious contrast to the powerful and often violent *Angst* of some current schools.

There is one more significant result of all this momentum: rising prices bring stellar collections to the market. The present world record for a single-owner Contemporary sale was set in 1988 when the wonderful Tremaine Collection, a highly important group of pictures, fetched $25.8 million (£14.4 million). Even before that, with the Ted Ashley sale in 1986, Christie's established its outstanding record with single-owner sales. The fall 1989 season offered two distinguished and well-known collections both from Chicago. The evening portion of the Robert B. Mayer Collection made $18.4 million (£11.6 million), making it the second most valuable single-owner Contemporary sale at auction (with additional works sold in subsequent sessions). Highlights of the collection were important works by Lichtenstein, Johns, Dubuffet, Artschwager, Diebenkorn, Kelly, Frankenthaler, Stella and Segal. The sale of contemporary art from the Manilow Collection focused attention on art from the 1970s, and achieved world record prices for works by Ryman, Baselitz, Moskowitz, Penck and Schnabel.

The spring round of sales set records for a Lichtenstein, and for works by Dubuffet, Francis, Marden and Still, among others. The sales included paintings from the collection of art dealer Virginia Dwan and from the distinguished collection of USX Corporation, Pittsburgh.

Any analysis of the season must note the broad appeal and strong performance at auction of major works by Pop artist Roy Lichtenstein, an artist with an unusual history of record-breaking sales at Christie's. In 1986 *Blang*, from the Ted Ashley Collection, sold for a record $792,000 (£546,206). In 1988, the Tremaine Collection offered *I Can See the Whole Room...and There's Nobody in It!*, which made a record $2 million (£1.1 million). *Torpedo...Los!*, the Lichtenstein in the sale of the Robert B. Mayer Collection in November 1989, brought $5.5 million (£3.5 million), and in May *Kiss II* was purchased by a Japanese collector for $6 million (£3.6 million), again breaking the Lichtenstein records, all set at Christie's.

Important works by Jean Dubuffet also made strong prices this season. *Monsieur Dhotel*, from the Mayer Collection, fetched a record $2.53 million (£1.6 million) in November. This record did not last long however; in May *Pèse cheveu* sold for a very strong $5.2 million (£3 million).

As in past years, Christie's exhibition of important works was taken to Japan. For the first time, however, in recognition of strong European interest, contemporary works were taken to a central European city, Düsseldorf, in the autumn. While levels of interest from different countries do fluctuate, it is clear that the appeal of contemporary art is now global, with buyers from many countries participating in saleroom transactions.

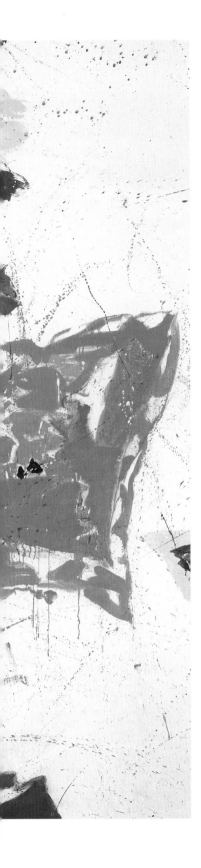

SAM FRANCIS
American b.1923
Round the World (detail)
Signed and dated '1958 to 1959
Paris'
Oil on canvas
108 × 136½ in. (274.3 × 321.3 cm.)
Sold 7 May 1990 in New York
for $1,870,000 (£1,119,760)
Record auction price for a work
by the artist

JEAN DUBUFFET
French b.1901
Pèse cheveu
Signed, inscribed and dated 62
Oil on canvas
76 × 59 in. (193 × 149 cm.)
Sold 7 May 1990 in New York
for $5,170,000 (£3,095,808)
From the Makler Family Collection
Record auction price for a work
by the artist

ROBERT RYMAN
American b.1930
Summit
Oil on linen
75½ × 72 in. (191.7 × 183 cm.)
Sold 7 November 1989 in New York for $2,310,000 (£1,462,025)
From the Manilow Collection
Record auction price for a work by the artist

ROY LICHTENSTEIN
American b.1923
Kiss II (detail)
Signed and dated '62
Oil on canvas
57⅛ × 67¾ in. (145 × 172 cm.)
Sold 7 May 1990 in New York for $6,050,000 (£3,622,754)
Record auction price for a work by the artist

THE COBRA MOVEMENT

Matthijs Erdman

The approach of 1992 and the newly gained freedom in Eastern Europe, both extra impulses for European unity, have helped to create a feeling of optimism that may have led to the success of the first sale entirely dedicated to the avant-garde Cobra Movement at Christie's Amsterdam on 22 May 1990. Cobra is a truly European movement and was founded by artists and writers mainly from Denmark, Belgium and Holland in Paris in 1948.

The name Cobra – the poisonous snake – is not only an acronym of the cities where the members lived and worked – Copenhagen, Brussels and Amsterdam – but also reflects the radical character of the group. The protagonists included great talents such as Jorn, Pedersen and Jacobsen from Denmark, Alechinsky and Dotremont from Belgium, and Appel, Constant and Corneille from the Netherlands, while the French painters Atlan and Doucet were also active in the group. They organized joint exhibitions and wrote theoretical manifestos that were published in the Cobra magazine to support their ideas for a new art in a new society. Some of these ideas were derived from Surrealism but the artists were also inspired by folk art and the artistic expressions of children and the mentally ill.

Out of the association of Cobra artists arose a distinctive Cobra style which continued to develop after 1951 when the movement was officially disbanded. A striking aspect of this vocabulary is the imaginary creatures that wander in the night, staring at us with penetrating eyes. 'A painting is not a construction of colours and lines, but an animal, a night, a cry, a person or all those at once,' wrote Constant in 1948 in the Dutch experimental magazine *Reflex*. This language of images has had a lasting effect on the later works of the majority of the artists involved, and indeed on European post-war art in general.

Alechinsky and Constant were particularly well represented in the sale, which consisted of 216 lots. Alechinsky's large *Les Grands Transparents* from 1958 sold for D.fl.862,500 (£273,202) to a member of the New York trade. Two early pictures by Constant, *Figures at Night* and *Two Birds*, from 1949, sold to the French actor Alain Delon for D.fl.345,000 (£109,280) and D.fl.644,000 (£203,991) respectively, the latter a world auction record for a work by the artist.

The sale was dotted with typically bright and bold works by Karel Appel, whose appeal continues to expand. His large wildly painted canvas *The Smiling Grasshopper*, 1960, sold on behalf of the St. Louis Museum of Art for D.fl.345,000 (£109,280).

CONSTANT
Dutch b.1920
Two Birds
Signed 'Constant '49'
Oil on canvas
31⅞ × 24⅝ in.
(81 × 62.5 cm.)
Sold 22 May 1990 in
Amsterdam for
D.fl.644,000
(£203,991)
Record auction price
for a work by the
artist

New records were also established for Lucebert (D.fl.195,500, £61,925), Anton Rooskens (D.fl.172,500, £54,640) and Eugene Brands (D.fl.161,000, £50,997). The buyers were assembled in two packed connected salerooms, and they reflected the international character of the sale. From the USA to Japan and from Denmark to France people had come to Amsterdam to witness the event.

Although works by Cobra artists are sold all around the world, this sale, which totalled D.fl.10,290,200 (£3,382,203), confirmed that Amsterdam is a vital and probably the most important market-place for this movement. The decision to bring together so many Cobra works showed clearly the enormous appeal Cobra has for a wide audience and gave an extra stimulus to an already strong market.

PIERRE ALECHINSKY
Belgian b.1927
Les Grands Transparents
Signed and dated
'Alechinsky VIII 58'
Oil on canvas
78¾ × 118¼ in.
(200 × 300 cm.)
Sold 22 May 1990 in Amsterdam for
D.fl.862,500
(£273,202)

KAREL APPEL
Dutch b.1921
Smiling Grasshopper
Signed and dated
'Appel 1960'
76¾ × 51¼ in.
(194.9 × 130.2 cm.)
Sold 22 May 1990 in
Amsterdam for
D.fl.345,000
(£109,280)
From the property of
the St. Louis
Museum of Art

HANS HARTUNG
German 1904–89
T–47–47
Oil on canvas
38 × 51 in. (97 × 129.5 cm.)
Sold 5 April 1990 in London for £330,000 ($561,000)

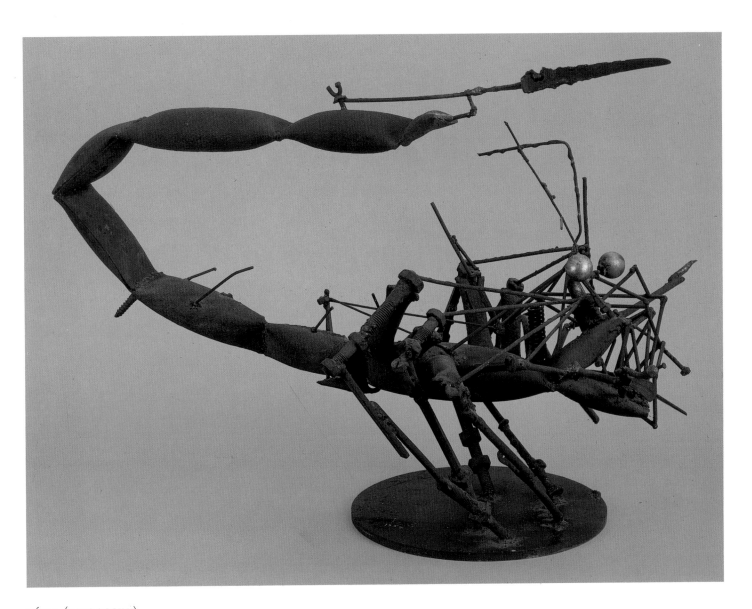

CÉSAR (BALDACCINI)
French b.1921
Le Scorpion
Signed and dated 1954
Welded iron
18½ × 25¼ in. (47 × 64 cm.)
Sold 28 June 1990 in London for £120,000 ($207,240)
Record auction price for a work by the artist

SERGE POLIAKOFF
French 1906–69
Composition abstraite
Signed
Oil on canvas
38⅛ × 51⅛ in. (97 × 130 cm.)
Sold 30 November 1989 in London for £462,000 ($725,340)

ERNEST WILHELM NAY
German 1902–68
Feuerklang
Signed and dated 59
Oil on canvas
39⅜ × 31½ in.
(100 × 80 cm.)
Sold 28 June 1990 in
London for £242,000
($417,934)
Record auction price
for a work by the
artist

ANTONI TÀPIES
Spanish b.1923
Porte grise sur fond noir
Signed and dated 1961
Oil and composition on canvas
32 × 39⅜ in. (81.4 × 100 cm.)
Sold 30 November 1989 in London for £506,000 ($794,420)

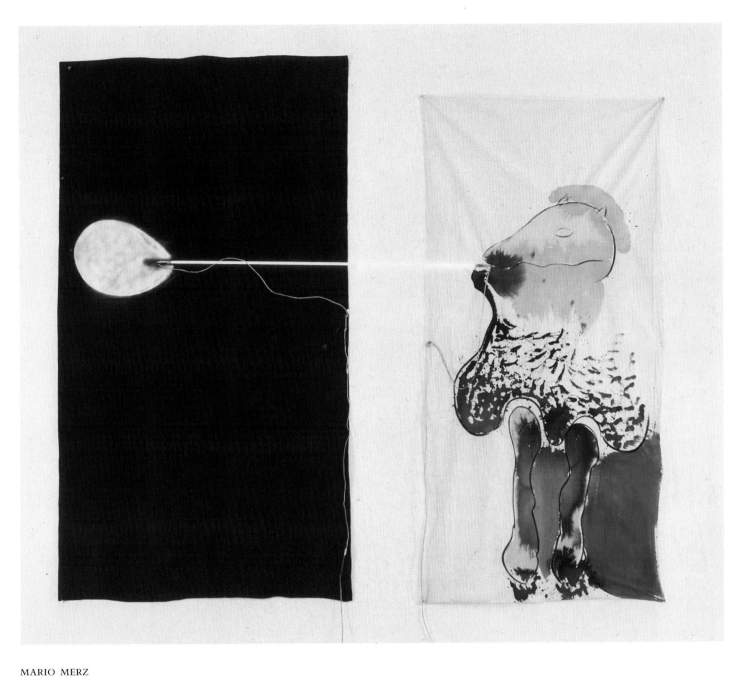

MARIO MERZ
Italian b.1925
Seifenblasende Kuh
Mixed media on canvas and neon light
104 × 118 in. (260 × 295 cm.)
Sold 5 April 1990 in London for £99,000 ($168,300)
Record auction price for a work by the artist

AFRO
Italian 1912–76
Figura, 1962
Oil on canvas
27½ × 39½ in. (70 × 100 cm.)
Sold 9 April 1990 in Rome for L.345,000,000 (£169,117)

Opposite:
JEAN DUBUFFET
French b. 1901
Bateau au fond jaune
Signed and dated 64
Oil on canvas
57½ × 44⅞ in. (146 × 114 cm.)
Sold 5 April 1990 in London for £1,210,000 ($2,057,000)

SIR WILLIAM ORPEN,
RHA, RA
Irish 1878–1931
Mrs St. George
Signed
1906
Oil on canvas
85 × 47 in.
(221 × 120 cm.)
Sold 7 June 1990 in
London for £220,000
($368,720)
From the property of
K.J. and J.C. Rowe

Opposite:
JOHN DUNCAN
FERGUSSON, RBA
Scottish 1874–1961
La Cocarde
Signed and inscribed
on the reverse
*c.*1910
Oil on board
26 × 22½ in.
(66 × 57 cm.)
Sold 7 December
1989 in Glasgow for
£352,000 ($551,584)
Record auction price
for a work by the
artist

LAURENCE STEPHEN LOWRY, RA
British 1887–1976
Bourton-on-the-Water
Signed and dated 1957
Oil on canvas
18 × 24 in. (45.7 × 61 cm.)
Sold 9 March 1990 in London for £104,500 ($177,650)
Record auction price for a work by the artist

CAREL WEIGHT, RA
British b.1908
Sunday-go-to-Meeting
1948
Oil on canvas
29½ × 24½ in.
(75 × 62 cm.)
Sold 8 June 1990 in
London for £31,900
($53,528)
Record auction price
for a work by the
artist

STANLEY SPENCER, 'THE RESURRECTION: WAKING UP'

Keith Bell

The recent extraordinary prices being paid at auction for the paintings of Stanley Spencer are a welcome indication that the often ambivalent relationship which collectors, critics and historians have had with Spencer's work is at last beginning to develop into a clearer recognition of his outstanding abilities as an artist. It is particularly appropriate that one of the paintings, *The Resurrection: Waking Up*, sold at Christie's on 9 March 1990, played an important part in rehabilitating Spencer's public reputation after a long period during which he was estranged from the Royal Academy and made the object of considerable critical hostility. The painting is part of a series, *The Resurrection, Port Glasgow*, which Spencer began to paint while he was in Glasgow as a war artist. The series was conceived in the artist's spare time while he was working on the *Shipbuilding on the Clyde* paintings (Imperial War Museum) for the War Artists Advisory Committee.

It is clear that Spencer had been thinking about a new series of religious paintings for some time. On 6 May 1943 he wrote to inform his dealer Dudley Tooth that he had spent several days attempting to develop these ideas, which he had 'had for several years', and which he now tried to draw out onto canvas. This early attempt was 'not right', but he was still working on the scheme when he wrote to Tooth two weeks later. During the next few months Spencer continued to develop the scheme, which now evolved from the rather general concept of a religious subject into the more specific one of a 'Resurrection' situated in Port Glasgow. The catalyst for this change was Spencer's well-known discovery of a hilltop cemetery one evening while he was out for a walk from Glencairn, his Glasgow lodging home. He later reported to his ex-wife Hilda that he 'went along a road until with the Clyde away below, gleaming in the last rays of later daylight', he saw 'stone bibles and large winged angels above the hedge'. The cemetery consisted of a spiral path which ascended the hill, with well-kept graves on either side, each decorated with a glass case filled with wax flowers. It was, Spencer reported, as if 'the dead were whiling away their time blowing out bubbles of glass'. The hilltop itself reminded him of the Hill of Zion, a scene which was later incorporated into the *Resurrection* series.

Spencer found the cemetery a place of wonderful ease and fulfilment. There were parallels for this in his earlier Resurrection paintings, notably the Tate Gallery's *Resurrection, Cookham* of 1927. The cemetery was, he told Hilda, a place where 'a man could put flowers on a girl's grave and not be accused of ruder advances'. This experience of the site, and the mystical way in which he had discovered the hill in the half-light of a northern late-summer's evening, provided Spencer with the stimulation that he needed to reconsider the stalled religious series. As Spencer explained on numerous occasions, his ideas for paintings required places with intimate personal associations (among these he listed Cookham and Macedonia), together with an approximate period of time, preferably several years, in which to absorb them properly into his imagination. By the summer of 1943, sufficient time had elapsed since his first visit to Port Glasgow for him to feel at home in the city. And with the discovery of the Port Glasgow cemetery, he had found a place through which his feelings for the area could be suitably expressed, in the same way that the churchyard in the village of Cookham had formed the spiritual home for his recollections of childhood and adolescence.

Spencer's initial plan for the *Resurrection* was for a painting three or more feet high and roughly fifty feet long. This was in keeping with his painting practice of the late 1930s, and closely resembled his early plans for the *Shipbuilding* series which he was working on concurrently in Port Glasgow. As in that series, however, Spencer was compelled, for both logistical and market reasons, to break down the single picture into a series of smaller works. Only the Tate Gallery's, *Resurrection, Port Glasgow* retained something of the artist's original concept of scale, although the painting is still much shorter than the earlier design. Not for the first time Spencer was compelled to fragment his original ground scheme, and to compromise by producing works which were autonomous to the extent that they could be both exhibited and sold separately.

Ever since he had painted the murals in the Sandham Memorial Chapel at Burghclere in the 1920s, Spencer had planned his figurative paintings as related series which were to hang together, preferably in a building of his own design. In the case of the Glasgow *Resurrection* series, the paintings were only brought together briefly at the Royal Academy Summer Exhibition in 1950, before being sold to a variety of different galleries or private owners. Long before this, however, Spencer must have abandoned any real hope that the paintings would be permanently displayed together, for there were numerous divergences in the size of the canvases, which would have made continuity of hanging impossible.

These difficulties were further compounded by the frequently controversial subject-matter to be found in his figure paintings. Since the early 1930s, Spencer's evolving philosophy on religion and sexuality had often meant that his pictures received a hostile reception from critics, buyers and public institutions. This sharp decline in the artist's popularity culminated in the rejection of two of his paintings, *St. Francis and the Birds* and *The Dustman or The Lovers*, from the 1935 Royal Academy Summer Exhibition, prompting his indignant resignation in protest. Subsequently, Spencer's dealer Dudley Tooth had found it increasingly problematic to sell what he termed the 'difficult' figure paintings, and he encouraged Spencer to concentrate instead on the popular and relatively high-priced landscape works. Spencer, who was in serious financial difficulties at the time, had little choice but to comply, although he continued to paint some figurative pictures in his spare time.

When Spencer told Dudley Tooth about his plans for the Glasgow *Resurrection* paintings, his dealer's response was, not unnaturally, extremely cautious. 'Unless you eliminate the elements which people object to', Tooth wrote, 'I can see little hope of the picture or pictures helping you to reduce your debts.' He went on to ask to 'see the compositions' before Spencer started to paint, and remarked that if the artist could see his way to avoiding the more controversial elements of his earlier paintings, he would 'rather have them than landscapes'. Tooth concluded on a positive note by encouraging Spencer 'to do what your inner feelings dictate'.

Spencer was fully aware that some of his figurative paintings 'put people off', as he admitted grudgingly to Tooth. But he went on to declare that he could 'give no guarantee…that I could or would do a figurative picture that would meet with the kind of approval…that was accorded to my early religious paintings'. However, the kind of extreme sexual imagery which characterized Spencer's earlier paintings of the 1930s no longer seemed so important to him by the end of that decade. This change had first been signalled by the *Christ in the Wilderness* series, whose more traditional imagery suggested a return to the less controversial paintings of Spencer's earlier career in the 1920s. Now, in the *Resurrection* series, Spencer returned to the calm relaxed atmosphere of his earlier pictures, with the figures emerging from their tombs as if preparing for an ordinary day. As he informed Tooth, 'the main trend is towards expressing the fulfilment and realisation of this present lives (*sic*) hopes and wishes. This causes the joy expressed at the Resurrection to be something felt and shared between the resurrecting people and shown in their meeting again.'

The painting in the Christie's sale of 9 March 1990, *The Resurrection: Waking Up*, was the first of the series to be completed. In an undated letter written in late 1944, Spencer reported to Tooth that he had completed the central and left-hand panels of the triptych. The letter also contains an interesting indication of the artist's working methods: Spencer explained that he needed reproductions of his landscape and flower paintings, so that they could be used as sources for the plant-life in his new picture. Despite their absence, however, he was able to include 'primroses, ivy that creeps about among the grass, violets, and convolvulus, and daisies'.

STANLEY SPENCER, RA
British 1891–1959
The Resurrection:
Waking Up
1945
Oil on canvas
Triptych: centre
panel 30 × 20 in.
(76 × 51 cm.),
side panels each
20 × 30 in.
(51 × 76 cm.)
Sold 9 March 1990 in
London for £770,000
($1,309,000)
From the property of
the Nevill Family

The painting represents the moment when the dead emerge from their graves amongst their friends and relatives who have come to visit the cemetery. This event, as the title suggests, is seen as being no more dramatic than the act of waking up on a normal day. There is no question of division between the good and the bad, and the atmosphere is a purely domestic one – a condition which Spencer loved. The ordinariness of the transition from one state of being into another is emphasized by the gardener in the centre of the painting, who is collecting leaves with his wooden boards, apparently oblivious to the momentous happenings going on around him. The event is, however, witnessed by the couple seated on the park bench, the man holding a bunch of roses as if intending to replenish a vase on one of the graves. The couple is in fact Stanley and Hilda Spencer, accompanied by one of their daughters, possibly Shirin. Spencer frequently included himself as well as members of his family and friends in his paintings in order to emphasize their personal and very domestic atmosphere.

The *Resurrection* paintings were first exhibited at the Royal Academy in the summer of 1950, Spencer and Dudley Tooth having earlier agreed to delay the showing of the series until the works could all be seen together. The exhibition also marked Spencer's return to membership of the Academy, from which he had resigned with such acrimony fifteen years before. While critical reaction was mixed (there were objections to perceived weaknesses in colour and design), the *Resurrection* series was generally well received, with the largest painting, *The Resurrection, Port Glasgow*, being purchased by the Tate Gallery for £2,000 . With the parallel success of his wartime *Shipbuilding on the Clyde* series (Imperial War Museum), Spencer's reputation was once again re-established outside the small group of friends, collectors, and, of course, his dealer Dudley Tooth, who had supported him during the period of diminished public reputation during the 1930s.

SIR ALFRED MUNNINGS, PRA
British 1878–1959
The Coming Storm
Signed
1910
Oil on canvas
40 × 50 in. (102 × 127 cm.)
Sold 8 November 1989 in London for £352,000 ($563,200)

SIR WINSTON SPENCER CHURCHILL, OM, HON. RA
British 1874–1965
Seascape near Antibes
Signed
*c.*1920
Oil on canvas
19 × 23½ in. (48 × 57 cm.)
Sold 8 March 1990 in London for £31,900 ($52,316)

SIR HERBERT JAMES GUNN, RA
British 1893–1964
Fishing Boats, Antibes
Signed and inscribed
Oil on canvas
13¾ × 17¾ in. (34 × 44.5 cm.)
Sold 7 June 1990 in London for £40,700 ($68,213)
Record auction price for a work by the artist

GLUCK
British 1895–1978
Medallion
Signed
1936
Oil on canvas
11½ × 13½ in.
(29 × 34 cm.)
Sold 9 November
1989 in London for
£63,800 ($102,080)
Record auction price
for a work by the
artist

Opposite:
GWEN JOHN
British 1876–1939
The Seated Woman
Painted between 1919
and 1926
Oil on canvas
10½ × 8½ in.
(27 × 22 cm.)
Sold 9 March 1990 in
London for £181,500
($308,550)
Record auction price
for a work by the
artist

DAME BARBARA HEPWORTH
British 1903–75
Mylor
1962–3
Slate
33½ in. (85 cm.) high
Sold 10 November 1989 in London for
£60,500 ($98,010)

HENRI GAUDIER–BRZESKA
French 1891–1915
Crouching Fawn
Conceived in 1913, cast between 1918 and
1924
Bronze
9 in. (22 cm.) high
Sold 10 November 1989 in London for
£20,900 ($33,231)
Record auction price for a bronze by the artist

DIEGO RIVERA
Mexican 1886–1957
Juanita Sentada
Signed and dated
1935
Tempera on masonite
31½ × 23½ in.
(80 × 59.5 cm.)
Sold 1 May 1990 in
New York for
$352,000 (£214,634)
From the property of
the St. Louis Art
Museum

Opposite:
DAVID ALFARO SIQUEIROS
Mexican 1896–1974
Niña Madre
Signed and dated
1936
Encaustic on panel
30⅛ × 24 in.
(76.5 × 61 cm.)
Sold 21 November
1989 in New York
for $363,000
(£229,746)
From the property of
the Santa Barbara
Museum of Art
Record auction price
for a work by the
artist

MATTA
Chilean b.1911
Sin Título
Signed
c.1938–9
Oil on canvas
28 × 36 in.
(71 × 91.4 cm.)
Sold 1 May 1990 in
New York for
$660,000 (£402,439)

JUAN O'GORMAN
Mexican 1905–82
Los Mitos Paganos
Signed and dated
1947
Tempera on panel
43 × 49 in.
(108 × 122 cm.)
Sold 21 November
1989 in New York
for $550,000
(£343,101)
Record auction price
for a work by the
artist

REMEDIOS VARO
Spanish 1900–63
Hacia La Torre
Signed
1961
Oil on masonite
48½ × 39⅜ in.
(123 × 100 cm.)
Sold 1 May 1990 in
New York for
$825,000 (£503,048)
Record auction price
for a work by the
artist

DRAWINGS, WATERCOLOURS AND PRINTS

GERRIT BATTEM
Dutch c.1636–84
A Wooded River Landscape with Woodcutters on the Bank and Drovers Crossing a Bridge
Bodycolour
11 × 16¾ in. (27.7 × 42.6 cm.)
Sold 21 November 1989 in Amsterdam for
D.fl.270,250 (£83,462)

AGOSTINO CARRACCI
Italian 1557–1602
Cupid Fighting a Satyr
(recto); *The Head of a
Monk* (verso)
Black and white
chalk on blue paper
13½ × 10 in.
(34.5 × 25.5 cm.)
Sold 4 July 1990 in
London for £93,500
($164,467)

A study for a fresco
on a chimney in
Palazzo Magnani,
Bologna, dating from
the early 1590s. The
use of black and
white chalk on blue
paper is relatively
unusual in Bolognese
drawings of the
period, and suggests
that Agostino had
seen studies by
Veronese and
Tintoretto on his
visits to Venice in the
1580s.

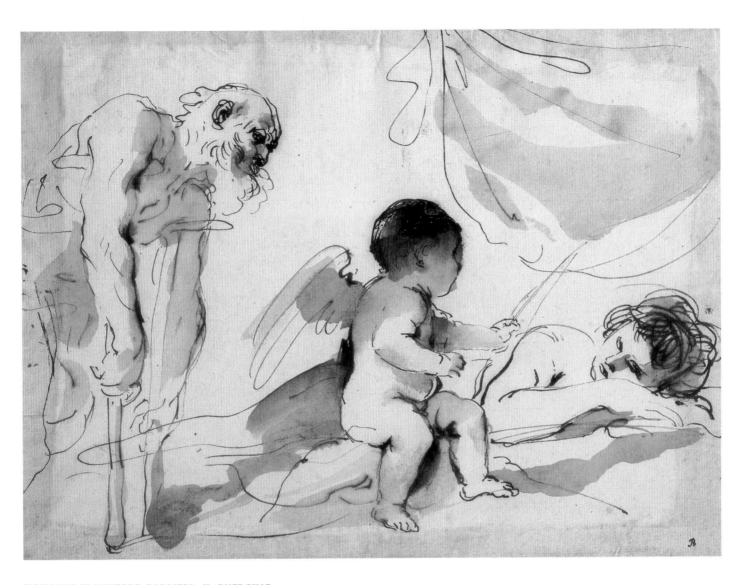

GIOVANNI FRANCESCO BARBIERI, IL GUERCINO
Italian 1591–1666
A Man on Crutches, Cupid and the Sleeping Venus
Black chalk, pen and brown ink, brown wash, watermark
encircled bird
7½ × 10¼ in. (19.3 × 26.1 cm.)
Sold 4 July 1990 in London for £104,500 ($183,816)

The vibrant penwork overlaid with wash is typical of drawings of
Guercino's period in Rome, 1621–3.

JEAN–LUBIN VAUZELLE
French 1776–?
A View of the Tuileries from the Champs-Elysées
Signed 'vauzelle ft'
Black chalk, pen
and brown ink, watercolour
10 × 14 in. (25.3 × 35.5 cm.)
Sold 5 December 1989 in
London for £22,000 ($34,298)

One of only two recorded pupils of Hubert Robert, Jean–Lubin Vauzelle specialized in picturesque views of France, Spain and Italy. He exhibited regularly at the Salon between 1799 and 1837. This view of the Palais des Tuileries, seen from the Champs-Elysées, shows the Place de la Concorde as it looked before the obelisk was erected.

LOUIS DE BOULLOGNE
French 1654–1733
Apollo and Daphne
Black chalk, pen and grey ink, grey wash heightened with white on blue paper
10 × 12¾ in. (25.8 × 33 cm.)
Sold 10 January 1990 in New York for $33,000 (£19,880)

Louis de Boullogne came from a family of artists. One of the most successful painters of his generation, he was appointed *Premier Peintre du Roi* in 1725. He treated the subject of Apollo and Daphne on a number of occasions.

JEAN–BAPTISTE GREUZE
French 1725–1805
*The Head of a Boy, in
Profile to the Left*
Red chalk
13¾ × 12 in.
(34.7 × 30.2 cm.)
Sold 4 July 1990 in
London for £49,500
($87,071)

JEAN–AUGUSTE–DOMINIQUE
INGRES
French 1780–1867
*Portrait of Gabriel
Foureau de Beauregard,
aged two*
Signed, inscribed and
dated 'Gabriellino
Foureau.', 'Ingres
fecit/flor. 1821'
Pencil
8½ × 6¼ in.
(21.3 × 16 cm.)
Sold 3 July 1990 in
London for £143,000
($251,537)

A portrait of the son
of Louis Foureau de
Beauregard,
Napoleon's physician,
who had left France
after Waterloo, and
settled in Florence.
This drawing was
probably given to
him by Ingres, in
gratitude for his
treatment of the fever
that had affected the
artist on his arrival in
Florence in 1821.

FRANCISCO JOSE DE
GOYA Y LUCIENTES
Spanish 1746–1828
La Bouillie
Black lead, brush and
black and grey wash,
fragmentary
watermark
8⅞ × 5¾ in.
(22.6 × 14.6 cm.)
Sold 10 January 1990
in New York for
$715,000 (£430,722)
Record auction price
for a drawing by the
artist

This title refers to the
soup given to the
poor by the
monasteries and
religious institutions.
The drawing may
date from 1811,
when Madrid was
gripped by famine.

JACOB CATS
Dutch 1741–99
A View of the Singel with Workmen at the Leidseveer
Inscribed 'SCHILDER' and 'ALLE SOORTEN WITW...'
Black chalk, brown wash, grey ink framing lines, watermark LC
11¼ × 15¼ in. (28.3 × 38.5 cm.)
Sold 20 November 1989 in Amsterdam for D.fl.146,000 (£14,206)
From the Leonhardt Collection

FERDINAND BOL
Dutch 1616–80
A Kneeling Woman in an Attitude of Surprise:
Study for an Annunciation
Black chalk, pen and brown ink, brown
wash, brown ink framing lines
7⅜ × 4½ in. (18.7 × 11.4 cm.)
Sold 31 May 1990 in New York for $60,500
(£36,011)
From the Norbert
L. H. Roesler Collection

Opposite:
ABRAHAM STORCK
Dutch *c*.1635–*c*.1710
The Frigate 'Piet en Paul' in Three Different
Positions on the IJ
Inscribed 'PIET EN' (recto) and 'PIET EN PAUL' (in
reverse, recto), and '.t 1712' (verso)
Pen and brown ink, grey and brown wash,
brown ink framing lines
16 × 22 in. (40.4 × 55.7 cm.)
Sold 20 November 1989 in Amsterdam for
D.fl.264,500 (£81,686)
From the Leonhardt Collection

Tsar Peter the Great came to Amsterdam in
1697, travelling incognito under the name of
Pieter Michaeloff. The Tsar worked in the
Dutch East India shipyards for several
months, and helped to construct the frigate
Piet en Paul. This drawing shows the Tsar
standing in the boat on the right, admiring
the frigate on the River IJ after the launch in
November 1697.

JOHANN ROTTENHAMMER
Dutch 1564–1625
Diana and Actaeon
Signed, dated and inscribed
'HR[monogram]ottenhamar/1595
Roma' and 'ACTAEON'
Red and black chalk
7⅛ × 8⅞ in. (18.1 × 22.6 cm.)
Sold 31 May 1990 in New York for $104,500 (£62,202)
From the Norbert L. H. Roesler Collection

Opposite:
HANS HOFFMANN
German *c*.1530–91/2
Two Squirrels, One Eating a Hazelnut
With Dürer monogram and date 1512
Black chalk, watercolour and bodycolour on vellum
10¼ × 10 in. (26 × 25.1 cm.)
Sold 3 July 1990 in London for £528,000 ($928,752)
Record auction price for a work by the artist
This drawing, long considered a work by Dürer, was
previously sold at Christie's on 12 June 1854 for 14 gns.

THOMAS GAINSBOROUGH, RA
British 1727–88
A Wooded Landscape with Travellers
Black chalk and stump, watercolour and oil paint on reddish-brown
paper, varnished
8⅜ × 11⅞ in. (20.4 × 30.2 cm.)
Sold 14 November 1989 in London for £59,400 ($95,040)

THOMAS ROWLANDSON
British 1756–1827
Old Smithfield Market
Pencil, pen and ink and watercolour
11¼ × 18½ in. (28.1 × 47 cm.)
Sold 10 July 1990 in London for £40,700 ($73,219)

JOHN LINNELL
British 1729–96
Design for a Chimneypiece
Inscribed and dated July 22 1754
Pen and grey ink, grey, blue and ochre wash
6¾ × 4⅜ in. (17.2 × 11.4 cm.)
Sold 19 December 1989 in London for £11,000 ($17,578)

EDWARD LEAR
British 1812–88
Figures on a Road near Galle, Ceylon
Signed with monogram, inscribed and dated Decbr. 1874
and 1876
Watercolour heightened with white
16 × 10⅜ in. (40.6 × 26.6 cm.)
Sold 20 March 1990 in London for £14,300 ($23,309)

JOHN MARTIN
British 1789–1854
The Thames near Richmond
Pencil and watercolour
11 × 27⅝ in. (27.9 × 69.9 cm.)
Sold 10 July 1990 in London for £41,800 ($75,198)

MYLES BIRKET FOSTER
British 1825–99
The Church of Santa Maria del Rosario or of the Gesuati, Venice
Signed with monogram
Pencil and watercolour heightened with white
8¼ × 12 in. (20.9 × 30.5 cm.)
Sold 31 October 1989 in London for £29,700 ($47,223)

WILLIAM RICHARD
LETHABY
British 1857–1931
*A Design for an
Interior in the Arts and
Crafts Style*
Pencil, pen and
brown ink,
watercolour and
coloured chalks
heightened with
white
13½ × 25⅝ in.
(34.3 × 64.8 cm.)
Sold 19 December
1989 in London for
£6,600 ($10,692)

GEORGE VICAT COLE, RA
British 1833–93
*Harvest Time near
Holmbury Hill, Surrey*
Signed and dated
1865
Watercolour
heightened with
white and gum arabic
19½ × 28½ in.
(49.5 × 72.4 cm.)
Sold 19 December
1989 in London for
£16,500 ($26,730)

ARCHIBALD THORBURN
British 1860–1935
Pheasants
Signed and dated
1922
Watercolour
14½ × 10½ in.
(36.8 × 26.7 cm.)
Sold 2 March 1990 in
London for £18,700
($31,229)

ARCHIBALD THORBURN
British 1860–1935
*The Close of Season:
Grouse on a Moor*
Signed, inscribed and
dated 1918
Watercolour
heightened with
white, on grey paper
14½ × 21⅝ in.
(36.8 × 54.7 cm.)
Sold 2 March 1990 in
London for £41,800
($69,806)
Joint record auction
price for a work by
the artist

JEAN FRANÇOIS MILLET
French 1814–75
Bucheron préparant des fagots
Signed
Pastel
19¼ × 13½ in.
(49 × 34 cm.)
Sold 25 October 1989
in New York for
$825,000 (£515,625)
Record auction price
for a pastel by the
artist

PAUL CÉSAR HELLEU
French 1859–1927
Portrait of Annette
Signed and inscribed
Pastel on canvas
25½ × 20½ in.
(64.8 × 52.1 cm.)
Sold 22 June 1990 in
London for £57,200
($97,698)

The sitter was Lord
Duveen's niece,
Mrs Miles Bingham

After HIERONYMOUS BOSCH
Flemish *c.*1450–1516
Die Blau Schuyte
(Hollstein 20)
*c.*1559
Engraving, first state (of two), a very fine impression of this rare print
P.8⅞ × 11⅝ in. (22.6 × 29.5 cm.)
Sold 28 June 1990 in London for £28,600 ($49,392)

Below, far left:
ALBRECHT DÜRER
German 1471–1528
The Martyrdom of St. Catherine (Bartsch 120)
1498
Woodcut, a very fine Meder a-b impression
L.15¼ × 10 in. (38.8 × 25.4 cm.)
Sold 28 June 1990 in London for £44,000 ($75,988)

Left:
JACQUES BELLANGE
French 1594–1638
Les Trois Maries au tombeau (Walch 46)
*c.*1630
Etching, second (final) state, a very fine impression
P.17¹³⁄₁₆ × 11⁹⁄₁₆ in. (45.2 × 29.3 cm.)
Sold 28 June 1990 in London for £49,500 ($85,487)

HENDRICK GOLTZIUS
Flemish 1558–1617
A Landscape with a Group of Trees, a Shepherd and Shepherdess
(Bartsch 243), *c*.1600
Chiaroscuro woodcut, a fine impression
L.4⅜ × 5¹¹⁄₁₆ in. (11.1 × 14.5 cm.)
Sold 28 June 1990 in London for £37,400 ($64,590)

Below right:
REMBRANDT HARMENSZ. VAN RIJN
Dutch 1606–69
A Young Man in a Velvet Cap
(Bartsch 268), 1637
Etching with touches of drypoint, second (final) state, an excellent impression
P.3¾ × 3¼ in. (9.6 × 8.3 cm.)
Sold 28 November 1989 in London for £52,800 ($82,896)

Far right:
REMBRANDT HARMENSZ. VAN RIJN
Dutch 1606–69
Diana at the Bath
(Bartsch 201), *c*.1631
Etching, a fine and early impression
P.7 × 6¼ in. (17.8 × 15.9 cm.)
Sold 28 June 1990 in London for £15,400 ($26,596)

EDVARD MUNCH
Norwegian
1863–1944
Madonna – Liebendes Weib
(Schiefler 33Ab2)
Signed in pencil
1896–1902
Lithograph with woodcut printed in colours, a very fine, early impression, on thin Japan
L.23¾ × 17½ in.
(60.4 × 44.5 cm.)
Sold 15 May 1990 in New York for $616,000 (£371,017)
Record auction price for a print by the artist

Opposite:
EMIL NOLDE
German 1867–1956
Junges Paar
(Schiefler, Mosel L52)
Signed, titled and inscribed in pencil
1913
Lithograph printed in colours, a very fine impression, on Japan
L.24⅛ × 19⅝ in.
(61.3 × 49.9 cm.)
Sold 29 June 1990 in London for £132,000 ($227,964)
Record auction price for a print by the artist

ERICH HECKEL
German 1883–1970
Männer und Frauen (Dube 192)
Signed and inscribed in pencil
1910
Woodcut printed in black and deep green, a fine,
richly-inked impression
L.10⅜ × 14⅞ in. (26.3 × 37.8 cm.)
Sold 29 June 1990 in London for £82,500 ($142,478)

JAMES ABBOTT MCNEILL
WHISTLER
American 1834–1903
Portrait of Whistler
(Kennedy 54)
1859
Drypoint, first state
(of two), a very fine
impression
P.8⅞ × 5⅞ in.
(22.6 × 15 cm.)
Sold 18 January 1990
in New York for
$52,800 (£32,124)

EDGAR DEGAS
French 1834–1917
La Sortie du bain (Reed and Shapiro 66)
1891–2
Lithograph, fifth (final) state, a strong impression
L.11¹³⁄₁₆ × 12³⁄₁₆ in. (30 × 31 cm.)
Sold 15 May 1990 in New York for $79,200 (£49,958)

CHARLES MERYON
French 1821–1868
Le Ministère de la marine, Paris (Detteil 45)
Dated 18 Fev. 65 in pen and brown ink
Etching with drypoint, second state (of six), an extremely
fine, delicate impression
P.6½ × 5¾ in. (16.5 × 14.5 cm.)
Sold 29 November 1989 in London for £33,000 ($51,810)
Record auction price for a print by the artist

GEORGES ROUAULT
French 1871–1958
Cirque de l'étoile filante
(Chapon and Rouault 240–258)
1934–5
Aquatints printed in colours,
title, text and set of 17 plates,
from the edition of 200, in
portfolio
Overall S.19$\frac{1}{16}$ × 15$\frac{1}{8}$ in.
(48.5 × 38.5 cm.)
Sold 29 June 1990 in London
for £77,000 ($132,979)

EDOUARD VUILLARD
French 1886–1940
La Cuisinière (Roger–Marx 42), 1899
Lithograph, a fine impression, from the edition of 100 on *Chine volant*
L.14 × 10$\frac{7}{8}$ in. (35.6 × 27.7 cm.)
Sold 29 November 1989 in London for £37,400 ($58,718)
Record auction price for a print by the artist

PABLO PICASSO
Spanish 1881–1973
La Suite des saltimbanques
(Bloch 1–15)
1905
Etchings with drypoint, the rare and complete set of 15 plates, from the edition of 29 after steelfacing on Japan
P.18⅛ × 14⅞ in. (46.1 × 37.7 cm.) and smaller
Sold 29 November 1989 in London for £605,000 ($949,850)

Opposite:
PABLO PICASSO
Spanish 1881–1973
Nature morte sous la lampe (Bloch 1102)
Signed in pencil, numbered 27/50
1962
Linocut printed in colours
L.25¼ × 20⅞ in. (64 × 53 cm.)
Sold 29 June 1990 in London for £176,000 ($303,952)

ROY LICHTENSTEIN and others
American b.1923
Hommage à Picasso
1973
Lithographs, silkscreens, etchings and aquatints, most printed in colours, text and set of 60 plates, from the total edition of 120, in portfolio
Sold 28 November 1989 in London for £55,000 ($86,350)

Opposite:
PABLO PICASSO
Spanish 1881–1973
Buste de femme au chapeau (Bloch 1072)
Signed in pencil, numbered 30/50
1962
Linocut printed in colours
L.24⅞ × 20¹⁵⁄₁₆ in. (63.1 × 53.2 cm.)
Sold 29 June 1990 in London for £198,000 ($341,946)

SUSAN ROTHENBERG
American b.1945
Untitled (Maxwell 1)
Signed in pencil, numbered 13/18
1977
Lithograph printed in colours with extensive hand colouring
S.11⅞ × 15½ in. (30.2 × 39.4 cm.)
Sold 21 November 1989 in New York for $46,200 (£29,247)

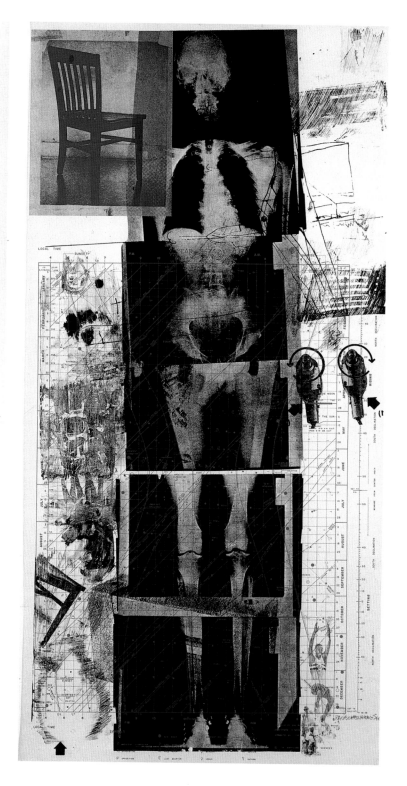

LOUISE BOURGEOIS
American b.1911
He Disappeared into Complete Silence
(Wye, pls. 29–37)
Signed and inscribed in pencil
1947
Set of nine engravings in portfolio
Overall S.11 × 7¹¹⁄₁₆ in. (28 × 19.5 cm.)
Sold 17 May 1990 in New York for $41,800
(£24,881)

ROBERT RAUSCHENBERG
American b.1925
Booster (Foster 47)
Signed in pencil, numbered 15/38
1967
Lithograph and screenprint in colours
S. 72 × 35½ in. (183 × 90.2 cm.)
Sold 17 May 1990 in New York for $165,000
(£98,214)

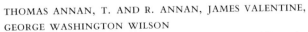

THOMAS ANNAN, T. AND R. ANNAN, JAMES VALENTINE,
GEORGE WASHINGTON WILSON
*Photographic Views of Ancient and Modern Buildings in
Glasgow and of Scenery and Houses in the Neighbourhood*
One from an album of 227 albumen prints of varying
sizes, several unpublished
1868–91
The largest size 12 × 14⅝ in. (30 × 37 cm.)
Sold 11 May 1990 in London at South Kensington for
£19,800 ($33,066)

ALVIN LANGDON COBURN
The White Bridge, Venice
Platinum and gum print
1905
14¾ × 11⅝ in. (37.9 × 29.3 cm.)
Sold 23 April 1990 in New York for $66,000 (£40,244)
Record auction price for a work by the photographer

ALFRED STIEGLITZ
Equivalents
Four from a set of
21 gelatin silver
prints, three series
of seven each
Signed, titled,
numbered and
inscribed 'To
Alma Wertheim,
Alfred Stieglitz'
c.1920
Each print
3½ × 4⅝ in.
(8.9 × 11.5 cm.)
Sold 30 October
1989 in New York
for $396,000
(£249,056)
Record auction
price for a single
lot of photography

EDWARD STEICHEN
George Frederick Watts
Waxed platinum print
Signed, titled and dated 1902
19½ × 15½ in. (49.5 × 39.4 cm.)
Sold 30 October 1989 in New York for $110,000
(£69,182)
Record auction price for a work by the photographer

ALEXANDRA FEODOROVNA
European Royal Holiday Album
One from an album of 94 panoramic gelatin silver prints
1907–12
3 × 10⅞ in. (7.6 × 27.8 cm.)
Sold 9 November 1989 in London at South Kensington
for £37,400 ($60,588)

Above:
HENRY PEACH ROBINSON
She Never Told Her Love
Albumen print
1857
7¼ × 9½ in. (18.4 × 24.1 cm.)
Sold 9 November 1989 in London at South Kensington
for £24,200 ($39,204)

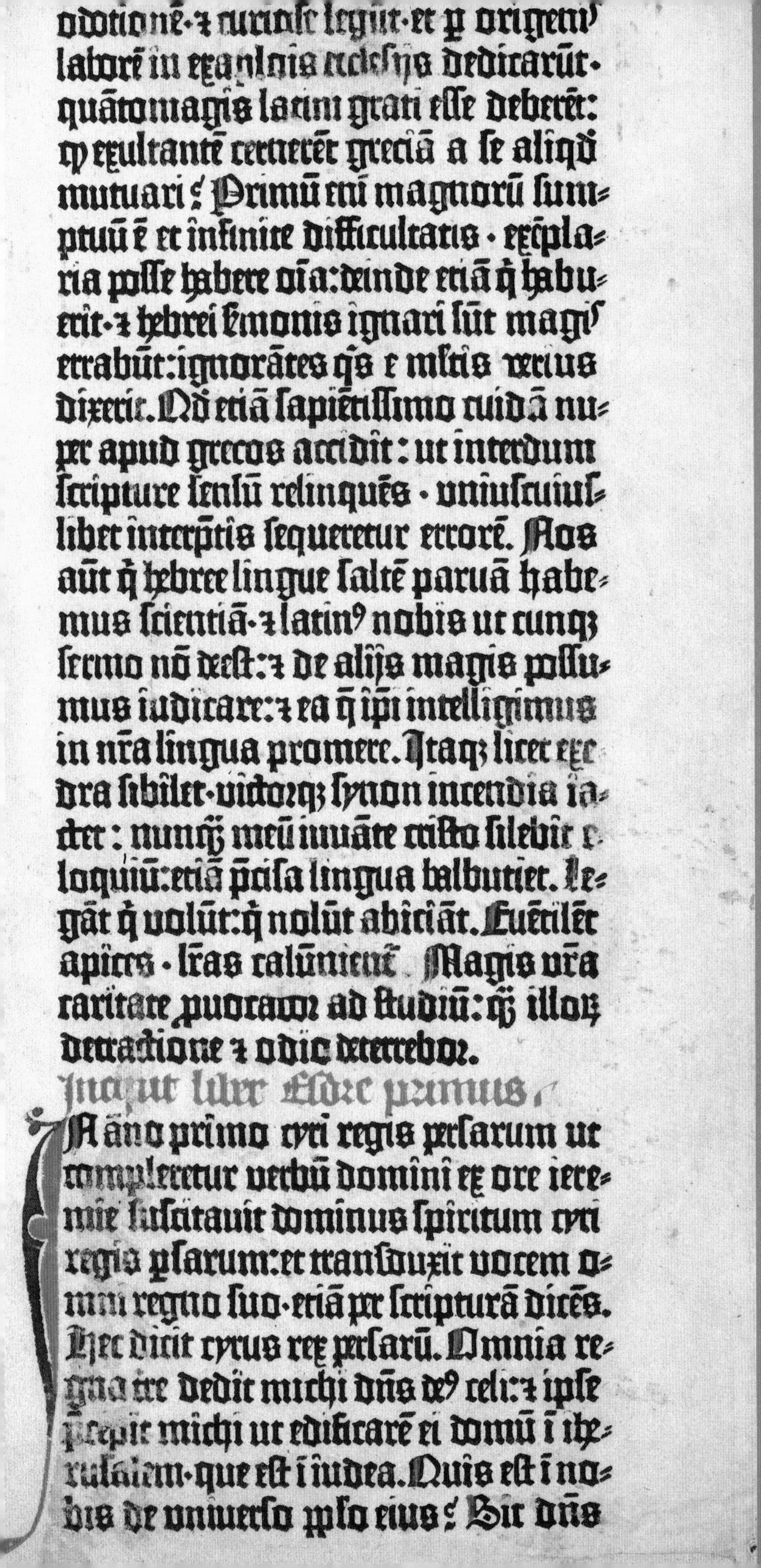
otione· ꝛ curiose legit· et p origenis
laborē in exaplois ecclesijs dedicarūt·
quātomagis latini grati esse deberēt:
q exultantē cernerēt greciā a se aliqd
mutuari? Primū eni magnorū sum-
ptuū ē et infinite difficultatis· exempla-
ria posse habere oīa: deinde etiā q habu-
erit· ꝛ hebrei smonis ignari sūt magis
errabūt: ignorātes q̄s e multis verius
dixerit. Qd etiā sapientissimo cuidā nu-
per apud grecos accidit: ut interdum
scripture sensū relinquēs· uniuscuius-
libet interpretis sequeretur errorē. Nos
aūt q hebree lingue saltē paruā habe-
mus scientiā· ꝛ latinꝰ nobis ut cunqz
sermo nō deest: ꝛ de alijs magis possu-
mus iudicare: ꝛ ea q ipi intelligimus
in nr̄a lingua promere. Itaqz licet exe-
dra sibilet· uictorqz synon incendia ia-
ctet: nunqz meū iuuāte cristo silebit e-
loquiū: etiā p̄cisa lingua balbutiet. Le-
gāt q uolūt: q nolūt abiciāt. Euentilēt
apices· lr̄as calūniēt. Magis ur̄a
caritate puocabor ad studiū: q illorū
detractione ꝛ odio deterrebor.
Incipit liber Esdre primus.
In āno primo cyri regis persarum ut
compleretur verbū domini ex ore iere-
mie suscitauit dominus spiritum cyri
regis psarum: et transduxit vocem o-
mni regno suo· etiā per scripturā dicēs.
Hec dicit cyrus rex persarū. Omnia re-
gna terre dedit michi dn̄s deꝰ celi: ꝛ ipse
p̄cepit michi ut edificarē ei domū i ihe-
rusalem· que est i iudea. Quis est i nobis de uniuerso pplo eius? Sit dn̄s

BOOKS AND MANUSCRIPTS

JOHANN GUTENBERG (printer)
Detail of a leaf from the *Gutenberg Bible* on vellum
Folio
Mainz, *c*.1450–5
Sold 8 December 1989 in New York for $63,800 (£40,226)

Book of Hours (Latin, use of Rome)
Illuminated manuscript on vellum
273 leaves with 15 large miniatures mostly by the Master of the Prayerbook and numerous marginal illustrations
Bruges, *c*.1500
3¾ × 2¾ in.
(9.4 × 6.8 cm.)
Sold 6 December 1989 in London for £308,000 ($483,560)

Opposite:
Nativity
Historiated initial 'P' cut from illuminated manuscript Gradual on vellum
Lombardy, *c*.1490
7¼ × 7¼ in.
(18.5 × 18.5 cm.)
Sold 6 December 1989 in London for £39,600 ($61,230)
From the collection of the late Mrs James B. Conant
Record auction price for a signed manuscript initial

Left:
Awetaran (Four Gospels, Armenian)
Illuminated manuscript on vellum
274 leaves
Constantinople, 1131
(AD 1682)
7¾ × 6 in.
(19.5 × 15.2 cm.)
Sold 20 June 1990 in London for £71,500 ($122,336)

LACTANTIUS (LUCIUS
COELIUS FIRMIANUS)
Opera
Subiaco: [Conrad
Sweynheym and
Arnold Pannartz]
29 October 1465
First edition, folio,
bound in
contemporary
Roman brown calf
Sold 20 June 1990 in
London for £220,000
($376,420)

PLINIUS SECUNDUS
(GAIUS), the elder
Historia Naturalis
First edition, folio,
bound in
contemporary Italian
blind–tooled brown
goatskin
Venice: Johannes de
Spira [before 18
September] 1469
Sold 8 June 1990 in
New York for
$242,000 (£143,195)

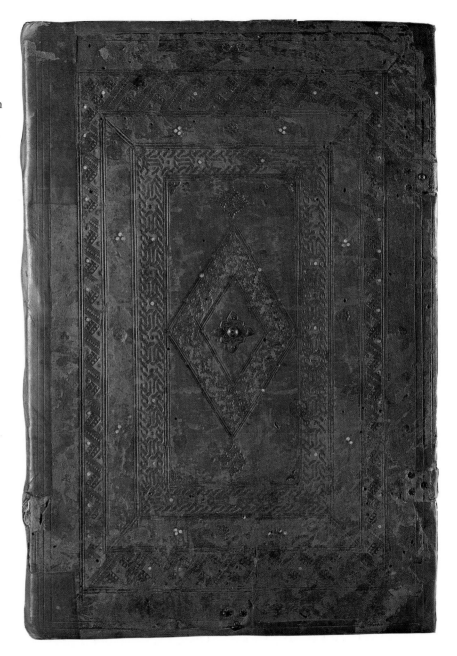

says it appears as if he had been designedly kept in the
Confusion. – But I will not torment myself with Conjectures
& suppositions; Facts shall satisfy me. – Frank had not heard
from any of us for ten weeks, when he wrote to me on the
12th of November, in consequence of Lord St. Vincent's being removed
to Gibraltar. – When his Commission is sent however, it will not
be so long on it's road as our letters, because all the Govern-
-ment dispatches are forwarded by Land to his Lordship from
Lisbon, with great regularity. – I returned from Manydown this
morning, & found my Mother certainly in no respect worse than

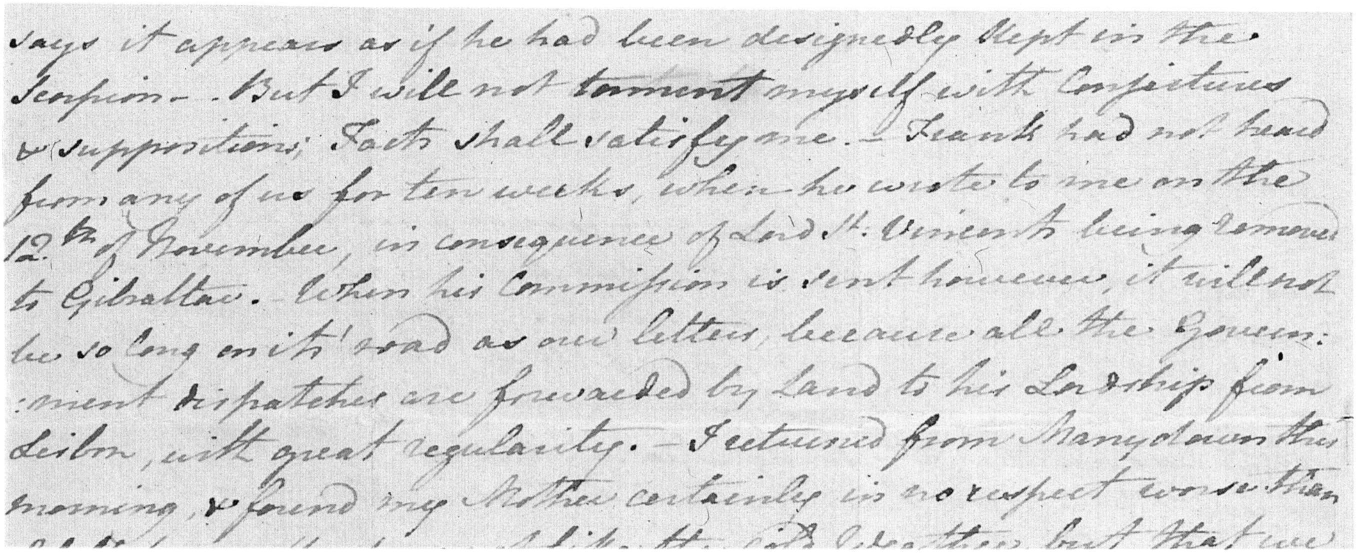

Above:
JANE AUSTEN
Autograph letter signed to her sister Cassandra
Four pages, quarto
Steventon, 14[–26] December [*c.*1798]
Sold 7 June 1990 in New York for $19,800 (£11,716)
From the Frederick R. Koch Foundation

Below:
GEORGE GORDON, LORD BYRON
Autograph manuscript of his poem *Maid of Athens ere we part*
Three pages, quarto
1810
Sold 7 June 1990 in New York for $37,400 (£22,130)
From the Frederick R. Koch Foundation

Song. Athens 1810. —
"Ζωη μου σας αγαπω" a Romaic expression of
tenderness, if I translate it I shall affront
the Gentlemen, as it may seem I supposed they could not, & if I do not I may affront the
Ladies, for fear of any misconstruction on their
part of the latter I shall do so, begging pardon of those
learned. – it means "My Life, I love you!" sounds

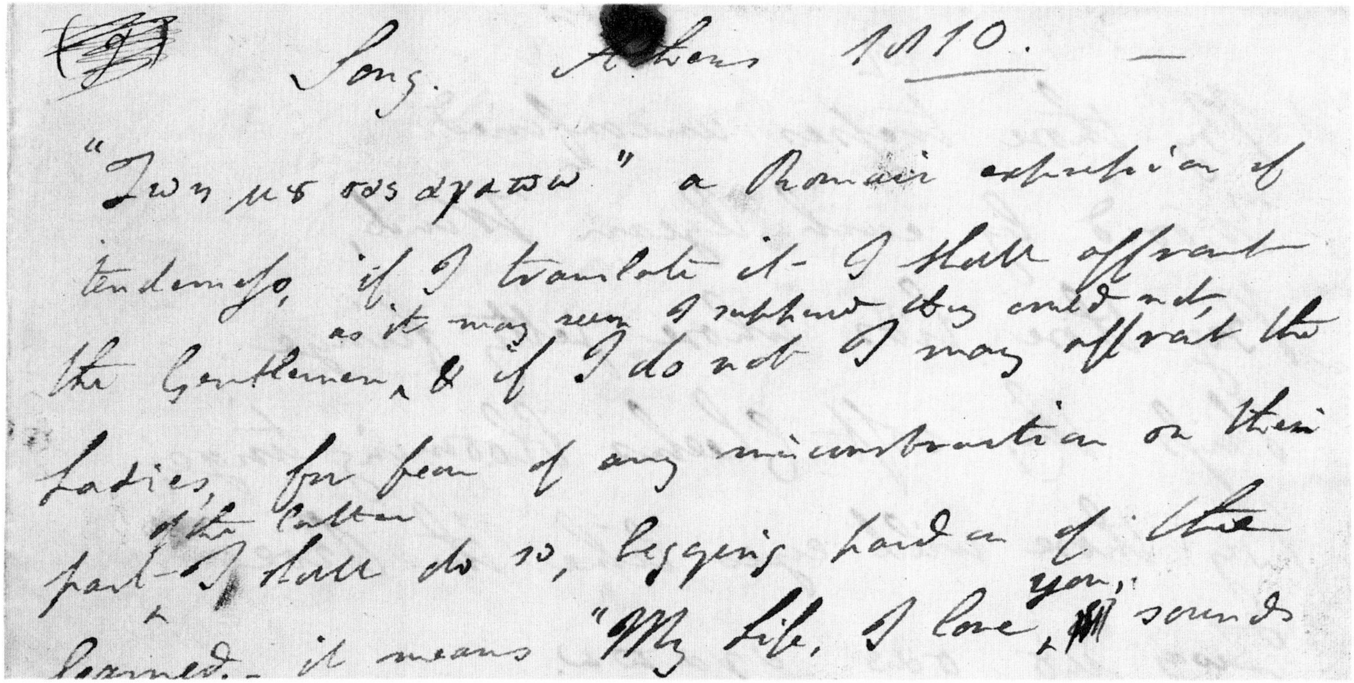

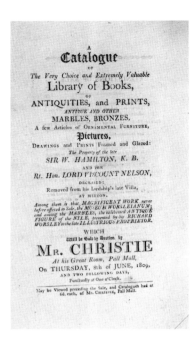

Far left:

HORACE WALPOLE
Catalogue of the library of Mr Horace Walpole at Strawberry Hill. 1763
Original manuscript, *c*.160 pages
Folio, bound in contemporary calf
Sold 6 December 1989 in London for £46,200 ($72,534)

Left:

JAMES CHRISTIE
A Catalogue of the Very Choice and Extremely Valuable Library of Books, Antiquities, and Prints from the Property of Sir W. Hamilton, K.B. and the Rt. Hon. Lord Viscount Nelson,
8 June 1809
Emma Hamilton's copy with James Christie's statement of account
Octavo
Sold 20 June 1990 in London for £4,400 ($7,528)
From the collection of Edwin Wolf 2nd

Below:

ADMIRAL HORATIO NELSON
Autograph letter signed to Lady Hamilton
2½ pages, quarto
17 February 1801
Sold 20 June 1990 in London for £4,400 ($7,528)
From the collection of Edwin Wolf 2nd

'Victory of the Nile' celebratory mug
1798
5¼ in. (13.5 cm.) high
Sold 20 June 1990 in London for £25,300 ($43,288)
From the collection of Edwin Wolf 2nd

Above:
ABRAHAM LINCOLN
Autograph letter about three of his poems to
Andrew Johnston of Quincy
Quarto
Illinois, 25 February 1847
Sold 8 June 1990 in New York for $143,000 (£84,615)

Below:
WILLIAM ELLERY
Autograph letter signed to his brother Benjamin Ellery
concerning the signing of the Declaration of Independence
Two pages, quarto
Philadelphia, 10 July 1776
Sold 8 June 1990 in New York for $121,000 (£71,598)

SAMUEL LANGHORNE CLEMENS (MARK TWAIN)
Autograph manuscript of Chapter 15 ('Down the River') from *A Tramp Abroad*
33 pages, octavo
1879–80
Sold 8 December 1989 in New York for $33,000
(£20,806)

LAFCADIO HEARN
17 autograph letters signed to his biographer
Elizabeth Bisland (Wetmore)
93 pages, octavo and 12mo
1887–1903
Sold 8 December 1989 in New York for $88,000 (£55,484)
From the estate of Pamela G. Reilly

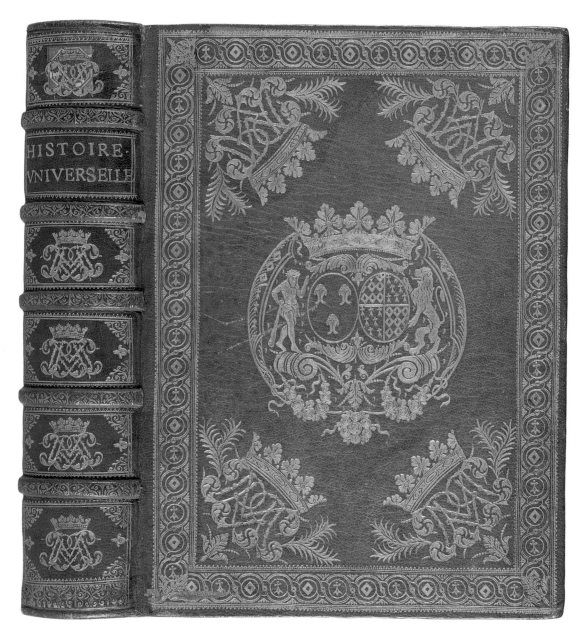

Opposite:
PAUL VALERY
Variété
Five volumes,
quarto, uniformly
bound in purple
morocco by
Pierre-Lucien Martin,
limited editions
1924–44
8¾ × 6¾ in.
(21.8 × 17 cm.)
Sold 8 June 1990 in
New York for
$25,300 (£14,970)

Opposite, top right:
VICTOR HUGO
Notre-Dame de Paris
Three volumes in
one, octavo, in a
cathedral binding of
Parisian purple
morocco by
Kleinhans
Paris, 1836
8½ × 5½ in.
(22.3 × 14.3 cm.)
Sold 8 June 1990 in
New York for
$10,450 (£6,183)

DUC DE FRONTENAY
Suite de l'abbregé de l'histoire universelle
Owned by Marguerite, Duchess of Rohan and Princess of Léon
(1617–84)
Autograph manuscript signed, 488 leaves
Quarto measure in an armorial binding of French red morocco, all
edges of the leaves decorated in the French manner
France, seventeenth century
11 × 8¼ in. (28 × 21 cm.)
Sold 8 June 1990 in New York for $44,000 (£26,035)

Below left:
CHARLES WHITE
'Martingale'
Sporting Scenes and
Country Characters
London, 1860
Octavo measure, in a
jewelled binding of
vari-coloured
morocco with 28
stones by Sangorski
& Sutcliffe
8 × 5¼ in.
(20 × 13.6 cm.)
Sold 8 December
1989 in New York
for $22,000 (£13,871)

Below right:
ALBERTO SANGORSKI
(calligrapher and
illuminator)
ABRAHAM LINCOLN and
WALT WHITMAN
The Gettysburg Speech
and The Second
Inaugural Address
London, 1928
Illuminated
manuscript on
vellum, quarto
measure, in a binding
of vari-coloured
morocco by
Riviere & Son
12¼ × 10¼ in.
(31 × 26 cm.)
Sold 8 December
1989 in New York
for $35,200 (£22,194)

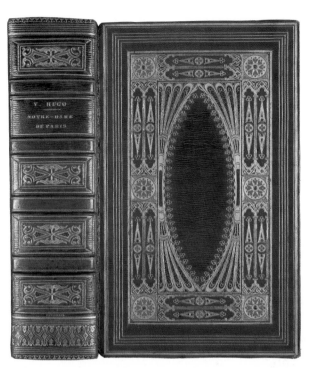

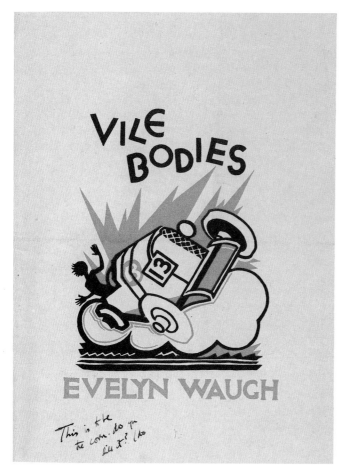

EVELYN WAUGH
Autograph manuscript signed of his second novel
Vile Bodies
142 pages, folio
1929
Sold 7 June 1990 in New York for $110,000 (£65,087)
From the Frederick R. Koch Foundation

WILLIAM SOMERSET MAUGHAM
Autograph manuscript signed of his short story collection
The Casuarina Tree: Six Stories
319 pages, quarto
c.1926
Sold 7 June 1990 in New York for $49,500 (£29,289)
From the Frederick R. Koch Foundation

WILLIAM BLAKE
Songs of Innocence
31 relief-etched plates coloured by hand, octavo
1789
Bentley's copy A
Sold 8 June 1990 in New York for $550,000 (£325,443)
From the collection of Joseph Scott McKell

SIR WILLIAM JACKSON HOOKER and WALTER FITCH
Victoria Regia
Double atlas folio, 4 coloured lithographed plates
London, 1851
Sold 8 June 1990 in New York for $10,450 (£6,183)

ALBERTUS SEBA
Locupletissimi rerum naturalium thesauri accurata descriptio
Four volumes, large folio, 449 coloured etched plates; signed by the colourist J. Fortuÿn
Amsterdam, 1734–65
Sold 25 April 1990 in London for £165,000 ($275,550)

JOHN GOULD
The Birds of Australia
Eight volumes,
including
Supplement, large
folio, 681 coloured
lithographed plates
1840–69
Sold 25 April 1990 in
London for £165,000
($275,550)

CACATUA GALERITA: *Vieill.*

El Khasné.

DAVID ROBERTS
The Holy Land...Egypt and Nubia
Six volumes, large folio, 241 coloured lithographed plates mounted on card
London, 1842–9
Sold 25 April 1990 in London for £104,500 ($174,515)

FURNITURE

One of a pair of ormolu three-branch
wall-lights
Stamped 'TH'
*c.*1820
48 in. (122 cm.) high
Sold 14 June 1990 in London for £55,000
($93,000)

Early nineteenth-century copies of lights
designed in the 1770s for Louis XVI, and
bearing the TH brand of the Tuileries Palace

THE BADMINTON CABINET

Charles Cator

The Badminton Cabinet
Florentine *pietra dura*, ebony and ormolu cabinet
Made for the 3rd Duke of Beaufort
152 in. (386 cm.) high; 91½ in. (232.5 cm.) wide; 37 in. (94 cm.) deep
Sold 5 July 1990 in London for £8,580,000 ($15,178,020)
Record auction price for a piece of furniture and for any item from the applied arts

During June and early July Christie's Great Rooms were dominated, in every sense, by the monumental Badminton Cabinet commissioned in 1726 by Henry, 3rd Duke of Beaufort from the Grand Ducal Workshops in Florence. Almost as remarkable as the magnificent Cabinet itself is the fact that the young Duke was aged only nineteen at the time and so made one of the grandest acts of patronage of the eighteenth century before he had even come of age. He was born in 1707 and succeeded his father in 1714 at the early age of seven. His great-grandfather, the 1st Duke, had rebuilt Badminton between 1664 and 1691, transforming the rambling fifteenth- and sixteenth-century house into an Inigo Jones/Palladian-style mansion more suited to his princely way of life. The 2nd Duke, who succeeded his grandfather in 1699, made few changes and it was not until his son, the 3rd Duke, returned from Italy that the major remodelling of Badminton began.

The young Duke was keenly interested in architecture and in 1725 he set off on the Grand Tour. He was accompanied by William Philips, his tutor, friend and artistic advisor. Sadly Philips' friendship later proved to be false and on their return in 1727 he tried to misappropriate some of Beaufort's Italian purchases. Another member of the Duke's household on the journey was Dominique du Four, who kept an account book of incidental expenses, which allows us to chart the party's progress through Europe.

Professor Alvar González-Palacios, the leading Italian furniture scholar who wrote the erudite monograph on the Cabinet for the catalogue, has discovered a wealth of new information not only about the Cabinet itself, but also about the Duke's extensive acquisitions in Rome. A very complete group of documents relating to the eventual shipping of the Cabinet in 1732/3 survives in the Badminton archives and, in addition, there is a series of letters from the Duke's agent in Rome, Giovanni Francesco Guernieri, an architect and stuccoist. Du Four's account book shows that the Duke's party left Paris in March 1726 and arrived in Florence on 27 April, remaining there until 2 May. It was almost certainly in this short period that the Cabinet was commissioned from the Grand Ducal Workshops (*Galleria dei lavori delle pietre dure*). The *Galleria*, originally set up by Grand Duke Ferdinand I de' Medici in 1588, was a court workshop entirely dedicated to producing sumptuous works of art in *pietre dure* for the Medici, either for their personal use or as ambassadorial gifts to eminent contemporaries. Cabinets had assumed a particular importance at the Florentine court as the largest and most spectacular vehicles for demonstrating the great skill of Florentine craftsmanship and for enhancing the exalted position of their owners. By 1726, however, the output of the *Galleria* was much reduced from the great days of Grand Duke Cosimo III, who had died in 1723. His successor, the last Medici Grand Duke, Gian Gastone, was a sick and disillusioned man without heirs. The Badminton Cabinet was certainly by far the most important work of art created in the *Galleria* during the late Baroque period and the commission must have brought a welcome renewal of activity. Beaufort's high rank and his well-placed connections in Rome, especially at the Vatican, no doubt facilitated this highly unusual and, indeed, unorthodox commission.

Professor González-Palacios has identified Girolamo Ticciati (d.1744) as the sculptor responsible for the models of the very beautiful attenuated statuettes of the Four Seasons which are placed at the upper angles. Ticciati's waxes and their moulds (which still survive) feature in an inventory of the models acquired by Carlo Ginori for the porcelain manufactory at Doccia founded in 1743. Ticciati was a pupil of Giovanni Battista Foggini, the man who, until his death in 1725, was director of the *Galleria dei lavori* during some of its most artistically successful and productive years. Professor González-Palacios sets the Duke's Cabinet in its appropriate context as a glorious fulfilment of the luxurious style created and developed by Foggini and he shows how it bears all the hallmarks of his sumptuous *oeuvre* executed in the twilight years of the Medici dynasty. The Cabinet is itself the most monumental piece of furniture ever produced in the *Galleria* and the three floral plaques in the centre and at the sides are themselves among the largest known; each stone is carefully chosen not only for its colour, but also for its subtle markings, which heighten the illusion of reality. The use of the three-dimensional chalcedony masks and hardstone fruit as well as the cabochon panels of lapis lazuli and agate all contribute further to the magnificent effect. The gilt-bronzes are also of remarkable richness and show great inventiveness; indeed, some of them were entirely new models. We know from Guernieri's correspondence that in 1728 the Duke's Florentine agent Thomas Tyrrel had intervened to increase the number of mounts, resulting in delay to the completion of the Cabinet, and this may account for the differences between the finely executed watercolour drawings prepared by the *Galleria* (which were sold with the cabinet) and the finished Cabinet.

The Duke's antiquarian interests encompassed an enthusiasm for heraldry, and it is no coincidence that his arms occupy such a prominent position at the pinnacle of his Cabinet. The Beaufort arms are the Royal Arms of England as used from 1406–1603, but differenced by a bordure compony of Argent and Azure, the Lancastrian colours. Their placing emphasizes the Beaufort family's illustrious descent from the Plantaganet Kings of England through John of Gaunt, son of Edward III, and may perhaps have contained an implied reference to their anti-Hanoverian and pro-Jacobite sentiments.

By August 1732 the completed Cabinet was in Leghorn awaiting shipment to London through the shipper John Winder of Winder and Aikman, who had handled the previous shipment of the Duke's acquisitions in Rome. On 21 August Captain Daniel Pullam and the *Oriana* sailed for London with 'five large cases…containing the severall parts of a large Cabinett of his Grace the Duke of Beaufort'. By early 1733 the *Oriana* had arrived in London and William May, the English shipping agent, arranged for the unloading of the five cases at a cost of £21 19s. 6d. and the payment of the customs charges, which totalled

£94 18s. 6d., with the Cabinet being valued at £500. Six years later, May petitioned the Duke through Michael Aiskew (who supervised his London household) that the Duke should reimburse Captain Pullam for the loss of £10 10s. that he had incurred during the shipping of the Cabinet. The captain had been forced 'not to take in any ballast that should damage the cabinet' and so had had to buy a large quantity of cork to ensure its safety, which he had subsequently resold in London at a loss.

It is almost certain that the Cabinet was always destined for Badminton, where it was placed in the Duke's newly created Cabinet Room on the east façade. The 1762 picture inventory shows how marvellously rich this room must have looked. Not only did it contain his stupendous Cabinet, but it was entirely hung with Beaufort's Grand Tour purchases and further enriched with some of the spectacular virtuoso carving Grinling Gibbons had created for the 1st Duke.

Professor González-Palacios's researches have also shed fascinating light on the 3rd Duke's activities and acquisitions in Rome, where he remained at length after Florence. He had extremely influential contacts there, particularly among highly placed dignitaries of the Catholic Church, and he was especially friendly with Cardinals Alberoni and Albani, as well as Cardinal Lercari. He is also recorded as having had a private talk with the King of England, as the Old Pretender was called in Rome. It is not clear how Beaufort obtained these introductions, but his great-uncle, the Duke of Ormonde, had strong sympathies with the Church of Rome and certainly the Beaufort family, as a whole, had done little to hide their Jacobite sympathies. He spent large sums – almost £5,000 – on important pictures by Claude, Salvator Rosa, Carlo Maratta, Pietro da Cortona, Reni and Poussin, as well as by others with high-sounding attributions such as Leonardo and Raphael. In addition, he acquired a number of table tops of precious marbles and a quantity of sculpture. One of his greatest treasures was the magnificent Alberoni sarcophagus, dating from the reign of Septimius Severus, which was given to him by Cardinal Alberoni. In 1733 William Kent designed a heroic plinth for it and it was placed in the splendid North Hall at Badminton.

Beaufort also made another extraordinary acquisition in Rome. Through Guernieri he commissioned a small room or *cabinet* entirely lined with inlaid marbles, which was shipped to London with some other items, including Cardinal Alberoni's sarcophagus, in ninety-six cases in September 1728. In the past this marble room (*cabinet*), which no longer exists, has been muddled with the Badminton Cabinet itself but this confusion was set right for the first time in our catalogue.

The evidence of the correspondence from Rome emphasizes further just what a remarkable collector and patron the 3rd Duke was. His vast range of acquisitions in the Eternal City reflects his omnivorous collecting tastes as well as his wisdom and connoisseurship. Not only did he patronize Francis Smith and James Gibbs as architects at Badminton and William Kent as a designer, but he also commissioned a celebrated series of sporting pictures from John Wootton and a silver service from Thomas Germain. However, his crowning achievement as a patron was undoubtedly the commissioning of his magnificent Cabinet, the last major piece to be produced by the great Grand Ducal Workshops of the Medici. It represents the quintessence of the Grand Tour and is a princely statement of Beaufort's role as a great antiquarian collector and patron of the arts, as well as a declaration of his ancient and noble lineage. It is perhaps the greatest work of decorative art to have been commissioned by a British patron in three hundred years.

PRICES, PROVENANCE, ROYAL FURNITURE AND A HARDSTONE CABINET

Ronald Freyberger

George IV
ormolu-mounted
ebony side cabinet
mounted with Italian
pietra dura plaques
The cabinet
attributed to Robert
Hume, the *pietra dura*
panels Italian, 17th
century
39½ in. (100 cm.)
high; 66 in. (168 cm.)
wide; 22 in. (56 cm.)
deep
Sold 26 April 1990 in
New York for
$770,000 (£469,512)

Hardstones and marbles have exerted an allure since antiquity, through the Middle Ages, into the Renaissance and post-Renaissance periods and up to the present. From the sixteenth century onward, *pietra dura*, as it was developed in Rome, Florence, Paris and other centres, was recognized as the unprecedented artistic and technical achievement that it was. The enlightened Grand Tourist's response to this fascinating art form is exemplified at the highest level by the Florentine hardstone cabinet commissioned by Henry, 3rd Duke of Beaufort, in 1726 (see pp.234–7). In late Georgian England the fashion for sumptuous furniture embellished with hardstone panels was prevalent among such well-known collectors as George IV, the 3rd Duke of Northumberland, William Beckford, the 10th Duke of Hamilton, and George Watson-Taylor.

George Watson-Taylor (1771–1841) was, for a time, one of the wealthiest and most discriminating English connoisseurs of art. After he encountered financial difficulties, however, the contents of his country seat, Erlestoke Park, near Devizes in Wiltshire, were auctioned in a house sale of twenty-one sessions that lasted from 9 July to 1 August 1832. The splendour that appealed to George Watson-Taylor is evident in the descriptions listed in the auction catalogue that was prepared for this event under the direction of George Robins.

The hardstone cabinet illustrated here, and its pair in the Brooklyn Museum, New York, are easy to identify on p.150 of that catalogue – among the luxurious furnishings of the Grand North Drawing Room at Erlestoke Mansion, as Erlestoke Park was sometimes called. The furnishings of the Ante Drawing Room at Erlestoke described in the auction catalogue are a further indication of George Watson-Taylor's love of magnificence, and, more important, of his extreme discernment in artistic matters. This room contained two of the most exquisite pieces of furniture that have ever been created: Marie Antoinette's black and gold lacquer *secrétaire* and commode by Riesener, which stood, before the Revolution, in the *Cabinet Intérieur de la Reine* at the Château de Saint Cloud.

All four pieces of furniture, the lacquer furniture and the hardstone cabinets, were among the purchases made at Erlestoke by Robert Hume of Hume & Son, the London firm of carvers, gilders and furniture-makers, whose clientele included the Crown, William Beckford, George Watson-Taylor and the 10th Duke of Hamilton. Robert Hume's full range of activities has yet to be properly researched, but preliminary evidence suggests that George Watson-Taylor's hardstone cabinets can be attributed to Hume & Son and can be

Louis XVI ebony, Japanese lacquer and gilded bronze *secrétaire à abbattant* By Jean Henri Riesener Formerly part of the furnishings of Marie Antoinette's *Cabinet Intérieur de la Reine* at the Château de Saint Cloud Sold by Christie's 10 July 1882 for £9,450 Now in the Metropolitan Museum of Art, bequest of William K. Vanderbilt, 1920

dated to *c.*1820–30. Evidence also suggests that in 1832 at Erlestoke Robert Hume acted on behalf of the 10th Duke of Hamilton in making these and other purchases. That the Duke of Hamilton considered Erlestoke Mansion as an appropriate source for additions to his own collection is not surprising.

Alexander Douglas-Hamilton, 10th Duke of Hamilton (1767–1852), was another very wealthy individual who was given to extravagance. His attraction to splendour and magnificence was expressed in his lifelong occupation and true calling, the enlargement and embellishment of Hamilton Palace, his ancestral home near the town of Hamilton in Lanarkshire, Scotland. For many years Robert Hume was engaged to oversee the realization of the Duke's dream.

The result was a stately edifice of imposing scale and regal grandeur in which the Duke assembled a collection of works of art that in many ways could rival a royal or national collection. In the history of art collecting, the Duke has too often been cast unjustly in the shadow of his near contemporary and father-in-law, the almost too highly publicized William Beckford (1760–1844). An attempt to establish the 10th Duke of Hamilton as a great connoisseur in his own right appeared in the article, 'Eighteenth-Century French Furniture from Hamilton Palace', *Apollo*, December 1981. The Hamilton Collections were sold at Christie's in the legendary Hamilton Palace sale of 1882. The remaining contents of Hamilton Palace were sold by Christie's in 1919, and over a ten-year period in the 1920s and 1930s Hamilton Palace was dismantled and demolished. The loss is a tragic one, and to stand on the grass where Hamilton Palace used to be is a poignant experience indeed.

Marie Antoinette's lacquer furniture and George Watson-Taylor's hardstone cabinets were at Hamilton Palace from the 1830s to 1882 and are traceable there in inventories; one of the hardstone cabinets is also recorded in a photograph. After the 1882 sale, the lacquer furniture and the hardstone cabinets followed different paths. It is interesting to monitor the changes in the monetary values that were attached to these magnificent works of art while they were together in two outstandingly great collections for fifty years or more during the nineteenth century.

In 1832 at the Erlestoke Mansion sale, Marie Antoinette's lacquer furniture, both pieces together, sold for £121. 16s. The hardstone cabinets together sold for £490. 15s. In the Hamilton Palace inventory of 1835, the two pieces of Marie Antoinette's lacquer furniture are valued together at £300; the hardstone cabinets are valued together at £800. The 1876 inventory is a listing with no monetary values. By 1882, at the Hamilton Palace sale, circumstances had changed radically. The two pieces of Marie Antoinette's lacquer furniture were sold together for the astounding price of £18,900, which remained a world record until well into the twentieth century. It is within the realm of probability that today Marie Antoinette's lacquer furniture could be worth as much as the Badminton Cabinet or perhaps even more than that. In 1882 the hardstone cabinets together sold for £903.

Marie Antoinette's lacquer furniture came to the Metropolitan Museum of Art in 1920 as a bequest from William K. Vanderbilt, who purchased it in 1882. The last seventy years mark the longest period of time in this furniture's history that these magnificent works of art have been in any one place. One trusts that they will remain there, safely, forever.

In 1882 the hardstone cabinets were bought by Samson Wertheimer, of New Bond Street, then one of Europe's leading *antiquaires*. It is not yet clear if Wertheimer bought these cabinets for his own stock, or in partnership with another dealer, or as agent for a private individual. Ongoing research has shown that the cabinets appeared at Parke-Bernet Galleries in 1953 as property from the estate of the late Mrs Charles de Genahl, whose residence was in White Plains, a suburban community in Westchester County, north of New York City. As at Erlestoke in 1832, the cabinets were offered as separate lots, which fetched $380 and $300 respectively. The purchaser was Mrs Marie Bitzer, a New Yorker who bequeathed them to the Brooklyn Museum in 1989. On 26 April 1990 one was sold at Christie's New York for $770,000 (£469,512). This auction record for a piece of nineteenth century furniture sold in America is a splendid affirmation of the excellent artistic judgement of George Watson-Taylor and the 10th Duke of Hamilton, an amazing return on Mrs Bitzer's investment, and a most munificent donation to the Acquisition Fund of the Brooklyn Museum.

George III harewood, marquetry and parcel-gilt side table
34½ in. (87 cm.) high; 64½ in. (163.5 cm.) wide; 27½
in. (69 cm.) deep
Sold 19 April 1990 in London for £121,000 ($202,070)

This richly inlaid D-shaped table, with its 'palmette' frieze
and reeded legs with golden flowered tablets, reflects the
'Grecian' style of the 1770s. The central feathered sunburst
is inspired by the design on the Sun God's ceiling in the
temple engraved in Robert Wood's *Palmyra*, 1753.

Opposite:
George III burr yew, harewood and marquetry cylinder
desk
Attributed to Mayhew and Ince
36½ in. (96 cm.) high; 32½ in. (82.5 cm.) wide; 25 in.
(63.5 cm.) deep
Sold 19 April 1990 in London for £220,000 ($367,400)

This elegant bureau, with marquetry tablets and
medallions inlaid with festooned 'Etruscan' vases and urns
in the fashionable classical style of the 1770s, relates to
one at Syon House, Middlesex. The latter was almost
certainly supplied by John Mayhew and William Ince,
leading cabinet-makers and upholsterers of Golden Square
and authors of *The Universal System of Household Furniture*.
In the early 1770s they supplied furniture to Elizabeth,
Duchess of Northumberland, for Northumberland House.

One of a pair of George III mahogany commodes
33½ in. (85 cm.) high; 48 in. (122 cm.) wide; 25 in. (63.5 cm.) deep
Sold 19 April 1990 in London for £231,000 ($385,770)

These handsome chests of drawers, 'commodes', were designed for
the window piers of a mid–18th-century bedroom apartment. Their
serpentine forms, embellished with garlanded scrolls and Roman
acanthus, and their rich ormolu mounts reflect the 'French' style
promoted by Thomas Chippendale in *The Gentleman and
Cabinet-Maker's Director*, 1754.

George III mahogany commode
33½ in. (85 cm.) high; 47 in. (120 cm.) wide; 26 in. (66 cm.) deep
Sold 16 November 1989 in London for £77,000 ($123,970)

This commode is richly carved with naturalistic foliage in the French
manner and fretwork inlay in the 'Chinese' manner, reflecting the
amalgamation of styles popularized by Thomas Chippendale.

George III ormolu-mounted rosewood, satinwood and
marquetry commode
In the manner of John Cobb
Labelled 'His Grace the Duke of Marlborough, Blenheim
Palace, Woodstock, Oxon'
35 in. (89 cm.) high; 49 in. (124.5 cm.) wide; 23 in.
(58½ cm.) deep
Sold 5 July 1990 in London for £264,000 ($467,016)

Opposite:
One of a pair of George III giltwood bergères
Attributed to Marsh & Tatham
37 in. (94 cm.) high
Sold 5 July 1990 in London for £242,000 ($428,098)

These 'Dolphin' bergère chairs were commissioned in the
1790s by William, 3rd Viscount Courtenay, later 9th Earl
of Devon (1768–1835), for Powderham Castle, Devon.

George III ormolu-mounted mahogany oval wine-cooler with the
Williams-Wynn 'Snowdonian' eagle crest
The design attributed to Robert Adam
18 in. (47 cm.) high; 34 in. (86 cm.) wide; 22 in. (56 cm.) deep
Sold 16 November 1989 in London for £55,000 ($88,000)
From the property of the 1987 Williams-Wynn Settlement

The neo-classical design of this wine-cooler, which is embellished
with a medallion displaying the Williams-Wynn 'Snowdonian' eagle
crest and strigil 'sarcophagus'-flutes, relates to Robert Adam's designs
of the early 1770s for the sideboard and its silver at 20 St. James's
Square, the London house of Sir Watkin Williams-Wynn, Bt. The
wine-cooler is now in the National Museum of Wales, Cardiff.

The Hope Vasi-Cippi
One of a pair of white marble
urns-on-pedestals
*c.*1800
82 in. (208 cm.) high; 24 in. (61 cm.) wide
Sold 16 November 1989 in London for
£93,500 ($150,535)

These neo-Greek vases on sepulchral
cippi-columns were conceived around 1800 by
the Francophile connoisseur, collector, patron
and designer Thomas Hope (d.1831). They
flanked the entrance of his Statue Gallery at
Duchess Street, London, and they were
illustrated in *Household Furniture and Interior
Decoration executed from designs by Thomas
Hope*, 1807. They were inspired by the
Barbarini Bacchic vase with swan-headed
handles illustrated by G.B. Piranesi, *Vasi,
Candelabri, Cippi, Sarcofagi*, 1778, and by the
French architect Charles Percier, *Palaces,
Houses of Rome*, Cahier 14, 1798. Hope later
moved the vases to his Surrey villa, the
Deepdene, from where they were sold by
Lord Francis Pelham Clinton Hope at
Christie's London salerooms, 24 July 1917.

One of a set of eight George III white-painted armchairs
Made for William Aislabie at Studley Royal, Yorkshire
Sold 5 July 1990 in London for £115,500 ($204,320)
From the property of Henry Vyner, Esq.

These garden chairs, designed in the 'antique' manner with 'sunflower' backs, furnished William Aislabie's (d.1781) Orangery/Banqueting House at Studley Royal, Yorkshire. They are attributed to the important firm of cabinet-makers and upholsterers, John Mayhew and William Ince of Golden Square, Soho.

One of a pair of George II black and gold japanned open armchairs
Made for the 4th Duke of Beaufort by William and John Linnell
40¾ in. (103.5 cm.) high; 26½ in. (67.5 cm.) wide
Sold 19 April 1990 in London for £198,000 ($330,660)

These armchairs furnished the state bedroom apartment of Charles Somerset, 4th Duke of Beaufort, at Badminton House, Gloucestershire. The room was decorated in the exotic 'Chinese' manner of the early 1750s. Their Chinese-fret backs with pagoda-sweep crests formed a rail round the walls, which were hung with colourful Chinese paper decorated with flowers and birds. The suite of eight armchairs, possibly originally polychromed, accompanied the pagoda-roofed 'kiosk' bed. A contemporary watercolour of the design is in the Victoria and Albert Museum, London.

One of a pair of Regency lacquer and japanned centre tables
29 in. (74 cm.) high; 36½ in. (92 cm.) wide; 21¾ in. (55.5 cm.) deep
Sold 19 April 1990 in London for £148,500 ($247,995)

These drawing-room tables with Grecian-lyre end-supports belonged to Henry Richard, 3rd Earl of Warwick (1779–1853), forming part of the Regency furnishings of Warwick Castle. They have japanned frames decorated with Chinoiserie landscapes to correspond with their ormolu-banded Chinese lacquer tops.

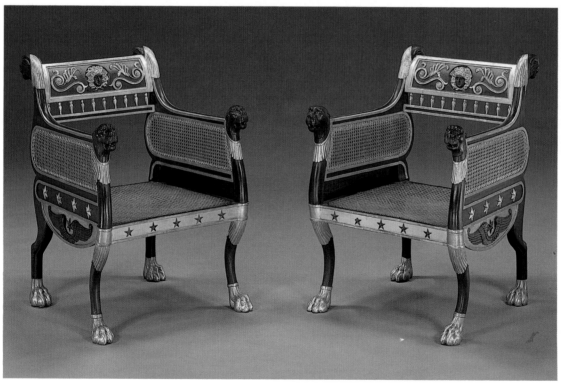

Pair of Regency simulated bronze and parcel-gilt bergères
After a design by George Smith
35½ in. (90 cm.) high; 24 in. (61 cm.) wide
Sold 16 November 1989 in London for £93,500 ($150,535)

These Grecian bergères, carved with leopard monopodia, Medusa masks and star-studded rails accompanied by the Egyptian *Ba*, reflect the classical style promoted by the connoisseur Thomas Hope at his Duchess Street mansion.

Pair of George III
walnut library
armchairs
Sold 27 January 1990
in New York for
$264,000 (£159,036)

Pair of George II
walnut and
beechwood library
armchairs
Sold 27 January 1990
in New York for
$396,000 (£238,554)

These chairs are from
a suite of seat
furniture, which
served as part of the
antique furnishings of
George IV's
Coronation
apartments at the
Palace of
Westminster in 1820.
The suite later
furnished the state
apartments of
Chatsworth,
Derbyshire, in the
1840s. The original
Aubusson tapestry
upholstery was
removed in the 1920s
for some Louis
XV-style chairs in
the Frick Collection,
New York.

One of a pair of George II grey-painted and parcel-gilt eagle console tables
32¾in. (83 cm.) high; 37¼ in. (94.5 cm.) wide; 17¾ in. (45 cm.) deep
Sold 27 January 1990 in New York for $308,000 (£185,542)
Formerly in the collection of Mr and Mrs Ronald Tree, Ditchley Park, Oxfordshire

The Siena marble slabs which form the table-tops are banded with gilt-brass and supported on scroll-console brackets fronted by eagles clasping scallop shells. The tables' Italian Baroque manner reflects the style introduced to English furniture by William Kent (d.1748).

One of a pair of George II grey-painted and
parcel-gilt mirrors
78 × 44½ in. (198 × 113 cm.)
Sold 27 January 1990 in New York for
$330,000 (£198,795)
Formerly in the collection of Mr and Mrs
Ronald Tree, Ditchley Park, Oxfordshire

These pier-glasses with their festooned
Greek–fret frames surmounted by baskets of
flowers between scroll pediments are in the
Palladian style associated with the architects
William Kent and James Gibbs.

Suite of George III mahogany and stained garden dining furniture
28½ in. (72.5 cm.) high; 61 in. (155 cm.) wide; 60½ in. (153.5 cm.) deep
Sold 7 April 1990 in New York for $308,000 (£187,805)

The suite is reputed to have been made for Frederick, Prince of Wales (d.1753), for Kew Gardens.

Elm and ash turner's tripod table
Early 18th century
26½ in. (67.5 cm.) high; 23½ in. (59.5 cm.) diameter
Sold 19 April 1990 in London for £14,300 ($23,881)

Elm and ash turner's tripod table
Early 18th century
25¾ in. (65.6 cm.) high; 19½ in. (49.5 cm.) diameter;
Sold 19 April 1990 in London for £14,300 ($23,881)

Mosaic table
Designed by William Burges for the Golden
Chamber, Tower House
The marble work by Burke & Co., the
cabinet-work attributed to Walden
32 in. (81.5 cm.) high; 36½ in. (93 cm.)
wide; 15½ in. (39.5 cm.) deep
Sold 19 April 1990 in London for £66,000
($110,220)

The artist and architect William Burges
(d.1881) designed this green-painted frame in
1879 for his Golden Chamber, a guest
bedroom at the Tower House, Melbury
Road, London. Its white marble top was
executed by Messrs Burke & Co. and
incorporates three Roman mosaic panels of
porphyry, serpentine and white marble,
banded by an incised ribbon bearing the date
1880 and a Latin inscription recording the fact
that they came from the floor of the Basilica
of Santa Maria in Trastevere, from the spot
where St. Paul preached to the Romans.

Regency penwork sideboard
The penwork attributed to Henzell Gouch
34¾ in. (88.5 cm.) high; 56 in. (142.5 cm.) wide; 18¾ in.
(47.5 cm.) deep
Sold 14 October 1989 in New York for $121,000 (£78,065)

This commode, with its exotic 'Indo-Chinese' and classical ornament,
relates closely to a sofa-table signed by Henzell Gouch and dated 1815,
which is now in the Victoria and Albert Museum, London.

Regency mahogany Carlton House desk
41½ in. (105.5 cm.) high; 64½ in. (164 cm.) wide; 34 in. (86.5 cm.)
deep
Sold 27 January 1990 in New York for $231,000 (£139,156)

One of a pair of Empire ormolu and bronzed candelabra Overall 75½ in. (192 cm.) high Sold 7 December 1989 in London for £115,500 ($182,490)

Ormolu centre table
Probably Florentine, late 19th century
33 in. (84 cm.) high; 41 in. (104.5 cm.) wide; 24¾ in. (63 cm.) deep
Sold 15 March 1990 in London for £44,000 ($70,400)

The *pietra dura* marble slab is decorated with butterflies and a 'fruits-of-the-sea' trophy wreathed with vines. It is supported on a neo-classical frame embellished with Bacchic panther heads.

Lapis lazuli veneered table top on an ormolu console table
Possibly Florentine, late 18th century, the base mid–19th century
37½ in. (95 cm.) high; 66 in. (168 cm.) wide; 22½ in. (57 cm.) deep
Sold 7 December 1989 in London for £82, 500 ($130,350)

The 18th-century slab, banded with ormolu and an inlaid Siena marble
guilloche border, is supported on a 19th-century 'Rococo' ormolu
console table, embellished with female heads and a cartouche bearing
the AR cypher of Augustus III, Elector of Saxony and King of Poland
(d.1763).

Italian Rococo
burr-walnut bureau
bookcase
Probably Milanese,
mid-18th century
86 in. (219 cm.) high;
35 in. (89 cm.) wide;
23 in. (59 cm.) deep
Sold 17 March 1990
in New York for
$264,000 (£162,963)

Genoese
ormolu-mounted
tulipwood
bureau-cabinet
18th century
94½ in. (240 cm.)
high; 43½ in.
(110 cm.) wide;
23⅝ in. (60 cm.)
deep
Sold 27 March 1990
in Rome for
L.322,000,000
(£158,620)

Central German Rococo walnut and marquetry bureau cabinet
Probably Erfurt, *c*.1760
95 in. (242 cm.) high;
64 in. (163 cm.) wide;
32½ in. (82 cm.) deep
Sold 26 April 1990 in New York for $330,000 (£201,220)

The distinctive marquetry of pastoral scenes set in elaborate rocaille cartouches with vigorous C-scrolls and rich foliage in stained and engraved woods relates closely to similar furniture made in Erfurt.

One of a pair of Louis XIV ormolu-mounted, marquetry and ebony armoires
83½ in. (210 cm.) high; 50 in. (127 cm.) wide; 22 in. (56 cm.) deep
Sold 7 December 1989 in London for £170,000 ($269,390)

The central 'Ionic' brass-inlaid pilaster and the ebony panels embellished with satyr-masked flower vases on claw-footed pedestals enriched with ormolu 'Apollo' masks reflects the late 17th-century fashion at the court of Louis XIV, popularized by Dutch craftsmen, such as Pierre Gole (died 1684), and particularly associated with the king's *ébéniste*, André-Charles Boulle (d.1732).

Louis XV ormolu-mounted marquetry
bureau-de-dame
32½ in. (82.5 cm.) high; 27 in. (68.5 cm.)
wide; 17 in. (43 cm.) deep
Sold 7 December 1989 in London for £88,000
($139,040)

The floral marquetry of this serpentined-
frame bureau can be compared to the work of
Pierre Roussel, *maître*, 1745.

Pair of Louis XV ormolu-mounted marquetry
bibliothèques basses
The feet and mounts English, 19th century
Sold 14 June 1990 in London for £90,200
($153,340)

These floral marquetry bookshelves,
purchased by the 2nd Earl of Bantry (d.1868)
for Bantry House, Cork, were thought to
have belonged to Queen Marie Antoinette.
The caster-blocks were added in Ireland.

Louis XV ormolu-mounted bureau plat
Stamped 'I.C. Ellaume'
30 in. (76 cm.) high; 62 in. (157.5 cm.) wide;
32 in. (81 cm.) deep
Sold 7 December 1989 in London for £55,000
($86,900)

The ends of this serpentined leather-topped
library bureau plat are appropriately
embellished with ormolu reclining female
figures of Astronomy, emblematic of one of
the liberal arts of secular learning. The piece
bears the brand of the *ébéniste* Jean-Charles
Ellaume, of rue Traversière-Saint Antoine,
maître in 1754, who is noted for his bureau
plats.

Louis XV ormolu-mounted marquetry
bibliothèque basse
Stamped 'J.F.Oeben'
*c.*1760
32½ in. (82.5 cm.) high; 43½ in. (111 cm.)
wide; 16¼ in. (41 cm.) deep
Sold 1 November 1989 in New York for
$165,000 (£105,566)

This marquetry bureau-cabinet reflects the
French neo-classical style of the 1760s. Its
frieze is fitted with small drawers flanking a
central hinged-fronted secretaire-drawer,
incorporating a leather writing panel above a
leather slide. The carcase bears the brand of
Jean-François Oeben (d.1763), who was
appointed Louis XV's *ébéniste privilégié* in
1754 and enjoyed the patronage of Madame
de Pompadour.

Louis XVI giltwood *tabouret de pieds*
Sold 14 June 1990 in London for £23,100 ($39,270)
Acquired by the Musée du Château Versailles

The canvas webbing bears the Château de Versailles stencil, and this may be the *tabouret* delivered for the use of the Comtesse de Provence, sister-in-law to Louis XVI, in 1787.

Louis XVI ormolu-mounted Japanese black-and-gold lacquer *commode*
à vantaux
By Adam Weisweiler
*c.*1785
36¾ in. (93.5 cm.) high; 58 in. (147.5 cm.) wide; 23 in. (58.5 cm.)
deep
Sold 1 November 1989 in New York for $264,000 (£105,566)

This neo-classical commode is likely to have been acquired by the 2nd
Earl Gower from the *marchand-mercier* Dominique Daguerre. It was
later acquired by the 1st Lord Carrington (d.1838) and it descended in
the Carrington family until it was sold at Christie's London salerooms
on 5 December 1928.

German Rococo walnut, marquetry and parquetry commode
Mid–18th century
31 in. (79 cm.) high; 52½ in. (133.5 cm.) wide; 24½ in. (62.5 cm.)
deep
Sold 23 September 1989 in New York for $264,000 (£167,088)

This serpentined commode, veneered with foliate-scrolled cartouches
with figurative marquetry flanked by trellis–work, relates to the
oeuvre of the Potsdam cabinet-makers J.F. and H.W. Spindler around
the time that they established their Berlin workshops in 1764.

Louis XVI ormolu-mounted mahogany commode
By David Roentgen
*c.*1785
33 in. (84 cm.) high; 52 in. (132 cm.) wide; 24½ in. (61.5 cm.) deep
Sold 14 June 1990 in London for £137,500 ($233,750)

This elegant commode reflects the French–Grecian style adopted by
the internationally celebrated Neuwied cabinet-maker David Roentgen
(d.1807) following his appointment as *ébéniste-mécanicien* to Louis XV
and his admittance as a *maître* to the Parisian *ébéniste* guild in 1780. It
relates to the furniture which he later provided to Tsarina Catherine II
of Russia, who recorded in 1785 that his 'two hundred cases have
arrived safely and at the right moment to satisfy my gluttony.' This
commode was formerly in the Lowenthal Collection, Berlin.

George III silver-gilt, silver and white marble mantel clock
Hallmarked 'Wm. Pitts and Jos. Preedy, 1795'; the later movement signed Grohé
17½ in. (44.5 cm.) high; 19 in. (48 cm.) wide
Sold 19 April 1990 in London for £57,200 ($95,524)
From the property of the late Michael Behrens, Esq.

This allegorical clock, with Calliope, the Muse of epic poetry, and her attendants celebrating at the altar of Apollo, god of poetry, relates closely to Louis XVI clocks in the Grecian manner of the 1790s. It bears the London assay mark for 1795, the year in which George, Prince of Wales (later George IV), celebrated his marriage. If reflects the Prince's taste for French furnishings, which was particularly encouraged by the Parisian dealer Dominique Daguerre, who had established premises in Sloane Street in the 1780s. The clock also bears the hallmarks of the celebrated silversmiths William Pitts and Joseph Preedy, who executed work for the Prince in the 1790s.

George III ormolu and Blue John candelabrum
By Matthew Boulton
14¼ in. (36 cm.) high; 14¼ in. (36 cm.) wide
Sold 21 December 1989 in Amsterdam for D.fl.82,800 (£27,000)
From the property of the late Mrs C.M. Cremers, Wassenaar

This Derbyshire 'Blue John' fluorspar 'egg', mounted as a neo-classical vase with winged female caryatid-therms bearing acanthus-scrolled branches for lights, is fitted with a foliate-lid terminating in a Bacchic pine-cone finial. This pattern was manufactured by Matthew Boulton of Soho, Birmingham, and was first mentioned in 1772, when examples were entered in Christie's and Ansell's sale.

Pair of German Rococo ormolu–mounted
Meissen porcelain candelabra
Mid-18th century
17½ in. (45 cm.) high
Sold 1 November 1989 in New York for
$88,000 (£56,302)

These highly decorative Chinoiserie
candlesticks, with festive boys wearing
ceremonial robes beneath the candle-nozzles
of triple-branched oak trees on scrolled
rock-work plinths, reflect the Rococo style of
the mid-18th century.

Florentine ormolu–mounted ebony and *pietra
dura* casket
13½ in. (34 cm.) high; 20½ in. (52 cm.)
wide; 14½ in. (37 cm.) deep
Sold 7 December 1989 in London for £29,700
($46,926)

The casket's tablets of flower vases and fruit
branches inhabited by birds and insects are
inspired by the late-17th-century designs of
Gian Battista Foggini for the *Opificio delle
Pietre Dure* at the Uffizi, Florence.

COLONIAL FURNITURE BY THOMAS TUFFT

Dean Failey

In early 1775, Philadelphia merchant and entrepreneur Richard Edwards (1744–99) placed an order for an impressive suite of furniture from local cabinet-maker Thomas Tufft. The purchase may have been in anticipation of his impending move to Lumberton, New Jersey, where he was to set up a store and begin an active trade between the outlying region and Philadelphia; or it may have been as a result of his recent marriage to Abigail Harrison.

Whatever the case, Edwards' account book entry for 24 March 1775 described the furniture as follows:

Thos Tuffts Acc't for my Furniture.	
To a pair of Mahogany Drawers Pitch head fret & Dentels	£22.
& a Table to Suit	£8.
To six Mahogany Chairs open backs an Elbow Chair to Suit	£13.8
To a Mahogany Table open fret Rails	£5.
To a Mahogany Clock Case Pitch head fret & dentels	£10.
I say settled this Account with Thos Tufft in full.	
19th 4 mo. 1776.	

Although he was a 'modest' Quaker, Edwards' order for case furniture designed with an architectural triangular or 'pitch head' pediment was extremely fashionable. The 'Mahogany Table [with] open fret Rails' was even more so, and it stands as a beautiful and unique survival today.

Little is known about the maker, Thomas Tufft. All that remains of his work is the surviving Edwards furniture together with a labelled dressing-table in the Philadelphia Museum of Art, and a labelled side chair in the Henry Francis du Pont Winterthur Museum. However, these pieces secure Tufft a significant place in the arts of colonial Philadelphia.

As is often the case, the table was located as a result of another auction: Christie's sale of the Edwards high chest of drawers and matching dressing-table, 28 May 1987, for $1.76 million (£1 million). To the delight and excitement of collectors and scholars, it was discovered at that time that all of the furniture had descended directly in the family.

Once again, provenance, documentation and aesthetic merit have proved a winning combination.

Richard Edwards Chippendale mahogany pier table By Thomas Tufft Philadelphia, c.1775–6 33¼ in. (85 cm.) high; 35½ in. (90 cm.) wide; 17⅛ in. (43.5 cm.) deep Sold 20 January 1990 in New York for $4,620,000 (£2,800,000) From the property of Mr Samuel Harrison Gardiner Record auction price for a table

Chippendale
mahogany side chair
Philadelphia, 1765–70
Sold 20 January 1990
in New York for
$418,000 (£253,333)
From the collection
of May and Howard
Joynt

Opposite:
The Cornelius
Stevenson
Chippendale
mahogany tea table
Attributed to
Thomas Affleck,
carving attributed to
Nicholas Bernard and
Martin Jugiez
Philadelphia, 1760–80
28¼ in. (72 cm.)
high; 35⅜ in.
(90 cm.) diameter
Sold 20 January 1990
in New York for
$1,320,000 (£733,333)

Federal inlaid and
flame birch veneered
mahogany chest of
drawers
New Hampshire,
1790–1810
37¼ in. (94 cm.)
high; 41 in. (104 cm.)
wide; 22½ in.
(57 cm.) deep
Sold 20 January 1990
in New York for
$220,000 (£133,333)

Chippendale
veneered mahogany
dressing bureau
Massachusetts,
1775–95
35 in. (89 cm.) high;
44 in. (111.7 cm.)
wide; 23 in. (58 cm.)
deep
Sold 20 January 1990
in New York for
$605,000 (£366,667)

Basel Gothic tapestry fragment woven with
the figures of a young woman and young
man in court dress
*c.*1430–40
76¾ × 37½ in. (195 × 93 cm.)
Sold 3 July 1990 in London for £638,000
($1,122,242)
Record auction price for a tapestry

During the fifteenth century the town of
Basel was the second most important trading
centre on the Upper Rhine, with a population
of 9,000. In 1431–8 the town was the seat of
the Council of Basel, convoked by Pope
Martin V in order to end the Great Schism
and bring about the reform of the Church.
The Council of Basel was supported not only
by the clergy, but also by the princes and
great universities. As a result, Basel was filled
with learned humanists, who may well have
encouraged and developed the native
iconography.

Throughout the Council, visitors were
astounded by the wealth and opulence of the
Basel burghers. Guests recorded that the
inhabitants of Basel decked their living and
reception rooms with magnificently coloured
tapestries.

Although the complex iconography of the
tapestries has yet to be clearly interpreted, the
first panel seems to mark a period in which
the medieval invention of the 'wildman', as
the personification of evil and violence, was
evolving into a gentler conception. Here the
wildman is the antithesis of civilized man and
the symbol of primitivism. The beasts in the
panel represent vices, probably envy and
barbarism, and are being urged forward by
their wild riders with flowering branches.

The courtly figures look apprehensively at
each other, as they resist the urge to give in
to their baser instincts. They stand in an
idealized meadow, symbolic of the earth's
riches, with a unicorn, a stag and rabbits
disappearing down and peeping out of their
burrows.

Brussels Gothic allegorical tapestry woven in silks and wools, depicting the winged figure of Fame trampling the Fates underfoot, surrounded by various allegorical figures
Monogrammed
CL SI
Early 16th century
13 ft. ½ in. × 11 ft. 8 in. (336 × 355 cm.)
Sold 14 June 1990 in London for £308,000 ($523,600)

This tapestry represents 'The Triumph of Fame', the fourth of six allegorical poems by Francesco Petrarch. The series described 'The Triumph of Love' leading to 'The Triumph of Eternity', and was a popular marriage theme during the Renaissance. The depiction of Fame as a winged female figure is taken from classical antiquity: Horace noted in the Odes that she flew on wings that never tired.

Franco–Flemish late
Gothic silk and wool
tapestry depicting the
Adoration of the
Magi
Late 15th or early
16th century
13 ft. 6 in. × 11 ft. 3 in
(405 × 338 cm.)
Sold 26 April 1990 in
New York for
$165,000 (£100,610)

Chinese Imperial dragon robe
Late 18th century
Silk embroidered with coloured silks and gilt threads
Sold 3 July 1990 in London at South Kensington for £15,400 ($27,104)
From the collection formed by Daniele Varé in the 1920s
Record auction price for a Chinese robe

The robe shows the twelve symbols of authority relating to the
sacrificial obligations of the Emperor

RARE EARLY TEXTILES

Susan Mayor

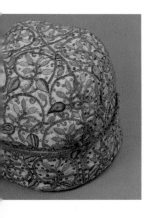

Gentleman's linen nightcap
*c.*1600
Embroidered in coloured silks, silver-gilt threads and sequins
Sold 19 June 1990 in London at South Kensington for £19,800 ($33,858)
Record auction price for a non-military hat

This season several highly important textiles appeared on the market at Christie's South Kensington. Most notably, on Tuesday 7 November, the Iklé Collection was auctioned raising £285,000 ($448,875). Leopold Iklé (1838–1922) began collecting one hundred years ago with the intention of forming a design archive for the machine lace manufactory, 'Iklé Frères', which he built up in St. Gall, Switzerland.

A Coptic tapestry panel from this sale realized the highest price of the season, £35,200 ($55,616). The only comparable examples known are in the Hermitage and Brooklyn Museums. A series of six fourteenth-century Lower Saxon panels embroidered with scenes of the Life of Christ, showing clothes worked in brightly coloured, almost modern, stripes, also realized £35,200 ($55,616).

Top prices spanned many cultures and many centuries. The second most important sale of the season (totalling £194,650, $330,905) was the Oriental and Islamic Textile sale on 23 April, which included part of the Kolz Collection from Michigan, USA, in particular a fine Moghul tent hanging or 'kanat', which realized £30,800 ($52,360). The most important sale of its type ever held at South Kensington, it also launched the Islamic Week in London and was consequently very well attended.

An eighteenth-century Chinese Imperial robe in another Oriental Textile sale realized a world record price of £15,400 ($27,104), but the most expensive article of dress sold at auction this year was a late Elizabethan nightcap which fetched £19,800 ($33,858). These nightcaps were of course worn by men, and were encrusted with sequins and sometimes with pearls. Among the less valuable items of costume were Paco Rabanne's 1968 armoured coat made of triangles of red suede, which sold at £1,870 ($3,179) and is now in the Ulster Museum. Spanning two cultures was an eighteenth-century dress made of Chinese embroidery selling at £5,280 ($8,976), even without its petticoat. This had been bought recently for the princely sum of £90 ($153).

The success of textiles generally might seem to overshadow fan sales. However, the fan market is still buoyant, even though a single fan has yet to reach five figures. This season we held four fan sales, which realized £242,279 (approximately $411,874) altogether. The top price was £3,960 ($6,732) for a fan from *c.*1720, painted with Diana the Huntress, which once formed part of the collection of Countess Beatrice Colonna in Rome.

Silesian linen altar cloth depicting the Adoration of Christ, with various other biblical scenes
Late 15th century
Worked in gilt, silver-gilt threads and coloured silks
34 × 30 in. (86.4 × 76.2 cm.)
Sold 7 November 1989 in London at South Kensington for £28,600 ($45,188)
From the Iklé Collection

Right:
Coptic tapestry panel depicting a nude female deity
Probably one of a pair
Late 4th or early 5th century
Framed and glazed
9½ × 9 in. (24.1 × 22.9 cm.)
Sold 7 November 1989 in London at South Kensington for £35,200 (£55,616)
From the Iklé Collection

Right:
Set of six North German linen panels depicting scenes from the Life of Christ
14th century
Embroidered with coloured silks, two of the panels framed and glazed
12 × 9 in. (30.5 × 22.9 cm.)
Sold 7 November 1989 in London at South Kensington for £35,200 ($55,616)
From the Iklé Collection

Fine cotton Mughal *kanat* printed
and painted with lilies and birds
Late 17th or early 18th century
Sold 23 April 1990 in London at
South Kensington for £30,800
($52,360)

Savonnerie carpet
19 ft. 7 in. × 13 ft. 1 in.
(595 × 399 cm.)
Sold 23 November
1989 in London for
£27,500 ($43,175)

Aubusson carpet
21 ft. 10 in. × 14 ft. 8 in.
(664 × 446 cm.)
Sold 23 November
1989 in London for
£41,800 ($65,626)

Kashan
'Mochtasham' carpet
13 ft. 6 in. × 10 ft. 4 in.
(412 × 314 cm.)
Sold 12 October 1989
in London for
£16,500 ($26,070)

Agra carpet
13 ft. 6 in. × 9 ft. 10 in.
(413 × 299 cm.)
Sold 23 November
1989 in London for
£55,000 ($86,350)

Dragon Soumac
carpet
Late 17th century
11 ft. 10 in. × 6 ft. 6 in.
(360 × 200 cm.)
Sold 12 October 1989
in London for
£71,500 ($112,970)

Slit tapestry silk rug
5 ft. 7 in. × 4 ft. 3 in.
(170 × 129 cm.)
Sold 7 April 1990
in New York for
$440,000 (£268,293)
Record auction price
for a Persian weaving

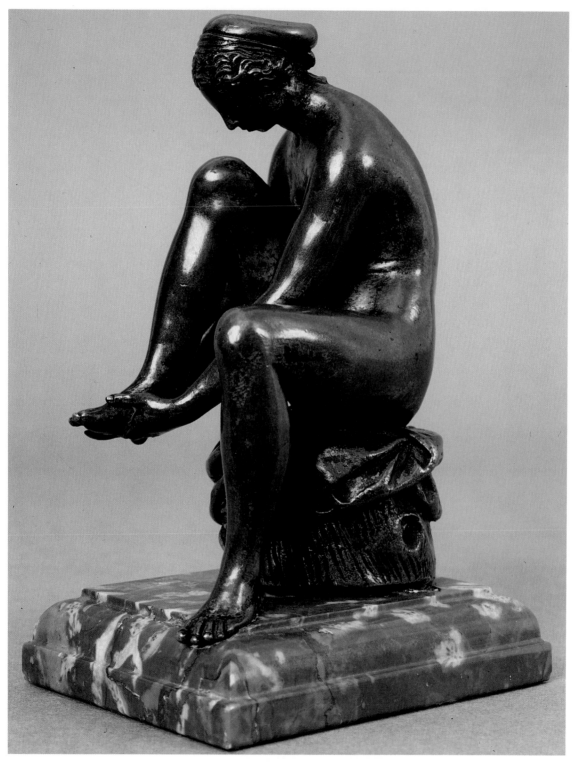

French bronze
statuette of a young
woman
Attributed Barthélémy
Prieur
Late 16th or early
17th century
4¼ in. (11 cm.) high
Sold 11 April 1990 in
London for £52,000
($89,760)

Florentine bronze
group of the rape of
a Sabine
By Giambologna
Signed 'Gio.
Bolonge'
Late 16th century
23¼ in. (59 cm.)
high
Sold 5 December
1989 in London for
£2,750,000
($4,400,000)
Record auction price
for a work by the
artist

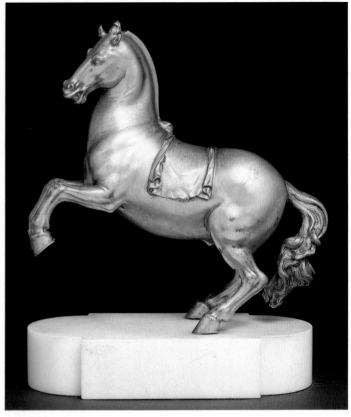

Terracotta model of a walking horse
By Artus Quellinus the Elder
Signed and dated 1638
11¼ in. (28.5 cm.) high
Sold 10 January 1990 in New York for $308,000
(£185,542)

Gilt-bronze statuette of a rearing horse
Attributed to Ferdinando Tacca
Mid-17th century
9½ × 8⅞ in. (23.5 × 22.5 cm.)
Sold 10 January 1990 in New York for $550,000
(£331,325)

Florentine bronze group of Diana discovered by Pan
Attributed to Ferdinando Tacca
Mid-17th century
13¾ × 15¾ in. (35.5 × 40 cm.)
Sold 3 July 1990 in London for £209,000 ($367,631)
Formerly in the collection of King Louis XIV of France,
inscribed with French Crown inventory number 282

Below:
Trapani gilt-copper and coral devotional pendant
Late 17th or early 18th century
12¼ in. (31 cm.) high overall
Sold 3 July 1990 in London for £22,00 ($38,698)

Far right:
Italo–Byzantine
(Venetian?) ivory
plaque of the
Annunciation
12th century
3⅞ × 3⅛ in.
(9.8 × 7.9 cm.)
Sold 8 January 1990
in New York for
$70,400 (£44,000)

English marble bust of William Pitt the Elder,
Earl of Chatham
By Joseph Wilton
Signed
Late 18th century
28¾ in. (73 cm.) high
Sold 5 December 1989 in London for
£115,000 ($184,800)

One of a pair of French white marble groups
of putti
Late 17th or early 18th century
40¾ × 42¾ in. (104 × 109 cm.)
Sold 5 December 1989 in London for £44,000
($70,400)

Painted plaster bust
of Robert Fulton
By Jean-Antoine
Houdon
Signed
27 in. (68.5 cm.)
high
Sold 1 December
1989 in New York
for $880,000
(£560,510)

French silvered bronze group of Hebe and Jupiter's eagle
Cast from a model by Albert-Ernest Carrier-Belleuse
Mid-19th century
19¾ in. (50 cm.) high
Sold 15 February 1990 in London for £33,000 ($56,100)

French bronze figure of a nereid
Cast from a model by Antoine-Louis Barye
Signed
Mid-19th century
12¼ in. (31 cm.) high
Sold 15 February 1990 in London for £36,300 ($61,710)

French silvered bronze bust of a *Nègre du Soudan en costume algérien*
Cast from a model by
Charles-Henri-Joseph Cordier
Signed
Mid-19th century
16¼ in. (42 cm.) high
Sold 10 May 1990 in London for £26,400
($44,352)

Roman micromosaic panel of the interior of
St. Peter's
By Augusto Moglia
Signed and dated 1899
28¼ × 20¼ in. (71.5 × 53 cm.)
Sold 10 May 1990 in London for £46,000
($77,616)

French tinted marble and bronze female figure
of a *Danseuse mauresque*
By Jean-Léon Gérôme
Signed
72 in. (182.9 cm.) high
Sold 22 May 1990 in New York $440,000
(£260,355)

French silvered bronze figure of Sappho
Cast by Victor Paillard from a model by
Jean-Jacques Pradier
Signed and dated 1848
33¾ in. (86 cm.) high
Sold 28 September 1989 in London for
£66,000 ($108,900)

Right:
Violin
By Tomaso
Balestrieri
Cremona, 1778
Length of back
13¹³/₁₆ in. (35.1 cm.)
Sold 28 March 1990
in London for
£93,500 ($154,275)
Record auction price
for a violin by the
maker

Far right:
Violoncello
By Francesco Rugeri
Cremona, 1667
Length of back
29¹³/₁₆ in. (75.6 cm.)
Sold 22 November
1989 in London for
£88,000 ($140,800)

Violin
By Giovanni Francesco Pressenda
Turin, 1847
Length of back 14 in. (35.6 cm.)
Sold 22 November 1989 in London for
£71,500 ($114,400)

Right:
Violin
By Joseph Rocca
Turin, 1841
Length of back 14 in. (35.6 cm.)
Sold 22 November 1989 in London for
£99,000 ($158,400)
Record auction price for a violin by the
maker

Far right:
Violin
By Francesco Rugeri
Cremona, 1677
Length of back 13^{15}⁄$_{16}$ in. (35.4 cm.)
Sold 22 November 1989 in London for
£71,500 ($114,400)
Record auction price for a violin by the
maker

THE SUMMERFIELD COLLECTION

Charles Ebrington

Ronald Summerfield was from Derby, and it was there that he first began to work as an antique dealer in 1935. During the pre-war years he ran a conventional antique business dealing in a wide range of goods. It was not until 1952, when his family moved to Cheltenham, that he started to collect with a fervour which in the course of the next thirty years enabled him to fill not just his shop and the flat above but also a large terraced house nearby. Summerfield bought extensively, buying anything if the price was right or paying over the odds if he wanted to prevent someone else from buying. The joy to him was the buying and hoarding of antiques rather than the actual trading. It was in fact extremely difficult to buy anything from Summerfield, as he really only sold just enough to finance further purchases. As the years passed he released even less and kept his shop open for purely intellectual stimulation – it gave him great pleasure to tantalize passers-by with a glimpse of something good, about which he would discuss the price, and then refuse to sell.

I first met him in 1985, and after a probationary period during which he would bring occasional pieces for Christie's to sell, I was finally asked to look at a picture in his home which was too large for him to move. It was a privilege few had been accorded. Walking through the front door one was faced by a sculptured wall of antiques surmounted by a plaster bust of Dante. Then one had to edge sideways down the narrow passage, ducking around the legs of a table, the surface of which had been long since buried by books and boxes.

Every room on each of the five storeys was filled to the ceiling with antiques of every conceivable nature. Although by then in his seventies, Summerfield would dart nimbly through the house. He would pick something up to show me and put it down again, insisting on replacing it himself – partly because he had an amazing memory for where everything was in the chaos, and partly because he had an uncanny knack of balancing everything so that nothing was ever broken.

Whole rooms had been blocked off by mountains of books which he bought to make barricades against possible intruders. Such was his success that there were at least two rooms that he had not been able to enter himself for over twenty years. One of these I helped him break into from a first-floor window, but the other was not opened until the mountain of books had been removed after his death.

Ron Summerfield died on Good Friday 1989, and owing to the publicity his death received and the makeshift security arrangements in existence, Christie's first priority was

Christie's staff clearing the unusual mix of items at Summerfield's house. (Photo: Robin Anderson)

to remove as much of value as soon as possible. Having been requested by him to arrange the disposal of his entire collection, we had considerable logistical problems to overcome.

We subsequently reckoned that the contents consisted of over 7,000 pictures, probably 25,000 pieces of porcelain, and large quantities of items from almost every specialist category that Christie's sells. Not surprisingly, it proved to be rather problematic to find a location for the auction. The garden was too small to hold a sale, and, anyway, it was full of his abandoned cars, which in turn were stuffed with yet more old and weathered books. It was obviously impractical to move everything up to London as there was simply not enough room even there.

After much searching, a suitable and secure warehouse was found where everything was taken from the house and sorted. We decided to hold a six-day sale on Cheltenham Racecourse, taking a selection of the best pictures and any piece of international interest to London. The rest of the chattels were given to the local auctioneers Bruton Knowles to sell in a series of sales lasting sixteen days.

During the summer the house was gradually cleared. The books went first to enable access, with a team of removal men following behind, who were packing and then unpacking at our temporary warehouse. Huge racks were assembled, where the porcelain was sorted, catalogued, lotted up, then repacked into containers. The pictures were sorted out as to their destination and those to be sold in Cheltenham were catalogued and stored. Throughout the summer a constant stream of experts came down from London to complete the cataloguing. The photography was done in a temporary dark-room at the back of the warehouse and by the beginning of August the catalogue had gone to the printers.

The sale itself started on 23 October. Huge numbers came to the viewing in a network of marquees in the shadow of the grandstand on Cheltenham Racecourse. Viewing was followed by a Charity Preview in aid of the National Art Collections Fund and the Sue Ryder Homes. This preview took place in gale-force winds – a forerunner of the winter storms. At the end of it every picture had to be removed from the wall and every piece of porcelain lain on its side to prevent damage. By nine o'clock the next morning everything had to be back in place for another day's viewing.

The bidding was very competitive. As well as the bidders in the room many commission bids were left and telephone bids were received from as far afield as Australia and Hong Kong. However, many lots were sold to local buyers, some of whom were bidding for lots they had narrrowly failed to buy twenty years previously when they had been outbid by Ronald Summerfield in local house sales. One man bought a large continental vase which Summerfield had adamantly refused to sell him, the pair to one he had bought in the same sale as Summerfield in 1959.

Over the six days £2,669,199 ($4,462,901) was raised and subsequent sales in London and Gloucestershire have raised the total to in excess of £6 million (approximately $10 million).

Summerfield had bought well and in large quantities. In the 1950s and 1960s, when many country house collections were being dispersed in an era before public awareness of the value of works of art was as acute as it is today, he bought pictures for a few pounds which today fetch thousands. In fact, the few purchase records that remain show the extent of the changes in price which have occurred over the years. *Milton Being Read to by His Daughter*, a

The exterior of Ronald Summerfield's house

Christie's Cotswolds representative, Charles Ebrington, takes on the challenge of sorting the Summerfield Collection. (Photo: Martin Reynolds)

painting from the circle of Edward Mathew Ward, fetched £4,180 ($6,496) in October 1989, whereas Summerfield had bought this item for £20 in the 1950s. Similarly, a pair of Henry Schafer watercolours of Caudebec sur Seine, originally bought for £10, was sold at Christie's for £1,760 ($2,943); and a watercolour by Emile Krause which Summerfield bought for 21 shillings in 1956 realized £1,320 ($2,207). The few records of Summerfield's purchases also included a picture of a ploughing match by Miles of Northleach, Gloucestershire, which shows a price of £2 12s. when bought some time in the 1950s. Christie's was to sell this for £14,200 ($23,742) in a Naive Paintings sale. Among the objects sold, there was a Chinese bronze figure of an eighteen-armed Bodhisattva, originally purchased by Summerfield for £4 and auctioned by Christie's for £5,280 ($8,828).

However, the most satisfactory sale was probably the monochrome portrait of a man in a turban attributed to Joseph Wright of Derby. This painting made £79,200 ($127,512) when it was included in an auction in London of Important British Pictures a month after the Cheltenham sale. It is believed that Summerfield bought this work in his home town during the 1930s.

Buried for a quarter of a century, the arrival of Summerfield's collection on the public market resulted in keen interest, and prices far exceeded all expectations. Perhaps Ron Summerfield's real achievement, though, was not to have amassed a collection worth millions, but to have collected and packed his terraced house with enough antiques to furnish half a dozen stately homes. The last time Christie's sold a property with so many lots was at Stowe Park in 1848!

NOSTELL PRIORY

Sir Nicholas Brooksbank, Bt., and John Hardy

In April 1990, two centuries after the Winn family called in James Christie (d.1807) to sell the contents of their St. James' Square house, they called in his firm once again to sell the contents 'surplus to requirements' of Nostell Priory near Wakefield. Both sales included furniture by Thomas Chippendale.

House sales are sometimes poignant occasions marking the end of a family's long tenure of an estate. The dispersal, in these circumstances, of the contents of an important house, always provokes great enthusiasm among dealers and collectors, who both welcome the rare opportunity of buying an object from the place for which it was originally made.

In recent years there have been fewer true dispersals and a growing number of 'attic' sales where unwanted and surplus contents have been offered for sale 'on the premises'. The Nostell sale, comprising over 750 lots of furniture, objects of art, garden ornaments, textiles, porcelain, prints, maps, arms and antiquities, showed how successful such occasions can be.

When the most widely read English saleroom correspondent arrived for a preview of the sale he asked, almost before he was out of his taxi, why the family was selling. He was told that the answer would probably be obvious before the end of his tour. By the time that Lady St. Oswald had trotted him round the house it was apparent to him that much of the palladian mansion, built in the mid-eighteenth century and furnished since by eight Rowland Winns, was packed with unwanted objects which had no future in either the public rooms or the family's private apartment.

Nostell is particularly renowned for the handsome furnishings supplied under the direction of the architects James Paine and Robert Adam for Sir Rowland Winn, 4th Baronet (d.1765), and his son the 5th Baronet (d.1786). Their patronage of Thomas Chippendale (d.1779) helped to earn him the title of the 'Shakespeare' of the English cabinet-making world (in Christopher Gilbert's *The Life and Work of Thomas Chippendale*, published by Studio Vista in association with Christie's in 1978). Considerable interest was shown in the various fine mahogany or oak pieces which could be ascribed to the Chippendale firm on stylistic grounds. The 5th Baronet's 'Four Seasons' marquetry wardrobe, attributed to Chippendale the Younger (d.1822) was finally acquired by Christopher Gilbert, Director of the Leeds City Art Gallery, for display at Temple Newsam House. Amongst the numerous items secured by the National Trust, to whom the house was presented in 1952, were a lead garden statue of Venus dating from the eighteenth century and a Roman marble head of a maenad, which formerly embellished one of the stone chimney pieces in the hall, where it was recorded in the 1818 inventory. However, a beautiful cinerary urn with spiral strigil fluting eluded them at £24,400 ($40,016), some five times above the original estimate. The market also applauded the taste of Charles Winn (d.1874), once described as a *collectionneur enragé*, whose considerable additions to the house furnishings included a collection of Etruscan vases which were sold at Christie's in 1975. These may originally have been displayed in his elegant Grecian breakfast room. A few years ago this room was re-decorated as an eighteenth-century bedroom following a serious fire which might have engulfed the entire house had it not been promptly discovered. The pink scar on the façade of the house is now the sole evidence of this narrowly averted catastrophe. The Regency furnishings from the breakfast room alone, comprising Grecian sideboard cabinets, a table, fender, pole screen and Pompeian chandelier, raised almost £100,000 (approximately $164,000).

When the Winn family bought the Nostell Estate in 1650 they moved into an adapted house surviving from the Augustinian Priory. In the mid-eighteenth century the fourth Sir Rowland demolished this medieval building, which stood at an awkward angle to his new house. A quantity of the stone presumably from this source, together with a number of carved beams which must have originated in the priory church, had long been stored at Nostell. The same store also contained the dismantled fragments of a Gothik folly. This was included in the sale and found a buyer who intends to re-erect it. Happily the fragments of old Nostell have been sold to the Nation by private treaty to ensure their long-term association with their original site.

Nostell Priory, Wakefield, Yorkshire, with Christie's marquee in the foreground

CLOCKS
AND WATCHES

Genevan gold, enamel and jewelled double
singing bird cage, with flying bird
automaton, clockwatch and music
By Frères Rochat and G. Rémond
Signed 'Fait à Genève per Strüber chez Jn.
Gge. Remond & Comp.'
*c.*1805–10
8½ in. (21.5 cm.) high
Sold 15 November 1989 in Geneva for
Sw.fr.825,000 (£323,529)

THE EAGLE AND THE DOVE:
A CONTRAST IN HIGH-FLYING AUTOMATA

Mayella Figgis

A double bill of singing birds set a milestone at Christie's Geneva on 15 November 1989. One of the two pieces took the form of a double-barrelled flintlock pistol, while the other was a double singing-bird cage. The pistol, the 'eagle' of the duo, broke the auction record set four years earlier by another ingenious automaton, the Fabergé sedan chair from the Sir Charles Clore Collection. By appearing side by side at auction this year, the eagle and the dove shifted attention from the Russian workshops of Fabergé to the earlier Swiss makers, Frères Rochat and Jean George Rémond.

Their names were first recorded *c.*1804, when they were working within Maison Leschot. Jaquet Droz and Jean Frédéric Leschot, originally from Neuchâtel, had settled in Geneva in 1787 and had become well known for producing and selling singing-bird boxes and watches on a commercial scale. Keenly aware of the very high reputation enjoyed by English workmanship, the partnership Droz and Leschot often misleadingly added the word London to Droz's signature, perhaps with the dubious justification that their agent Henri Maillardet resided there. In fact all their work was manufactured to the highest standard in Switzerland, but at lower, competitive prices.

If the first mechanical singing birds were rather crude, they had this much in common with their sophisticated successors: they brought surprise and delight. As the novelty of the early boxes became exhausted through extensive export not only to England, but also to China and India, greater elaboration had to be devised.

From the Leschot springboard the Rochat brothers went on to exploit this need, becoming the most famous makers of automata after they set up independently *c.*1810. Both the present examples date from about then. Of the two, the birdcage is probably the earlier as lacking the initials 'FR', found both on the movement of a related cage of 1815 (also sold at Christie's Geneva, 11 November 1987) and on the pistol.

In their standard work on the subject, *Le Monde des automates*, Chapuis and Gelis consider that 'of objects incorporating a singing bird, those presenting the greatest difficulties, both in their conception and execution are…pistols'. This enforces the view that the pistol postdates the singing-bird cage. It also explains the scarcity of these technically highly complex automata and the degree to which they were coveted by dilettanti.

Three grades of pistol have been identified in a total production that can have amounted to no more than a dozen, and all are the work of the Rochat brothers. In the simplest type, pulling the trigger releases from the single barrel a bunch of flowers previously concealed

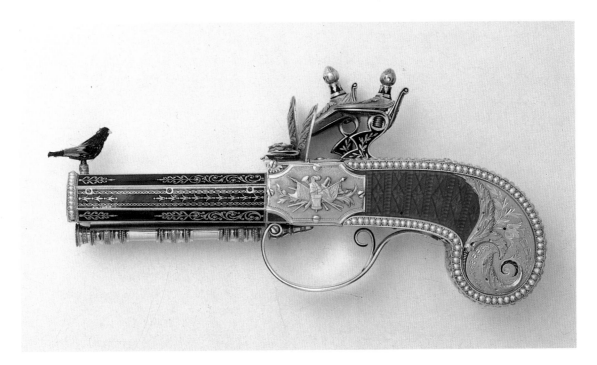

Genevan gold and
enamel singing bird
automaton, in the
form of a flintlock
box-lock pistol
By Frères Rochat
Stamped 'FR'
c.1810
6¼ in. (16.2 cm.)
long
Sold 15 November
1989 in Geneva for
Sw.fr.1,760,000
(£690,196)
Record auction price
for an automaton and
for any Swiss object
of vertu

by a medallion; it disappears again without a tune having been played. In a more complex type a bird is released, but remains still. With the most complex type, of which the present pistol is an example, the bird is catapulted out of the muzzle onto the end of the barrel, where it sings its tune while moving wings, tail and beak, turning its head and swivelling on its perch, finally snapping back into the barrel. These functions are achieved through the interaction of four springs, two of which are wound during play. Until the recent discovery of this unrecorded example, only two singing-bird pistols of this size and complexity were known; none had ever been sold at auction.

If the pistol is one of only three, the birdcage is, as far as we know, uniquely complex. It is constructed with paired columns at the angles, rather than the four single columns of other known examples, two of which have only a single bird. But most important, this is the only example where the lower bird takes to the air: when the upper bird ceases its song, the cage doors open and the lower bird 'flies' on a concealed extension of the perch bar and sings a different song before returning to its perch to end the action in a duet. In addition to the three movements in the base – operating clock, music and bird song – the accessory movement required to create the 'flying' effect is particularly intricate, as the bird continues to turn, flap its wings and move beak and tail, regardless of its position in the cage.

Both automata excelled on the day, but the pistol, on the first ever appearance of its *genre* at auction, sang the highest note without ruffling a single feather: it achieved a world record auction price for any automaton or Swiss object of vertu of Sw.fr.1,760,000 (£690,196). Bought by Patek Philippe as the ultimate example of Swiss craftsmanship of the period leading up to the establishment of their own business in 1830, it deservedly holds a place of honour in their museum in Geneva.

Far left:
Empire ormolu mounted mahogany clock and pedestal
Signed 'Breguet' and the enamel signed 'Dubuisson', the case by Denière
*c.*1810
35 in. (89 cm.) high
Sold 26 April 1990 in New York for $66,000 (£40,244)

Left:
French mahogany mantel regulator with equation of time
Signed 'Champion à Paris'
Dated 1823
22¾ in. (57.5 cm.) high
Sold 26 April 1990 in New York for $55,000 (£33,537)

Pair of George III gilt musical clocks in the form of camels
In the manner of James Cox
*c.*1780
22 in. (56 cm.) high
Sold 28 October 1989 in New York for $462,000 (£294,268)

Opposite, below left:
Queen Anne small bracket clock with alarm
Signed 'Cha. Gretton London', *c.*1710
12 in. (30.5 cm.) high
Sold 4 July 1990 in London for £17,600 ($31,170)

Right:
The Lonsdale
Tompion: a Charles II
diminutive travelling
timepiece alarm
Signed 'Tho:
Tompion Lon.' and
numbered '23', *c.*1680
8 in. (20 cm.) high
Sold 4 July 1990 in
London for £275,000
($487,025)

Far right:
William and Mary
miniature bracket
clock
Signed 'Tho.
Tompion Londini
Fecit'and numbered
'270', *c.*1690
10¼ in. (26 cm.)
high
Sold 4 July 1990 in
London for £198,000
($350,658)

Far right:
George I grande
sonnerie bracket
clock
Signed 'Dan.
Delander London'
*c.*1720
17½ in. (44.5 cm.)
high
Sold 4 July 1990 in
London for £82,500
($146,108)
From the Rous Lench
Collection

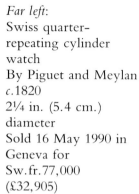

Far left:
Swiss quarter-repeating cylinder watch
By Piguet and Meylan
c.1820
2¼ in. (5.4 cm.) diameter
Sold 16 May 1990 in Geneva for Sw.fr.77,000 (£32,905)

Left:
French early verge tulip form watch
By Sermand, *c*.1640
1½ in. (3.8 cm.) long
Sold 4 July 1990 in London for £33,000 ($58,443)

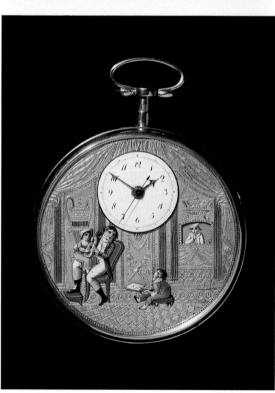

Far left:
Genevan gold and enamel musical automaton verge watch
By Isaac Daniel Piguet
c.1800
2¼ in. (5.8 cm.) diameter
Sold 4 July 1990 in London for £23,100 ($40,910)

Left:
Franco-Dutch watch case
Signed 'JT', attributed to Jean Toutin the Younger
c.1650
1¾ in. (4.6 cm.) diameter
Sold 15 November 1989 in Geneva for Sw.fr.77,000 (£30,196)

Right:
Swiss world-time watch with enamelled dial
Signed 'Patek Philippe & Co., Genève, No. 930837', *c*.1949
1¾ in. (4.4 cm.) diameter
Sold 28 October 1989 in New York for $71,500 (£45,541)

Below right:
One of a pair of English gold and enamel duplex watches for the
Chinese market
Signed 'Ilbery, London, No.2709', *c*.1820
2¼ in. (5.4 cm.) diameter
Sold 16 May 1990 in Geneva for Sw.fr.55,000 (£23,504)

Below:
Swiss gold and enamel keyless lever dress watch
Signed 'Vacheron & Constantin, Genève, No. 440280', *c*.1930
1¾ in. (4.7 cm.) diameter (photograph enlarged)
Sold 16 May 1990 in Geneva for Sw.fr.57,200 (£24,444)

Left:
Swiss gold square wristwatch with calendar and moonphase
By Audemars Piguet, retailed by Cartier and numbered '56735'
c.1940
⅞ in. (2.3 cm.) wide
Sold 16 May 1990 in Geneva for Sw.fr.132,000 (£56,410)

Top right:
Swiss gold chronograph wristwatch
Signed 'Audemars Piguet, Genève'
c.1945
1¼ in. (3 cm.) diameter
Sold 16 May 1990 in Geneva for Sw.fr.50,600 (£21,623)

Right:
Swiss gold calendar chronograph wristwatch
Signed 'Rolex Oyster Chronograph Antimagnetic, No. 6036 917818'
c.1952
13⅞ in. (3.5 cm.)diameter
Sold 22 June 1990 in London at South Kensington for £27,500 ($46,750)

Left:
Swiss gold wrist chronograph with perpetual calendar
Signed 'Patek Philippe & Co., Genève, No. 867733'
c.1950
1½ in. (3.7 cm.) diameter
Sold 28 April 1990 in New York for $154,000 (£94,478)

Far left:
French gold chronograph wristwatch
Signed 'Breguet'
c.1945
1¼ in. (3 cm.) diameter
Sold 15 November 1989 in Geneva for Sw.fr.71,500 (£28,039)

Left:
Swiss gold split-second chronograph wristwatch
By Patek Philippe, No.868327, for Serpico y Laino, Caracas
c.1953
1¼ in. (3.3 cm.) diameter
Sold 28 March 1990 in Rome for L.281,750,000 (£138,793)
Record auction price for a wristwatch sold in Italy

Right:
Swiss white gold rectangular calendar wristwatch
Signed 'Audemars Piguet & Co., Swiss, No. 38751'
c.1928
1¼ in. (3.4 cm.) long
Sold 16 May 1990 in Geneva for Sw.fr.33,000 (£14,103)

Above:
Swiss gold centre seconds wristwatch with perpetual calendar
Signed 'Patek Philippe & Co., Genève, No. 888168'
c.1960
1¼ in. (3.3 cm.) diameter
Sold 28 April 1990 in New York for $93,500 (£57,361)

Far left:
Swiss yellow gold perpetual calendar and
moonphase wristwatch
Signed 'Patek Philippe, Genève, No. 964559'
c.1948
1¼ in (3.3 cm.) diameter
Sold 22 June 1990 in London at South
Kensington for £55,000 ($93,500)

Left:
Swiss yellow gold officer's campaign watch
Signed 'Patek Philippe, Genève, 150e
Anniversaire, 1839–1989, No. 768838'
Completed 1989
1¼ in. (3.2 cm.) diameter
Sold 22 June 1990 in London at South
Kensington for £19,800 ($33,660)

Swiss lady's diamond and pearl bracelet watch
Signed 'Cartier' and 'E.W. & C. Co Inc.
Swiss', numbered '15390–10131'
c.1913
1¼ in. (3 cm.) wide
Sold 21 February 1990 in St. Moritz for
Sw.fr.30,800 (£12,320)

Right:
Swiss gold triple complicated
keyless lever pocket watch
Signed 'Audemars Piguet &
Cie., Genève, No. 5407'
c.1900
2 in. (5 cm.) diameter
Sold 16 May 1990 in Geneva for
Sw.fr.219,000 (£93,589)

Far right:
Swiss gold one–minute
tourbillon lever watch
Signed 'Patek Philippe & Co.,
Genève, Swiss, No. 198412'
c.1932
1⅞ in. (4.8 cm.) diameter
Sold 16 May 1990 in Geneva for
Sw.fr.440,000 (£188,034)

Right:
Swiss gold minute repeating
watch with perpetual calendar
and moonphase
Signed 'Patek Philippe & Co.,
Genève, No. 80266'
Completed 1888
2¼ in. (5.6 cm.) diameter
Sold 28 October 1989 in New
York for $110,000 (£70,064)

Far right:
Swiss gold independent jump
seconds keyless lever watch
Signed 'Patek Philippe & Co.,
Genève, No.34094'
c.1870
2¼ in. (5.4 cm.) diameter
Sold 15 November 1989 in
Geneva for Sw.fr.176,000
(£69,020)

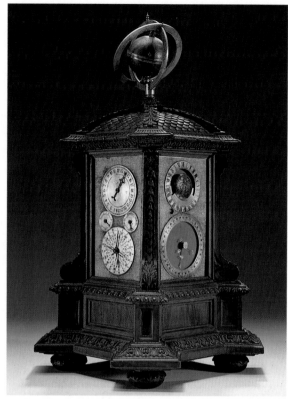

South German gilt-metal Meisterstück tabernacle clock
In the manner of Jeremias Metzger
Dated 1566
11½ in. (29.4 cm.) high
Sold 4 December 1989 in London for £93,500 ($146,795)

Above right:
Tyrolean carved walnut small astronomical clock with perpetual
calendar, equation of time, planetarium and orrery
Signed 'Joh. Uberbacher, Brixen, Tirol'
Mid-19th century
18½ in. (47 cm.) high
Sold 28 April 1990 in New York for $93,500 (£57,361)

Right:
Gilt-metal champlevé enamel and micromosaic grande sonnerie
carriage clock
Inscribed 'Roma Christmas MDCCCLXXXVI'
Dated 1887
7¼ in. (18.5 cm.) high
Sold 4 July 1990 in London for £8,250 ($14,108)

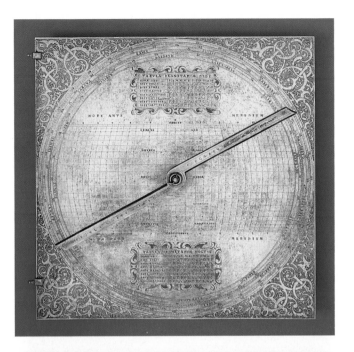

Above:
Spanish gilt-brass and silver universal equinoctial dial
Signed 'Juanin Cocart fecit en Madrid'
Dated 1600
2⅛ in. (5.4 cm.) long
Sold 29 March 1990 in London at South Kensington for
£38,500 ($63,525)

Top right:
South German gilt-copper astrolabe quadrant
Signed 'Christophorus Schissler Geometricus ac Artifex
Augusta Vindelicorum'
Dated 1576
11⅝ × 11⅝ in. (29.5 × 29.5 cm.)
Sold 28 September 1989 in London at South Kensington for
£187,000 ($304,810)

Right:
German brass astrolabe
Signed 'Andreas Becker'
Dated 1607
8⅜ in. (21.2 cm.) diameter
Sold 28 September 1989 in London at South Kensington for
£29,700 ($48,411)

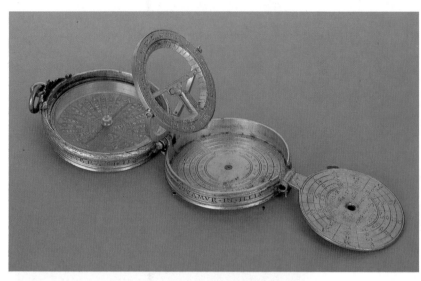

Elizabethan gilt–brass pocket astronomical
compendium
Signed 'Humfrey Cole'
Dated 1579
2¼ in. (5.6 cm.) diameter
Sold 29 March 1990 in London at South
Kensington for £115,500 ($190,575)

Below:
Dutch celestial globe on a painted wooden
stand
Signed 'Ger et Leon Valk, Amstelaedamenses
Cum Privilegio'
Dated 1700
15⅝ in. (39 cm.) diameter
Sold 29 March 1990 in London at South
Kensington for £8,800 ($14,520)

English silver
terrestrial globe
Early 19th century
7⅝ in. (19.4 cm.)
high; the globe
3½ in. (8.9 cm.)
diameter
Sold 29 March 1990
in London at South
Kensington for
£14,300 ($23,595)

JEWELLERY

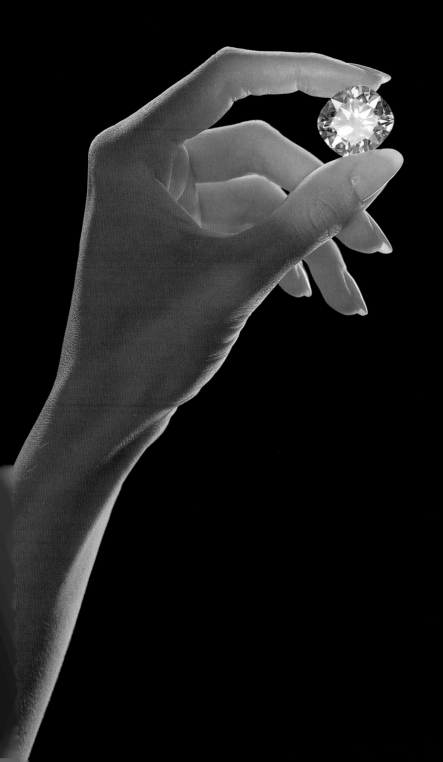

THE AGRA DIAMOND
Cushion-shaped fancy light pink diamond
weighing 32.24 carats
Sold 20 June 1990 in London for £4,070,000
($6,959,700)
Record auction price for a pink diamond

THE AGRA DIAMOND

Raymond Sancroft-Baker

A new world record price for a pink diamond was obtained in London on 20 June when 'the Agra' fetched £4,070,000 ($6,959,700); it also became the third most expensive diamond ever to be auctioned.

Judging by its soft pink colour and innate purity, the stone must have been mined in the Golconda region of the State of Hyderabad, India, where deposits were first exploited in the fifteenth century. This supposition is reinforced by the fact that one of the earliest owners of the stone was the Rajah of Gwalior. In 1526 he was defeated at the battle of Gwalior by Babur (son of the King of Turkestan), who received gifts including the Agra and Koh-i-Noor for his clemency shown in sparing the lives of the Rajah's family.

It is probable that the Agra passed to subsequent Mogul Emperors and it is reputed that Akbar (1556–1605) wore the diamond in his turban. The jewel remained in India until the early nineteenth century, when it was purchased by a London firm of diamond dealers called Blogg & Martin, who sold it to the eccentric Duke of Brunswick in 1844 for F.fr.348,000 (£13,670). In the duke's own catalogue compiled in 1860 the Agra was shown to be the equal fourteenth most important diamond in the world. The duke, who lived in Paris, made security his top priority – to the extent that he slept in the same room as his diamonds. The bedroom had only one small window and its iron lock could only be opened by those who had been specially instructed. The duke's bed was placed in front of the wall-safe containing the diamonds and a complicated mechanism had been devised whereby any attempt to open the safe activated four guns which would certainly have killed any burglar on the spot. Just to be sure, the guns also triggered an alarm that rang in every room of the house. As a last resort, a case with twelve loaded revolvers stood by the duke's bed. Despite such excessive precautions, the demented duke was robbed of nine million francs worth of jewels by his valet (who was eventually arrested at Boulogne). When the duke died in 1873 part of his collection was sold in the following year by Roussel & Fils, and the Agra realized Sw.fr.70,600 (£2,824).

In 1891 Edwin Streeter, the London jeweller and author of *Great Diamonds of the World*, bought the Agra from the Parisian dealer Bram Hertz, who had cut the stone from 41.75 carats to its present weight of 32.24 carats in order to eliminate internal flaws. It remained in Streeter's collection until he retired in 1904 and his stock was sold by his successors, the Parisian firm of Lacloche Frères, at Christie's in 1905, when the Agra realized £5,100, the purchaser being Max Meyer of Hatton Garden. The sale drew a large crowd of people,

THE AGRA DIAMOND
Cushion-shaped
fancy light pink
diamond weighing
32.24 carats
Sold 20 June 1990 in
London for
£4,070,000
($6,959,700)
Record auction price
for a pink diamond

which, according to a report in *The Times* on the following day, included 'a number of Indian gentlemen, attracted doubtless by the historical interest of the famous Agra diamond'.

Shortly afterwards it was acquired by Mr Louis Winans, who lived in Brighton and commissioned a firm of jewellers called Lewis & Sons to help him form his superb collection of coloured diamonds. Louis Winans had inherited a fortune from his father, an American railroad engineer who built Russia's first commercial railway from St. Petersburg to Moscow during the years 1843–51.

The collection was inherited by the present owner in 1927 and at the outset of World War II she asked her local blacksmith to make an iron casket into which she put the Agra, along with all her other jewels, burying it in her garden for the duration of the war.

On 20 June 1990 lot 232, described as 'A magnificent unmounted cushion-shaped fancy light pink diamond of 32.24 carats', sold to the Siba Corporation of Hong Kong, with Mr Laurence Graff as underbidder. The Agra diamond, along with its companion the 'Golden Drop', had been exhibited in many different countries both publicly and privately. The response everywhere was overwhelming, with dealers, industrialists, film stars and royalty all marvelling at their splendour. The first evening jewellery sale to be held at King Street was a glittering occasion and marked a sentimental return for the stone that first dazzled St. James's eighty-five years ago.

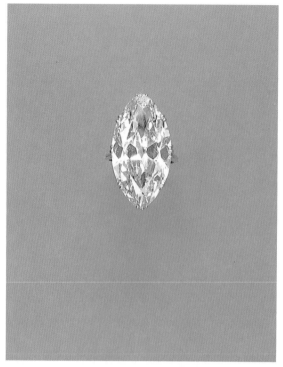

Far left:
Single-stone diamond ring weighing 14.02 carats, E colour and VS1
Sold 6 December 1989 in New York for $473,000 (£299,367)

Left:
Single-stone diamond ring weighing 25.06 carats
Sold 16 November 1989 in Geneva for Sw.fr.1,430,000 (£562,992)

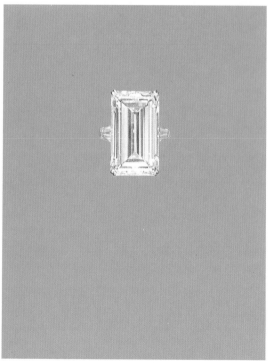

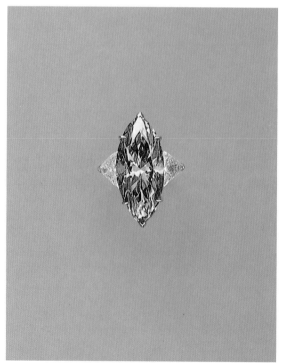

Far left:
Single-stone diamond ring weighing 22.43 carats, D colour and VVS2
Signed by Van Cleef & Arpels
Sold 16 November 1989 in Geneva for Sw.fr.1,265,000 (£498,031)

Left:
Single-stone fancy grey diamond ring weighing 17.79 carats
Sold 16 November 1989 in Geneva for Sw.fr.1,045,000 (£411,417)

Right:
Fancy pink, blue and
yellow diamond
pendant
Signed by Van Cleef
& Arpels
Sold 25 April 1990 in
New York for
$506,000 (£311,001)

Centre right:
THE GOLDEN DROP
Pear-shaped fancy
intense yellow
diamond weighing
18.49 carats
Sold 20 June 1990 in
London for
£2,200,000
($3,762,000)
Record auction price
for a yellow diamond

Far right:
Three-stone brown-
pink, yellow and
white diamond ring
Sold 25 April 1990 in
New York for
$374,000 (£229,870)

Right:
Single-stone fancy
yellow diamond ring
weighing 24.53 carats
Sold 6 December
1989 in New York
for $682,000
(£431,646)

Far right:
Fancy blue diamond
ring weighing 7.37
carats
Sold 24 October 1989
in New York for
$1,265,000 (£790,625)

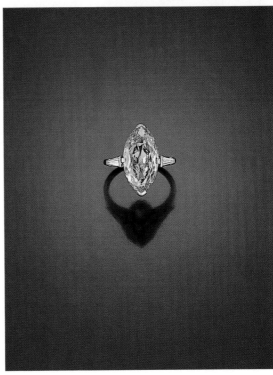

Diamond necklace with pear-shaped diamond weighing 30.08 carats, D colour and VS2
Sold 16 November 1989 in Geneva for Sw.fr.2,112,000 (£831,496)

Pair of diamond ear pendants weighing in total 29.50 carats, ranging from D to F colour and VS1 to SI2
Sold 25 April 1990 in New York for $330,000 (£202,827)

Diamond necklace
with five diamonds
weighing in total
29.56 carats
By Harry Winston
Sold 13 June 1990 in
New York for
$682,000 (£398,830)

Centre:
Pair of diamond ear
pendants, the
pear-shaped
diamonds weighing
10.53 and 12.05
carats
By Harry Winston
Sold 13 June 1990 in
New York for
$572,000 (£334,503)

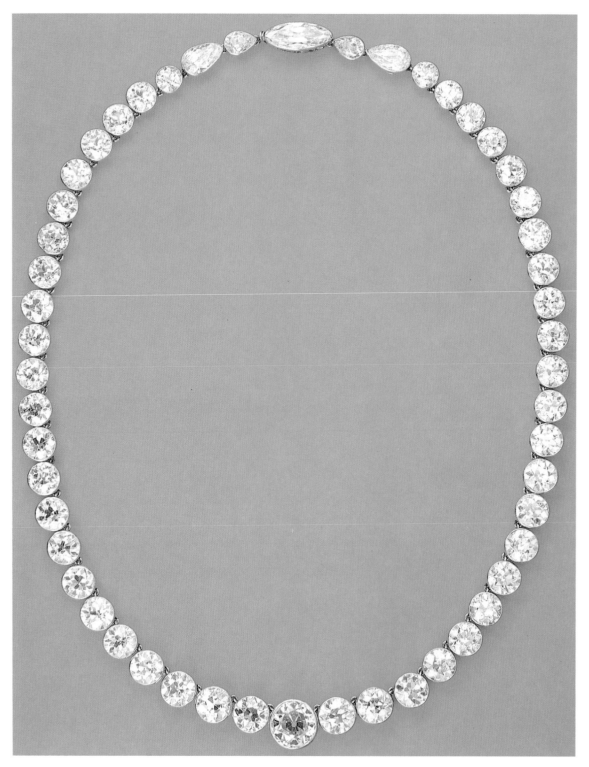

Diamond Riviere necklace
Sold for Sw.fr.825,000 (£324,803)

Below:
Briolette-cut diamond drop weighing 20.07 carats
Sold for Sw.fr.935,000 (£368,110)

Bottom:
Single-stone diamond brooch weighing 24.39 carats
Sold for Sw.fr.715,000 (£281,496)

Cabochon emerald
tiara with 19 emerald
drops weighing in
total 209.38 carats
Sold for Sw.fr.2,860,000
(£1,125,984)

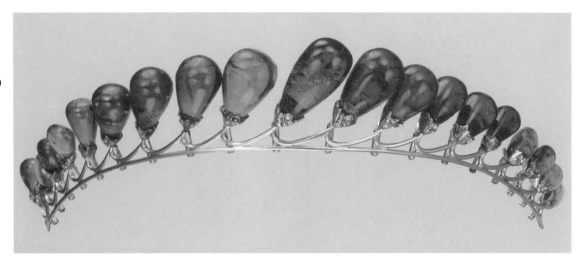

Art Deco emerald and diamond pendant brooch, the
emeralds weighing 16.74 and 21.65 carats
Signed by Boucheron
*c.*1920
Sold for Sw.fr.550,000 (£216,535)

Right:
Edwardian diamond bow brooch
*c.*1910
Sold for Sw.fr.330,000 (£129,921)

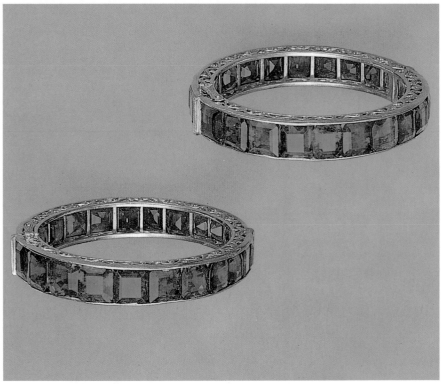

Above, left to right:
Pair of square-cut emeralds
Sold 22 February 1990 in St. Moritz for
Sw.fr.1,760,000 (£704,000)

Pair of emerald and diamond pendants
Sold 22 February 1990 in St. Moritz for
Sw.fr.682,000 (£272,800)

Single-stone emerald ring, 21.47 carats
Signed by Harry Winston
Sold 22 February 1990 in St. Moritz for
Sw.fr.1,045,000 (£418,000)

Single-stone imperial jade ring
Sold 17 May 1990 in Geneva for
Sw.fr.374,000 (£159,829)

Opposite:
Antique emerald and diamond necklace
c.1810
Sold 20 June 1990 in London for
£396,000 ($677,160)
From the collection of the late Dowager
Marchioness of Cholmondeley

Victorian emerald and diamond brooch
c.1880
Sold 20 June 1990 in London for
£528,000 ($902,880)

Pair of Indian emerald and gold bangles
Sold 16 November 1989 in Geneva for
Sw.fr.2,750,000 (£1,082,677)

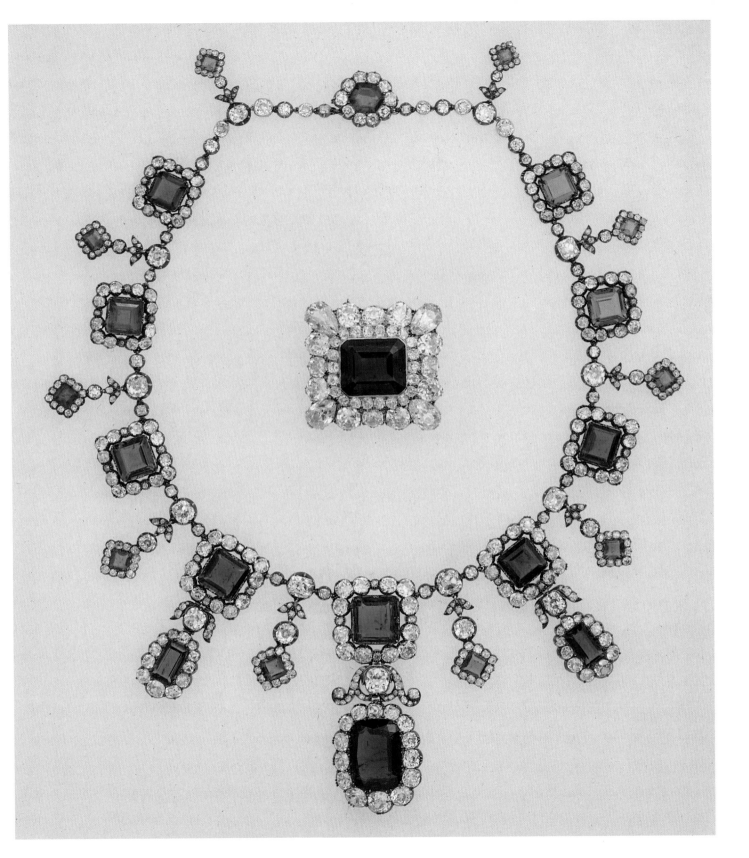

Sapphire and diamond necklace, the sapphires weighing in total
55.93 carats
Signed by Van Cleef & Arpels
Sold 17 May 1990 in Geneva for Sw.fr.1,540,000 (£658,119)

Top:
Single-stone sapphire
ring weighing 18.11
carats
Signed by Cartier
Sold 13 December
1989 in London for
£242,000 ($387,200)

Single-stone sapphire
ring weighing 19.28
carats
Signed by Cartier
Sold 16 November
1989 in Geneva for
Sw.fr.704,000
(£277,165)

Right:
Single-stone sapphire ring, 38.00 carats
Signed by Sterlé, Paris
Sold 22 February 1990 in St. Moritz for
Sw.fr.308,000 (£123,200)

Far right:
Single-stone sapphire ring, 10.15 carats
Signed by Boucheron
Sold 22 February 1990 in St. Moritz for
Sw.fr.341,000 (£136,400)

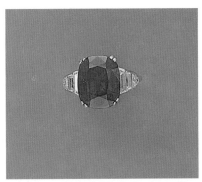

Sapphire and
diamond bracelet
Sold 31 May 1990 in
Rome for
L.143,750,000
(£68,779)

Right:
Sapphire and
diamond leaf brooch
Signed by Cartier
Sold 22 February
1990 in St. Moritz
for Sw.fr.176,000
(£70,400)

Far right:
Pair of sapphire and
diamond ear pendants
Signed by Cartier
Sold 22 February
1990 in St. Moritz
for Sw.fr.198,000
(£79,200)

Left:
Edwardian pearl and diamond stomacher brooch
c.1910
Sold 20 June 1990 in London for £418,000 ($714,780)
Below:
Pair of diamond cluster earrings
Signed by Harry Winston
Sold 20 June 1990 in London for £154,000 ($263,340)

Bottom:
Diamond bracelet
Signed by Van Cleef & Arpels
Sold 20 June 1990 in London for £68,200 ($116,622)

Pair of diamond
earrings
Signed by Van Cleef
& Arpels
Sold 20 June 1990 in
London for £220,000
($376,200)

Diamond necklace
Signed by Van Cleef
& Arpels
Sold 20 June 1990 in
London for £715,000
($1,222,650)

Left:
Art Deco diamond and black onyx jabot pin
Signed by Cartier
Sold 22 February 1990 in St. Moritz for
Sw.fr.209,000 (£83,600)

Below:
Retro gold and diamond tulip clip brooch
By René Boivin
Sold 22 February 1990 in St. Moritz for
Sw.fr.22,000 (£8,800)
From the collection of HRH Princess Irène of
Greece and Denmark

Bottom:
Ruby and diamond bracelet
By Harry Winston
Sold 22 February 1990 in St. Moritz for
Sw.fr.187,000 (£74,800)

Right:
Single-stone ruby ring weighing 12.20 carats
Signed by Bulgari
Sold 17 May 1990 in Geneva for
Sw.fr.880,000 (£376,068)

Far right:
Single-stone ruby ring weighing 10.37 carats
Sold 17 May 1990 in Geneva for
Sw.fr.792,000 (£338,462)

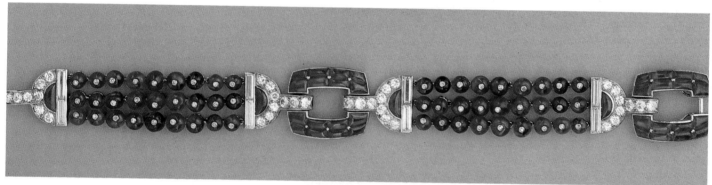

Ruby and diamond bracelet
Signed by Cartier
Sold 13 December 1989 in London for
£51,700 ($83,237)

Ruby, emerald and diamond chimera bangle
Signed by Cartier
Sold 22 February 1990 in St. Moritz for
Sw.fr.88,000 (£35,200)

Above:
Victorian emerald and diamond tiara
*c.*1850
Sold 20 June 1990 in London for £275,000 ($470,250)
From the collection of the late Dowager Marchioness of
Cholmondeley

Below:
Antique drop pearl necklace
*c.*1860
Sold 13 December 1989 in London for £148,500
($237,600)

Black cultured pearl and diamond necklace, the pearls measuring 12.0 to 15.2 mm. Sold 24 October 1989 in New York for $880,000 (£550,000)

Art Deco 'water clock' of jade, black marble, lapis lazuli, coral, aventurine quartz, mother-of-pearl and enamel
Signed by Cartier
*c.*1929
8½ in. (22 cm.) diameter
Sold 25 April 1990 in New York for $187,000 (£114,935)

Art Deco elephant 'mystery clock' of jade, coral, diamond, mother-of-pearl and onyx
Signed by Cartier
*c.*1928
7¾ in. (19.5 cm.) high
Sold 25 April 1990 in New York for $748,000 (£459,741)

Art Deco coral, emerald and diamond brooch
Signed by Cartier
*c.*1920
Sold 20 June 1990 in London for £66,000
($112,860)

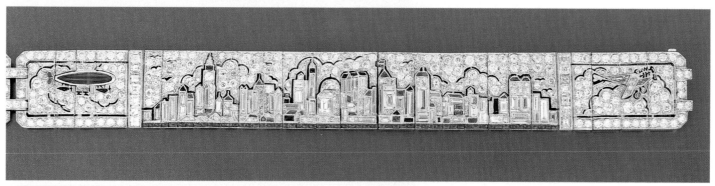

Art Deco diamond and gem-set 'skyline'
bracelet
Sold 13 June 1990 in New York for $79,200
(£46,316)

Art Nouveau diamond, pearl and enamel
pendant
Signed by Lalique
*c.*1895
Sold 13 December 1989 in London for
£46,200 ($74,382)

Left, top to bottom:
Jewelled and enamelled gold memento mori gimmel ring
Germany, *c.*1615
Sold 13 December 1989 in London for
£33,000 ($52,800)
From the Phyllis Phillips Collection

Gold and enamel armorial ring
Italian, *c.*1568
Sold 13 December 1989 in London for
£26,400 ($42,240)
From the Phyllis Phillips Collection

Sardonyx cameo with the head of Pallas
Athene
Inscribed 'LAV. R. MED.'
The cameo 18th century, the mount early
19th century
Sold 13 December 1989 in London for
£26,400 ($42,240)
From the Phyllis Phillips Collection

Louis XIV jewelled and enamelled gold ring
*c.*1680
Sold 13 December 1989 in London for
£20,900 ($33,440)
From the Phyllis Phillips Collection

Top right:
Spanish Armada jewelled and enamelled gold
earring
Inscribed 'The first gift to Mary'
*c.*1588
2½ in. (6 cm.) high
Sold 13 December 1989 in London for
£27,500 ($44,000)
From the Phyllis Phillips Collection

Right:
Diamond and enamelled gold case containing
miniature of Friedrich Wilhelm, Elector of
Brandenberg *c.*1647
*c.*1647
Sold 13 December 1989 in London for
£30,800 ($49,280)
From the Phyllis Phillips Collection

SILVER
AND
OBJECTS OF ART

Part of the Regency buffet from the Al-Tajir
Collection, including the Shield of Achilles
modelled by John Flaxman and made by
Philip Rundell, 1822

THE GLORY OF THE GOLDSMITH: MAGNIFICENT GOLD AND SILVER FROM THE AL-TAJIR COLLECTION

Charles Truman

The *Glory of the Goldsmith* exhibition at Christie's during January 1990 presented an unparalleled opportunity, not only to show some great masterpieces of the goldsmith's art, but to re-create the spirit in which the plate was originally displayed. The Great Rooms at King Street were transformed by George Carter and his team to create a series of lavishly decorated room settings, laid out in more or less chronological order, into which the visitors could gaze with a mixture of envy and admiration.

The exhibition was drawn from the magnificent collection of gold and silver amassed over the last twenty years by His Excellency Mohammed Mahdi Al-Tajir. It began with an intimate 'cabinet of curiosities' in which some of the rarest and most costly pieces from His Excellency's collection were shown. In the sixteenth and seventeenth centuries it was fashionable to have on hand a dwarf to show off natural and man-made curiosities. At King Street a silver dwarf, reputed to be a model of Sir Jeffery Hudson, Court Dwarf to Charles I, stood in the *Schatzkammer* to welcome our guests. Around him were the earliest pieces in the collection, an Aragonese ewer of about 1500, three Elizabethan pieces, a tankard of 1575, a tigerware jug of 1577 and the Braikenridge Tazza of 1571, some splendid Dutch and German silver of the sixteenth and seventeenth centuries and that *tour de force* of goldsmithing, the van der Haer ewer and basin made by Christian van Vianen in Utrecht in 1632. Arguably the single most important group in the Al-Tajir collection, the ewer and basin are not only a triumph of design, they are also technically extraordinary, being raised from single sheets of metal. In the same room stood three of His Excellency's finest clocks, including the Augsburg ivory clock of about 1640, which sold in our Rooms in 1984, and the Orpheus clock of about 1570, which we had sold in Geneva some two years later. These clocks represented only a tiny fraction of a large and comprehensive collection. Displayed alongside them in the 'Treasury' was a selection of gold boxes, gold mounted rock crystals and jewels. Here was the 'Pearl of Asia' – reputedly the largest pearl in the world – the Gothic *sautoire* worn by the Empress Marie-Louise, second wife of Napoleon I, and a rare selection of English gold plate. Notable pieces included the Walpole Cup by David Willaume, made in 1739, a Queen Anne race cup of about 1710, and the Rutland Salver of 1801 by Paul Storr.

From the Treasury the visitor progressed through a wide corridor flanked by three room settings showing toilet services and two with buffets of plate suitable for late seventeenth or early eighteenth-century dining-rooms. Of the toilet services, one Charles II and two Huguenot, that by Benjamin Pyne, dated 1708 and originally in the collection of the Dukes of Norfolk, is probably the most complete example to have survived. The service by Pierre Platel of 1700 showed the grandeur of Louis XIV's silver before that monarch took the desperate step of melting his plate to pay for his wars against Marlborough. Set on white damask, the services glittered as they would have done in the state bedrooms of the great Georgian houses. Also displayed on damask, but with a delightful verdure tapestry behind, was a splendid Baroque buffet. Based on a massive wine cistern by Jakob Drentwett, the buffet comprised an enormous papal presentation dish and some English silver in the luscious floral style of the reign of Charles II.

It was in the dining-room that silver really came into its own. The buffet of plate was a symbol of power and riches, whilst the decoration of the table showed the festive side of eating. The Al-Tajir collection contains, in virtually complete form, the dinner service ordered from George Wickes in 1745–7 by the Earl of Kildare, later the Duke of Leinster. This offered the opportunity to dress a table as it would have been when the earl sat down to dine off his newly acquired plate. With a flower-filled epergne in the centre, the tureens, covered dishes, cruets, salvers and sauceboats, sugar bowls and spice jars were arranged formally over the table for the 'premier service', with two tureens on the sideboards intended for the remove dishes. It is only sad that the opportunity did not arise to sit down and enjoy, if that is the right word, a dinner with eighteenth-century recipes.

On from this was a buffet composed entirely of silver by Paul de Lamerie, England's best-known goldsmith. Trays, salvers, baskets and tureens, themselves of great beauty and technical skill, paled beside one of the greatest pieces of English silver, the Lesquesne coffee pot of 1738. Transcending mere goldsmith's work, it is an astonishing spiralling sculpture in precious metal, which at the same time has perfect functional form. Of almost equal splendour, and displayed opposite, was George Wickes's Rococo ewer and basin made as a gift from the City of Bristol to Judge John Scrope in 1735. In the same case were a pair of sauceboats and a pair of candlesticks by another great master of the Rococo, Nicholas Sprimont. Although better known as the owner of the Chelsea porcelain factory, Sprimont began his career as a goldsmith first in Liège and then in London. His silver is so rare that some collectors value his work above that of Paul de Lamerie.

Passing cases of Neo-Classical French and English silver, the visitor to the exhibition was able to enjoy one of the glories of the Regency period. The early nineteenth century was a time of vast and conspicuous consumption. Massive displays of plate, much of it supplied by Rundell, Bridge and Rundell, were put on at great occasions such as the coronation of George IV, or the dinner celebrating Waterloo, when the Prince Regent, the King of Prussia and the Tsar of Russia sat down to dine at the Guildhall. Such settings were re-created in this exhibition in a huge buffet of silver-gilt massed from floor to ceiling against a sideboard of rich red velvet. Although to the modern eye such an extravagant display may seem overpowering, this would have been precisely the impression sought by a Regency nobleman when assembling such a group of silver. At the centre was that icon of Neo-Classicism, the Shield of Achilles, modelled by John Flaxman following the description in Homer. It is one of four made by Rundell, Bridge and Rundell in silver-gilt, the others being in the collection of Her Majesty the Queen, the National Trust and the

The Leinster Service
By George Wickes
London, 1745–7
Displayed as it would
have been arranged
for use by the 1st
Duke of Leinster
From the Al-Tajir
Collection

Huntington Library, San Marino. This was flanked by a pair of huge dishes by Paul Storr after a design by Thomas Stotthard, candelabra after the same artist, wine coolers after Piranesi, huge trays and salvers, and surmounted by an extraordinary piece of neo-Mannerism, a vase by Paul Storr after a seventeenth-century design by Jacques Stella. The effect was of a tumult of sculpture in silver-gilt.

The service supplied by Rundell, Bridge and Rundell to Sir Richard Sutton presented another opportunity to decorate a dining-room as it would have been about 1820. Compared to the light, almost frivolous Leinster service, here was the massive self-confident silver of the Regency. Additional displays showed virtually the full range of the royal goldsmith's design repertoire.

However, amongst the most breathtaking settings was that which showed Mr Al-Tajir's astonishing collection of French Empire silver. In one dining-room were displayed examples from the vast dinner service made for Count Nicolai Demidoff, pieces from Grand Duke Michael Pavlovitch's service and, perhaps of the greatest historical interest, a large part of the service made by Odiot for Madame Mère, Napoleon's formidable mother. In the same room was the inkstand also by Odiot which Madame Mère sent to her son Joseph Bonaparte, King of Spain, in 1812.

The exhibition concluded with some of the massive Victorian racing trophies and centrepieces for which the Al-Tajir collection is well-known. Such sculptural pieces formed a contrast to the restrained elegance of the Empire, and served to highlight the comprehensive nature of this spectacular assemblage of plate.

The exhibition, which was open for only twenty-one days, was seen by 11,000 visitors, the majority of whom made generous donations to the 'Save the Children Fund', in whose aid the exhibition was held. Christie's was proud to be able to send the Fund a cheque for nearly £27,000, a happy conclusion to the most spectacular exhibition ever held at Christie's.

Opposite:
Set of four George III silver-gilt candlesticks
By John Scofield
1791–2
13¾ in. (35 cm.) high
Sold 7 March 1990 in London for £165,000 ($280,500)

Pair of George III silver-gilt chamber candlesticks
By John Scofield, the snuffers by Wilkes Booth
1791–2
Sold 7 March 1990 in London for £16,500 ($28,050)

Pair of Queen Anne wine coolers
By David Willaume
c.1710
9½ in. (24 cm.) high
Sold 23 May 1990 in London for £770,000 ($1,293,600)
The arms are those of Wentworth, Baron Raby and 3rd
Earl of Strafford, and his wife Anne, only daughter and
heiress of Sir Henry Johnson of Bradenham,
Buckinghamshire, whom he married in 1711

Queen Anne ewer and basin
Engraved with the royal arms, supporters and motto of
Queen Anne
By David Willaume
1705
The basin 26 in. (66 cm.) diameter; the ewer 14¼ in.
(36 cm.) high
Sold 23 May 1990 in London for £374,000 ($628,320)

George IV silver by John Bridge
Engraved with the crest of Campbell
Two-handled campana-shaped wine coolers, pair of wine coasters and a pair of two-handled oval sauce tureens and covers
1825
The coolers 10¾ in. (27.5 cm.) high
Sold 25 Octover 1989 in London: the coolers for £33,000 ($54,440); the coasters for £7,150 ($11,798); the tureens for £17,600 ($29,040)

Silver-mounted maplewood mazer bowl
By Omar Ramsden
1937
10¼ in. (26 cm.) diameter
Sold 23 May 1990 in London for £19,800 ($33,264)

Right:
James II Chinoiserie monteith
By George Garthorne
London, 1688
11⅜ in. (28.9 cm.) diameter
Sold 18 October 1989 in New York for
$286,000 (£182,166)

Below:
One of a pair of George III two-handled oval
soup tureens, covers and stands
By Thomas Pitts
1772
The stand 23½ in. (59.7 cm.) long;
13 in. (33 cm.) high overall
Sold 25 October 1989 in London for £137,500
($226,875)

A SILVER FOUNTAIN
BY GIUSEPPE D'ANGELO

Christopher Hartop

Sicilian table fountain
By Giuseppe
d'Angelo
Messina, c.1670
Based on Giovanni
Angelo Montorsoli's
Fountain of Orion
22 in. (56 cm.) high
Sold 19 April 1990 in
New York for
$1,980,000
(£1,201,860)
Record auction price
for a piece of silver

The cultural richness of Messina during the seventeenth century is in such contrast to its political turmoil that one cannot but be reminded of Harry Lime's scathing comments about cuckoo clocks in *The Third Man*. Traditionally, Messina had always looked more towards the Italian mainland than to its sister cities on Sicily, regarding itself as a cosmopolitan centre. But Messina's disputes with her neighbours, particularly with her long-standing rival, Palermo, meant that the region, and especially its silk industry, had suffered greatly in the middle of the seventeenth century. Bread riots had become so common in Messina that by 1674 events led to a revolution which resulted in the expulsion of the small Spanish garrison and an invitation from the city nobles for Louis XIV of France to take control of the city.

The new French Viceroy, the Duke of Vivonne, observed that the Messinese nobles were for the most part untaxed and enjoyed unrivalled riches. In four centuries of rule, it seems that the Spanish had never succeeded in discovering where their secret wheat stores were held. As patrons of the arts, the Messinese were unrivalled.

But the French regime was short-lived. By 1678 Louis realized that he could not support a garrison on Sicily and withdrew, leaving most of the leading citizens no choice but to flee to France with whatever assets they could muster. The Spanish returned in triumph and appointed a new Viceroy, General Gonzaga, who tore down the town hall and, as a symbolic gesture, ploughed up the site and sowed it with salt, thereby rendering the land sterile.

Given the pride of the Messinese, it is hardly surprising that one of them should have commissioned, at about this time, a silver table fountain in the form of their most splendid public monument and the greatest symbol of their former maritime might: the Fountain of Orion. This had been sculpted by Giovanni Angelo Montorsoli between 1547 and 1553 and erected in the square in front of the cathedral, one of two fountains commissioned by the city from the great Florentine sculptor. But, significantly, those parts of the original fountain's complex iconography which refer directly to the Habsburgs, such as the four flanking river gods symbolic of the Tiber, Nile, Ebro and Camaro, are absent from the silver version.

The silver fountain bears the maker's mark of Giuseppe d'Angelo, a member of a distinguished family of Messinese silversmiths who were not only related to the Juvara family, but were also frequent collaborators with them. Their greatest works in collaboration are perhaps the magnificent candlesticks in the treasury of Messina Cathedral, dating from 1671. This fountain appears to be part of a series of related sculptural table ornaments, one of which, a salt cellar in the Victoria and Albert Museum, bears the mark of Sebastiano Juvara. This salt and another, unmarked, example in the Museum of Decorative Arts, Oslo, have similar maritime motifs, indicating that they were probably made for the same patron in the 1660s or 70s.

Silver table fountains appear in a number of Sicilian inventories from the second half of the seventeenth century, but the identity of the patron who commissioned this example, and possibly the two related salt cellars, remains uncertain. However, the most likely candidate is Antonio Ruffo, a Sicilian nobleman whose palazzo in Messina was renowned at the time as a centre of cultural life. Ruffo, the youngest son of the Duke of Bagnara, appears to have weathered the political storms particularly well. For us today, he is perhaps best known as an enthusiastic patron of Rembrandt – he commissioned three paintings from the artist, including *Aristotle Contemplating the Bust of Homer.*

The subsequent history of the fountain is unknown until it appears in the collection of J. P. Morgan in 1936. It was included in the sale of part of Morgan's silver collection in New York in 1947, when it fetched $1,500. Interestingly, the fountain appeared in the sale catalogue incorrectly assembled, and it remained so for more than forty years, even appearing in a number of recent publications with two circular dishes incorrectly placed. On arrival at Christie's in the autumn of 1989, however, comparison with a photograph of the original fountain in Messina enabled it to be reassembled to follow exactly the form of Montorsoli's model.

Its appearance on the auction block in New York in the spring of 1990 caused a considerable stir and it was ultimately purchased, after much spirited bidding, by the London dealer Armitage for $1,980,000 (£1,201,860), a world record price for any piece of silver.

Salt cellar
By Sebastiano Juvara
Messina, *c.*1670
11 in. (28 cm.) high
(Reproduced by
courtesy of the Board
of Trustees of the
Victoria and Albert
Museum)

Opposite:
*The Fountain of
Orion*, Piazza del
Duomo, Messina
By Giovanni Angelo
Montorsoli
1547–53
Marble

American teapot and stand
By Paul Revere II
Boston, *c.*1790
The teapot 6 in. (15.2 cm.) high; the stand
7½ in. (19 cm.) long
Sold 2 June 1990 in New York for $165,000
(£98,214)
Record auction price for silver by Paul Revere

Canadian four-piece tea service and sugar
castor
By John Peter Arnoldi
Montreal, *c.*1790
The teapot 5⅜ in. (13.7 cm.) high
Sold 19 April 1990 in New York: the tea
service for $40,700 (£24,667), the sugar castor
for $4,180 (£2,538)

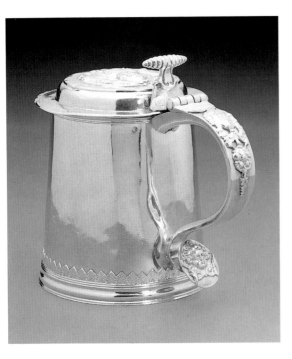

Above:
American tankard
By Charles le Roux
New York, *c*.1725
7 in. (17.8 cm.) high
Sold 19 January 1990 in New York for $242,000
(£146,667)

Above right:
Belgian pear-shaped teapot
By Olivier Franckson
Liège, 1751
Sold 15 May 1990 in Geneva for Sw.fr.132,000 (£56,410)

George II coffee-pot
Engraved with the arms of Molyneux impaling Sefton
By John Swift
London, 1739
11½ in. (29.2 cm.) high
Sold 18 October 1989 in New York for $60,500 (£38,535)

Set of eight Louis XV trencher salts
By Noël Léonard
Paris, 1719 and 1720
2¾ in. (7 cm.) long
Sold 6 December 1989 in London for £77,000 ($120,890)

George III gold cup and cover
By William Stroud
1801
10¾ in. (27.2 cm.) high
Sold 7 March 1990 in London for £104,500 ($177,650)

Set of four German candlesticks
Engraved with the coat of arms of George I of England as
Elector of Hanover
By Conrad Hermann Mundt
Hanover, 1726
6⅝ in. (16.2 cm.) high
Sold 18 October 1989 in New York for $93,500 (£59,544)

Parcel-gilt flagon
By David Ehekirch
Augsburg, *c*.1610
11 in. (28 cm.) high
Sold 15 May 1990
in Geneva for
Sw.fr.165,000 (£70,513)

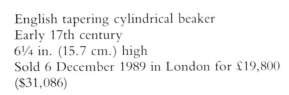

English tapering cylindrical beaker
Early 17th century
6¼ in. (15.7 cm.) high
Sold 6 December 1989 in London for £19,800
($31,086)

Pair of Charles II silver-gilt baluster vases and
covers
By Thomas Jenkins
c.1670
13 in. (33 cm.) high
Sold 7 March 1990 in London for £132,000
($224,400)

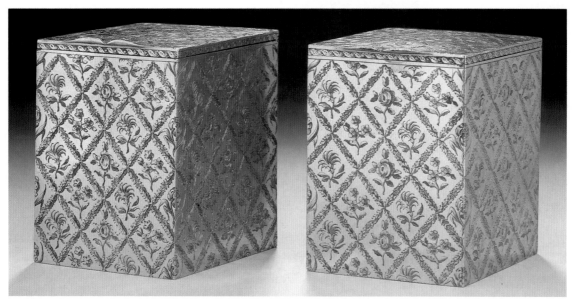

Pair of George III
silver-gilt tea caddies
By Pierre Gillois
London, 1768
4¼ in. (10.9 cm.)
high
Sold 19 April 1990 in
New York for
$44,000 (£26,708)

Above left:
Swiss enamelled gold musical singing-bird
box
By J.G. Rémond & Cie, the movement by
Frères Rochat
Geneva, *c*.1810
Sold 15 May 1990 in Geneva for Sw.fr.85,800
(£36,666)

Above right:
George II cartouche-shaped gold snuff box
Attributed to George Daniel Gaab
Set with a miniature of Mary, Countess of
Bute by C.F. Zincke
c.1750
2¾ in. (7 cm.) wide
Sold 11 July 1990 in London for £39,600
($71,280)

Left:
Swiss jewelled enamelled gold musical
penknife
Geneva, *c*.1810
5¾ in. (14.5 cm.) long
Sold 23 May 1990 in London for £15,400
($25,872)

Right:
PETER OLIVER
British *c*.1594–1647
Lady Anne Clifford,
Countess of Pembroke
Signed with initials
Sold 10 July 1990 in
London for £20,900
($37,599)

Far right:
RICHARD GIBSON
British 1615–90
Sir Henry Blount
Inscribed 'Sir H
B/Aetat/58'
Sold 10 July 1990 in
London for £19,800
($35,620)

Centre:
FRANS POURBUS
Dutch 1545–81
Portrait of a
Noblewoman
Signed with initials
and dated 1570
Sold 20 March 1990
in London for
£39,600 ($64,548)

Far right:
SAMUEL COOPER
British 1609–72
Portrait of a Young
Gentleman
Signed with monogram
Sold 10 July 1990 in
London for £19,800
($35,620)

Right:
JOHN HOSKINS
British *fl. c*.1645
Lady Mary Glemham
Signed with initials
and dated 1648
Sold 10 July 1990 in
London for £19,800
($35,620)

ISIDOR KAUFMANN
1853–1921
Young Boy with Arba Kanfot
Signed
Oil on panel
12 × 9¾ in. (30.5 × 24.8 cm.)
Sold 6 December 1989 in Amsterdam for D.fl.103,500 (£32,961)

Silver-gilt Torah case containing a Torah scroll
Maker's mark 'WA'
Lemberg, late 18th century
16¾ in. (42.2 cm.) high
Sold 20 June 1990 in Amsterdam for D.fl.299,000 (£92,857)

AUSTRIAN SCHOOL
Synagogue Service
Signed with
monogram 'PS' and
dated 1868
Oil on canvas
31½ × 39½ in.
(80 × 100 cm.)
Sold 20 June 1990 in
Amsterdam for
D.fl.92,000 (£28,571)

MANÉ KATZ
1894–1962
The Wedding
Signed
Oil on canvas
32 × 39 in.
(81 × 99 cm.)
Sold 6 December
1989 in Amsterdam
for D.fl.287,500
(£91,560)
From the property of
the late Prime
Minister of Israel,
Mrs Golda Meir

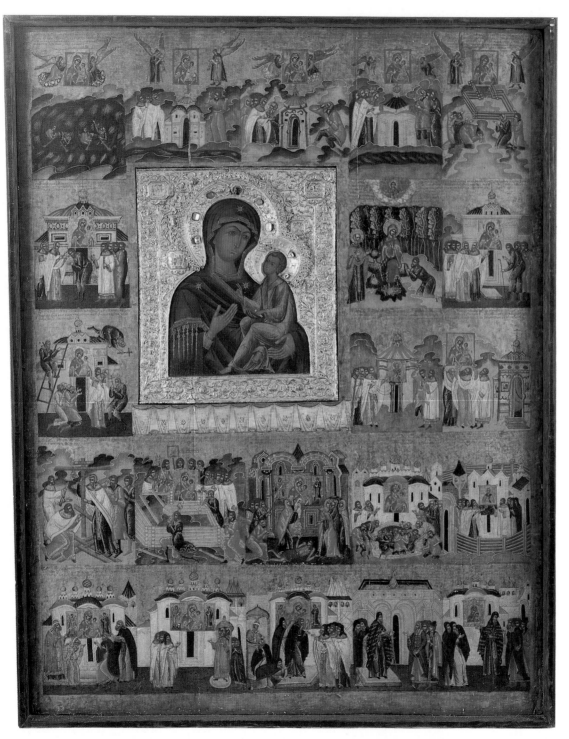

Icon of the Mother of God Tikhvinskaia with scenes from the history of the icon Central Russia, early 17th century 52 × 39¼ in. (132 × 99.7 cm.) Sold 27 April 1990 in London for £52,800 ($89,760)

IL'IA EFIMOVICH REPIN
1844–1930
*Portrait of Aleksandr
Fedorovich Kerenskii*
Signed and dated
1917
Oil on linoleum
45¼ × 33⅛ in.
(115 × 84.4 cm.)
Sold 27 April 1990 in
London for £57,200
($97,240)

IVAN IVANOVICH
SHISHKIN
1832–98
Summer Landscape at Valaam
Dated 1858
Oil on canvas
26 × 36½ in.
(65.8 × 93 cm.)
Sold 5 October 1989
in London for
£38,500 ($61,985)

KONSTANTIN IVANOVICH
GORBATOV
1876–*c*.1929
Landscape with Birch Trees
Signed and dated
1922
Oil on canvas
31½ × 37½ in.
(80 × 95.3 cm.)
Sold 5 October 1989
in London for
£24,200 ($38,962)

KONSTANTIN ANDREEVICH
SOMOV
1869–1939
*The Young Woman
Sleeping*
Signed and dated
1915
Oil on canvas
11½ × 17 in.
(29 × 43.2 cm.)
Sold 5 October 1989
in London for
£28,600 ($46,046)

BORIS MIKHAILOVICH
KUSTODIEV
1878–1927
Reclining Nude in Bed
Signed and dated
1919
Oil on canvas
13¾ × 18⅝ in.
(35 × 47.4 cm.)
Sold 5 October 1989
in London for
£20,900 ($33,649)

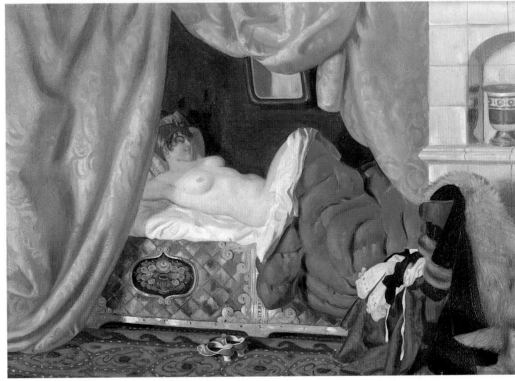

Gold-mounted nephrite desk barometer
Marked Fabergé, workmaster Henrik Wigström, St. Petersburg
1899–1908
4⅜ in. (11.1 cm.) high
Sold 19 April 1990 in New York for $33,000 (£20,120)
From the estate of Dorothy Schiff

Below right:
Enamelled gold and hardstone scent-flask in the form of an owl
Marked Fabergé, workmaster Karl Gustav Arnfelt, St. Petersburg
c.1885
1¼ in. (3.1 cm.) high
Sold 16 May 1990 in Geneva for Sw.fr.44,000 (£18,920)

Above:
Jewelled platinum-mounted rock-crystal snowflake pendant
By Fabergé
c.1914
Sold 16 May 1990 in Geneva for Sw.fr.46,200 (£19,743)

Left:
Imperial yellow-metal and enamel cigarette case
Marked Fabergé, workmaster Henrik Wigström
Inscribed in Cyrillic 'To Dear Nicki from Mummy, Christmas 1915'
3½ in. (8.7 cm.) wide
Sold 5 October 1989 in London for £38,500 ($61,985)

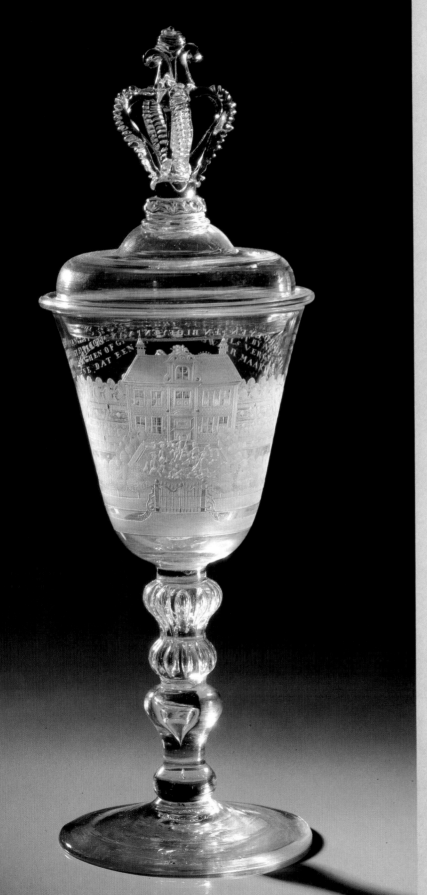

CERAMICS
AND GLASS

Armorial topographical light-baluster hunting
goblet with crowned cover
By Jacob Sang
Inscribed, signed and dated 1759
14 in. (35.5 cm.) high
Sold 6 June 1990 in Amsterdam for
D.fl.80,500 (£25,117)

Left:
London Delft inscribed Royal portrait wine bottle
*c.*1660
6¼ in. (16 cm.) high
Sold 29 May 1990 in London for £154,000 ($259,940)
From the Rous Lench Collection

Below left:
London Delft salt
Dated 1676
7½ in. (19.5 cm.) high
Sold 29 May 1990 in London for £176,000 ($296,560)
From the Rous Lench Collection
Record auction price for British ceramics and Delftware

THE ROUS LENCH SALE

Anton Gabszewicz

To many, the announcement of a second Rous Lench sale came as a surprise. The first sale held in 1986 had attracted frenzied interest, producing astounding prices and world records for English pottery and porcelain. It was hard to imagine that such excitement and commensurately high prices would be achieved again.

The collection was acquired by Thomas Burn, the owner of Rous Lench Court. A remarkable collector, Tom Burn was able to appreciate both the robust early slipwares of the seventeenth century, so naturally suited to the timbered interior of Rous Lench Court, and also the delicate and sophisticated porcelains of the eighteenth century.

The final dispersal on 29 and 30 May 1990 was truly representative of this extraordinary range of taste. The first morning's session was to see the new world record for a single lot of British pottery: £176,000 ($296,560) for the London Delft dated salt of 1676, followed within five minutes by the second most expensive lot of English pottery, a London Delft wine bottle with a three-quarter-length portrait of Charles II at £154,000 ($259,940). A new record for slipware was set by the 'Cat and Mouse' dish by Ralph Simpson which realized £93,500 ($157,548). It was, however, not only the inscribed and dated or documentary pieces that were to achieve the highest prices; a naturally modelled owl of Whieldon type realized £60,500 ($101,943), while its saltglaze counterpart made £71,500 ($120,478).

The afternoon sessions of both days were devoted to the dispersal of the Worcester porcelain, of local interest to the former owner of Rous Lench Court. The prices, although not as heady as those for the pottery, reflected a marked interest in the earliest pieces: a rare early blue and white soup-tureen and cover made £28,600 ($48,191).

The most stimulating session was on the second morning. The mysterious white candlesticks attributed to the 'Girl in a Swing' factory changed hands for a new world record of £93,500 ($157,548), they were previously sold in these rooms in 1962, when they realized £472. 10s. From Chelsea a white crayfish salt, one of Sprimont's masterpieces, made £10,450 ($17,608). From Bow a pair of white figures of the actor and actress Henry Woodward and Kitty Clive made £35,200 ($59,312).

Of all the treasures from Rous Lench one of the most pleasing and one in which the art of sculpture and the science of porcelain manufacture are so successfully combined is the white bust of George II thought to have come from Richard Chaffer's Liverpool factory. It fetched £35,200 ($57,433), showing a healthy return on the £1,150 it cost in 1956.

The sale totalled £2,923,030 ($4,925,306) – a record for any British Ceramics sale.

Staffordshire slipware 'Cat and Mouse'
charger
By Ralph Simpson
*c.*1680
18½ in. (47 cm.) diameter
Sold 29 May 1990 in London for £93,500
($157,548)
From the Rous Lench Collection
Record auction price for slipware

Documentary Staffordshire slipware
press-moulded clock-face dish
By Samuel Malkin
Dated 1712
14¼ in. (36 cm.) diameter
Sold 29 May 1990 in London for £49,500
($83,408)
From the Rous Lench Collection

Saltglaze model of an owl
c.1750
7¾ in. (20 cm.) high
Sold 29 May 1990 in London for £71,500 ($120,478)
From the Rous Lench Collection

Creamware model of an owl of Whieldon type
c.1750
8¾ in. (22.5 cm.) high
Sold 29 May 1990 in London for £60,500 ($101,943)
From the Rous Lench Collection

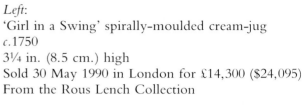

Left:
'Girl in a Swing' spirally-moulded cream-jug
c.1750
3¼ in. (8.5 cm.) high
Sold 30 May 1990 in London for £14,300 ($24,095)
From the Rous Lench Collection

Below left:
Bow large pierced circular basket
c.1760
11¾ in. (30 cm.) diameter
Sold 30 May 1990 in London for £14,300 ($24,095)
From the Rous Lench Collection

Pair of 'Girl in a
Swing' white
candlestick-figures
c.1750
8¼ in. (21 cm.)
high
Sold 30 May 1990 in
London for £93,500
($157,548)
From the Rous Lench
Collection
Record auction price
for English porcelain

Opposite:
Chelsea lobed
baluster vase
c.1750
5¼ in. (13 cm.)
high
Sold 30 May 1990 in
London for £5,280
($8,923)
From the Rous Lench
Collection

Bow documentary
cylindrical ink-pot
Painted by James
Welsh
Signed
*c.*1758
3¾ in. (9 cm.)
diameter
Sold 9 October 1989
in London for
£13,200 ($21,648)

Chelsea acanthus-leaf
moulded teapot and
cover
Incised triangle mark
1745–9
4¾ in. (12 cm.)
high
Sold 9 October 1989
in London for
£24,200 ($39,688)

Creamware botanical
part dinner-service
Perhaps Staffordshire,
*c.*1805
Sold 21 May 1990 in
London for £60,500
($102,245)

Worcester
fable-decorated bowl
Painted in the atelier
of James Giles
*c.*1765
9¼ in. (23.5 cm.)
diameter
Sold 29 May 1990 in
London for £15,400
($25,949)
From the Rous Lench
Collection

Vincennes
watering-can
1755
11¾ × 9¼ in.
(30 × 24 cm.)
Sold 3 December
1989 in Monaco for
F.fr.532,800
(£55,824)

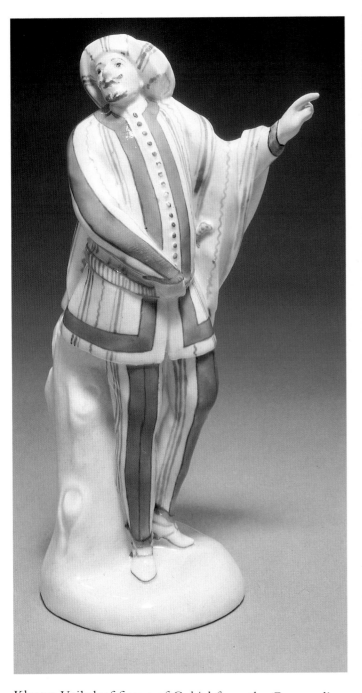

Kloster Veilsdorf figure of Gobiel from the Commedia dell'Arte
Modelled by Wenzel Neu, *c*.1765
6¼ in. (16 cm.) high
Sold 14 May 1990 in Geneva for Sw.fr.44,000 (£18,803)

Nymphenburg figure of a mushroom seller
Modelled by Franz Anton Bustelli
c.1755
7½ in. (19.5 cm.) high
Sold 14 May 1990 in Geneva for Sw.fr.93,500 (£39,957)

Meissen gold-mounted turquoise-ground
cartouche-shaped snuff-box
c.1740
3¾ in. (9 cm.) wide
Sold 14 May 1990 in Geneva for
Sw.fr.275,000 (£117,521)

Meissen candlestick from the Swan service
Modelled by J.F. Eberlein and J.J. Kändler
c.1739
9¼ in. (24 cm.) high
Sold 13 November 1989 in Geneva for
Sw.fr.82,500 (£32,226)

Right:
Capodimonte
polychrome group
Modelled by
Giuseppe Gricci
1750–5
9¾ in. (24.5 cm.)
high
Sold 29 November
1989 in Rome for
L.63,250,000
(£31,157)

Far right:
Naples (Real Fabbrica
Ferdinandea) figure
of a lady
c.1790
6¼ in. (16 cm.)
high
Sold 12 March 1990
in London for £7,700
($12,705)

Six Naples (Real
Fabbrica Ferdinandea)
portrait coffee-cans
and saucers, painted
with members of the
Bourbon family
c.1800
Sold 2 July 1990 in
London for £41,800
($72,857)

Opposite:
One of a pair of Dutch Delft tulipières
From the factory of Pieter
Adriaenszoon Kocks
c.1700
10¾ in. (27 cm.) high
Sold 15 November 1989 in Amsterdam for
D.fl.71,300 (£21,511)

Deruta waisted portrait albarello
c.1525
9 in. (22.5 cm.)high
Sold 12 March 1990 in London for £19,800 ($32,670)

Faenza famiglia gotica cylindrical albarello
1480–1520
10 in.(25.5 cm.) high
Sold 29 May 1990 in London for £52,800 ($88,968)
From the Rous Lench Collection

Castelli large dish,
the Mystic Marriage
of St. Catherine
Painted in the Grue
workshop
Late 17th/early 18th
century
16½ in. (42 cm.)
diameter
Sold 12 March 1990
in London for
£27,500 ($45,375)

Urbino istoriato dish, Christ appearing to Mary Magdalene Painted in the workshop of Orazio Fontana
*c.*1540
16¾ in. (42.5 cm.) diameter
Sold 2 July 1990 in London for £63,800 ($111,203)

Central European
'glass-blower's' flask
Inscribed and dated
1767
6½ in. (16.5 cm.)
high
Sold 13 February
1990 for £12,100
($20,570)

Venetian enamelled
dish
c.1500
9¾ in. (25 cm.)
diameter
Sold 13 February
1990 in London for
£14,300 ($24,310)

Amber-tinted ring
beaker
Germany, 17th
century
6½ in. (16.5 cm.)
high
Sold 13 February
1990 in London for
£8,800 ($14,960)

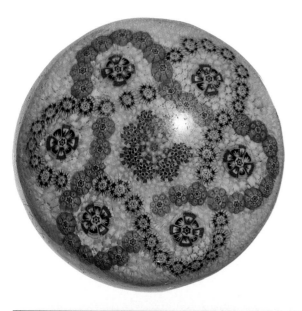

Far left:
Baccarat
carpet-ground
millefiori weight
Mid-19th century
3 in. (7.8 cm.)
diameter
Sold 13 February
1990 in London for
£5,500 ($9,350)

Left:
Baccarat pink gentian
weight
Mid-19th century
3 in. (7.5 cm.)
diameter
Sold 13 February
1990 in London for
£8,800 ($14,960)

Opaque-white
candlestick and pair
of tapersticks with
enamel drip-pans
South Staffordshire
*c.*1760
9¾ in. (25 cm.) and
7¼ in (18.5 cm.)
high respectively
Sold 30 May 1990 in
London: the
candlestick for £3,080
($5,190), the pair of
tapersticks for £6,600
($11,121)
From the Rous Lench
Collection

ORIENTAL CERAMICS AND WORKS OF ART

Famille rose and
doucai moon flask
Qianlong
six-character mark
and of the period
20 in. (51 cm.) high
Sold 1 June 1990 in
New York for
$825,000 (£491,071)

Blue and white
'dragon' vase
Yongzheng
six-character mark
and of the period
20½ in. (52.1 cm.)
high
Sold 20 March 1990
in Hong Kong for
HK$5,170,000
(£403,276)

Pair of Imperial
famille verte bowls
Kangxi Yuzhi marks
and of the period
4¼ in. (10.7 cm.)
diameter
Sold 20 March 1990
in Hong Kong for
HK$2,640,000
(£205,928)

CHRISTIE'S SWIRE HONG KONG: 1989/90

Colin Sheaf

Far left:
Green-glazed
black-ground baluster
vase
Yongzheng
six-character mark
and of the period
7 in. (17.8 cm.) high
Sold 26 September
1989 in Hong Kong
for HK$1,540,000
(£124,394)

Left:
Underglaze-blue
yellow-ground vase
Yongzheng
six-character mark
and of the period
8 in. (20.4 cm.) high
Sold 20 March 1990
in Hong Kong for
HK$5,500,000
(£429,017)

This season has been by far the most successful ever enjoyed by the Group's International Chinese department, thanks largely to the auctions in Hong Kong. The small office established in the mid-1980s has greatly expanded, and this season, under the direction of Alice Piccus, two series of sales were held instead of one. The figures show the scale of local growth: in 1989/90 the office sold £20,000,000 ($32,000,000) worth of art, twenty times the amount sold in 1986.

At present the objects sold fall into a narrow range of categories reflecting local demand: Chinese paintings of the nineteenth and twentieth centuries, jade carvings and jadeite jewellery, and of course Chinese porcelain – but only examples made during the period *c*.1300–1900. However, a stated objective of the new office is to widen the scope of auctions, and we began this season with a sale of China Trade paintings.

As the season progressed, Christie's set a string of new Group records. This was largely a result of Taiwanese demand, long unsatisfied, for the brightest and boldest examples of Chinese art we could supply. Sales of paintings in September and March, organized from New York by K.S. Wong, successively achieved the highest-ever totals for auctions of modern Chinese paintings. New world records were established for a host of individual modern artists, and March saw a new record for any modern Chinese painting sold at auction. Ceramics and jades auctions, organized jointly by Theow-Huang Tow and Colin Sheaf, also broke numerous records. A blue and white 'palace' bowl, *c*.1470, sold for HK$10,450,000 (£815,133), the highest price ever paid at Christie's for a ceramic object.

A major impetus to growth in the area has been the joint venture with John Swire and Sons, launched in May 1989. Unprecedented in the art world, the venture seeks to combine the political and administrative resources of Swire with the art expertise of our specialists. The experience of Swire under Baroness Lydia Dunn will continue to be of vital importance in an area where the financial and political climate is often unstable. Christie's will be best poised to take advantage of the continuing interest in local culture promoted by the region's Buddhist tradition. This should ensure that Christie's offices in Hong Kong, Taipei, and Tokyo will have a major strategic importance for the foreseeable future.

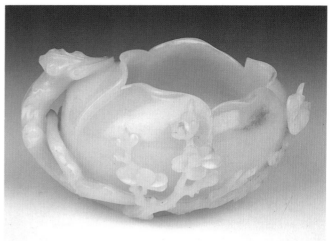

Jadeite censer and
cover
8¾ in. (22.3 cm.)
high
Sold 21 March 1990
in Hong Kong for
HK$5,720,000
(£446,178)

Opposite:
Far left:
Jadeite carving of a
dog in an arbour
6⅛ in. (15.5 cm.)
high
Sold 25 September
1989 in Hong Kong
for HK$1,650,000
(£133,279)

Above:
White jade floral
brush-washer
Qianlong
4¾ in. (12 cm.)
wide
Sold 20 March 1990
in Hong Kong for
HK$880,000
(£68,643)

Below:
Imperial jadeite
necklace with 89
beads
Sold 21 March 1990
in Hong Kong for
HK$6,600,000
(£514,821)

haic bronze square baluster vessel and
er, fanghu
ring states
n. (50.2 cm.) high
11 June 1990 in London for £132,000
8,988)

osite left:
ly Ming gilt-bronze figure of Avalokitesvara
ed Xuande 10th year (AD 1435) and of the
od
4 in. (78.5 cm.) high
11 December 1989 in London for
,000 ($225,082)

osite right:
nted wood figure of a court lady
g dynasty
n. (58.4 cm.) high
2 December 1989 in New York for $165,000
5,095)

g gilt-bronze cloisonné enamel beaker vase
in. (18.5 cm.) high
2 December 1989 in New York for
4,000 (£98,089)

Amber and
straw-glazed
pottery camel
Tang Dynasty
31½ in. (80 cm.)
high
Sold 1 June 1990 in
New York for
$440,000 (£261,904)

Opposite:
Pair of Ming
stoneware figures of
Buddhistic lions
16th century
69 in. (175 cm.) high
overall
Sold 1 June 1990 in
New York for
$264,000 (£157,143)

Famille verte dish
Kangxi
24 in. (61 cm.) diameter
Sold 17 June 1990 in Monaco for F.fr.666,000 (£68,307)

Pair of famille verte
bottle vases
Kangxi
11¾ in. (29.5 cm.)
high
Sold 15 May 1990 in
Amsterdam for
D.fl.34,500 (£11,694)

ANGLO–CHINESE SCHOOL
*View of the Bund,
Shanghai*
*c.*1860
Oil on canvas
29 × 39 in.
(73.7 × 99 cm.)
Sold 26 September
1989 in Hong Kong
for HK$748,000
(£45,896)

One of a pair of
garden scenes
19th century
Oil on canvas
22½ × 34¼ in.
(57 × 87 cm.)
Sold 10 October 1989
in Amsterdam for
D.fl.97,750 (£29,621)

CHARLES WIRGMAN
1832–91
*The Race Course,
Happy Valley, Hong
Kong*
Inscribed and dated
Feb. 18th 58
Pencil and
watercolour
heightened with
white
9⅝ × 13¾ in.
(24.3 × 35 cm.)
Sold 26 September
1989 in Hong Kong
for HK$264,000
(£21,002)

CHARLES WIRGMAN
1832–91
*Marriage Procession
near Manila*
Signed
Pencil and
watercolour with
white heightening
8 × 10½ in.
(20.4 × 26.6 cm.)
Sold 26 September
1989 in Hong Kong
for HK$605,000
(£48,130)

CHARLES WIRGMAN REDISCOVERED IN THE SALEROOM

Colin Sheaf

CHARLES WIRGMAN
1832–91
*Gillman's Bazaar,
Hong Kong*
Signed and dated
Nov. 3rd 57
Pencil and
watercolour
13 × 10 in.
(33 × 25.4 cm.)
Sold 26 September
1989 in Hong Kong
for HK$330,000
(£26,253)

In response to a circular announcing a forthcoming auction in Hong Kong of China Trade art, two large albums of drawings and watercolours arrived at Christie's. Little was known about the contents, and even less about the artist until subsequent research unearthed the fascinating story of a forgotten war artist.

Charles Wirgman was Swedish by ancestry. Essentially a sketcher with a knack for capturing atmosphere, he was perfectly suited to be the topical illustrator for a magazine. Not for him the elaborate, painstaking ritual of painting in oil; his skill lay in capturing a fleeting moment of war, a brief lull in the fighting, a rush of galloping camels in the desert, or a hilarious moment during a horse race in Hong Kong.

Wirgman's career took off when he set out for China around Christmas 1856 as an official illustrator and reporter for the *Illustrated London News*. Although specifically employed to cover the deteriorating international relations between Britain and China, Wirgman dealt with a wide range of subjects. Hong Kong Island was his playground, and he enjoyed the sub-British characteristics: the military bands, the Protestant church services, but above all, the bustling street community life. Many of his drawings capture the atmosphere of crowded, confused bustle which is still entirely the spirit of Hong Kong today.

Like any civilized Brit on the island, Wirgman went to Happy Valley racecourse. This beautiful bay had been developed initially as the island's residential centre, but it proved too malarial and the population moved westward. The huge open space was then turned into a vast race-track, with an expatriates' cemetery conveniently nearby for those who succumbed to malaria, fortified wines or over-excitement. Manila was another well-known (Spanish) colonial spot to visit, and Wirgman enjoyed the city, for it was full of human activity. His albums contain representations of a football game, a cockfight, the local 'Indian' billiard room, card games and musical soirees.

Wirgman's drawings in Hong Kong and Canton capture a moment of great importance in the shifting Sino-British diplomatic relationships, as Western imperialism began to impinge on a decaying Chinese administration. Ceded only a few years before Wirgman's visit, Hong Kong is shown in all its 'Britishness', but Wirgman's inquisitive eye penetrates the veneer and enjoys the contrast of two very different cultures. The sale in Hong Kong was intended to appeal to those who still find this contrast fascinating, and the extensive viewing showed that the venue for the sale was well-chosen.

TANG YIN
1470–1523
Scenes of Hermits' Long Days in the Quiet Mountains
Hanging scroll, ink and colour on silk
43 × 24¼ in. (109 × 62.5 cm.)
Sold 31 May 1990 in New York for $352,000
(£209,524)
Record auction price for a hanging scroll by the artist

Opposite, top to bottom:
YAN GENG
Late 13th/early 14th century
A Night Excursion of the Drunken Zhong Kui and his Sister
Handscroll, ink on silk
9¾ × 99¾ in. (24.4 × 253.4 cm.)
Sold 31 May 1990 in New York for $462,000
(£275,000)
Record auction price for a work by the artist

XIA CHANG
1388–1470
Bamboo Growing by a River, in the Spring Rain
Handscroll, ink on paper
15¾ × 488 in. (40 × 1,240 cm.)
Sold 31 May 1990 in New York for $440,000
(£261,905)
Record auction price for a work by the artist

DING GUANPENG
Active *c.*1742–54
Sixteen Luohans
Signed 'Painted by Imperial Order following the brushwork of Ding Yunpeng, Chen Ding Guanpeng'
Handscroll, ink and colour on paper
10⅝ × 255¼ in. (27 × 648.5 cm.)
Sold 4 December 1989 in New York for $605,000 (£380,503)
Record auction price for a Qing dynasty Imperial court painting

SHI LU
1919–82
Lotus in the Rain
Signed
Hanging scroll, ink and colour on paper
68½ × 36 in. (174 × 91.5 cm.)
Sold 25 September 1989 in Hong Kong for
HK$935,000 (£74,860)

ZHAO ZHIQIAN
1829–84
Flowers
One of a set of four hanging scrolls, ink and
colour on paper
54¼ × 27¼ in. (138 × 69 cm.)
Sold 19 March 1990 in Hong Kong for
HK$3,520,000 (£274,570)
Record auction price for a single lot of
modern Chinese paintings

JAPANESE SCREENS AT AUCTION

Sebastian Izzard

The tradition of decorative screen painting has a long and distinguished history in Japan. In the 1989–90 season Christie's sold several major sets of screens, making record prices for Japanese art.

The first set of screens portrayed the battle of the Uji Bridge, fought during the wars of the Heike between the Minamoto clan and the Taira. The screens, read from right to left, portrayed all the main events of this action, with the same group of warriors appreaing three times across the screens. The screens sold for what was then a world record for a pair of screens – $495,000 (£313,887).

This record was broken by two sets of screens sold in New York in March. The first of these depicted a panorama of the city of Kyoto and its environs. *Rakuchu Rakugai* 'screens in and out of the capital', became very popular during the seventeenth century, when they were often purchased as souvenirs of visits to the capital. All four seasons were portrayed, as were the famous buildings, beauty spots and festivals that characterized the city. The present pair was sold to a Japanese museum for $1,760,000 (£1,071,840), the highest price ever achieved for any pre-1900 Japanese work of art at auction.

Two lots later, a pair of Rimpa School flower screens were sold for $1,210,000 (£736,890). They show, from right to left, the pine shoots of early winter, and pass through the flowers of spring, early summer, late summer, and autumn, ending with chrysanthemums. The cumulative effect is of walking through a flowering meadow. This genius for handling the complexities of nature and transmuting them into a decorative dialogue makes the work of this school justly famous.

The last major pair of screens was sold in London in June. They depicted scenes from *The Tale of Genji*, the world famous eleventh-century literary masterpiece by Murasaki Shikibu. The screens describe twenty chapters of the story in a continuous panorama, the various scenes linked by a stylized cloud pattern. The combination of rich design and gold leaf epitomized the decorative traditions of Japanese painting. Of all the legends and stories portrayed by the Japanese screen painters *The Tale of Genji* was the most popular, and it seems appropriate that this splendid example made a record price for this subject-matter when it was sold for £198,000 ($330,000).

All four sets of screens returned to Japan, and if the Japanese economy remains as strong as it did during the 1980s the record prices achieved during the last season may soon by broken.

Rakuchu rakugai zu
Pair of six-panel screens
Early 17th century
Each 61 × 139½ in.
(154.4 × 353.2 cm.)
Sold 29 March 1990 in New York for $1,760,000 (£1,071,840)
Record auction price for a Japanese screen prior to 1900

RIMPA SCHOOL
Flowers and Grasses of the Four Seasons
Pair of six-panel screens
17th century
Each 62 × 137½ in. (157.5 × 348.2 cm.)
Sold 29 March 1990 in New York for $1,210,000 (£736,890)

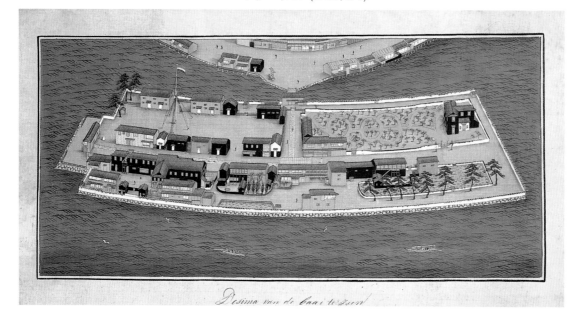

Deshima Island
Inscribed
19th century
Watercolour on silk
18 × 9½ in.
(45 × 24 cm.)
Sold 15 May 1990 in
Amsterdam for
D.fl.92,000 (£31,186)

Top:
'The Battle of Uji Bridge' from *The Tale of
the Heike*
Pair of six-panel screens
c.1610
Each 60½ × 139¾ in. (153 × 354.2 cm.)
Sold 17 October 1989 in New York for
$495,000 (£312,303)

Above:
Scenes from *The Tale of Genji*
Pair of six-panel screens
17th century
Each panel 67 × 24½ in. (170 × 62 cm.)
Sold 6 June 1990 in London for £198,000
($330,000)

MUNAKATA SHIKO
1903–75
One from a set of the *Judai deshi hanga saku*
(The Disciples of Buddha)
41 × 16 in. (102.2 × 39.7 cm.)
Sold 29 March 1990 in New York for
$990,000 (£607,362)
Record auction price for a work by the artist

Opposite:
UMEHARA RYUZABURO
1888–1986
Mount Fuji
Signed and dated 1949
Ink and mineral pigment on gold paper
14⅞ × 11¾ in. (37.8 × 29.8 cm.)
Sold 17 October 1989 in New York for
$1,430,000 (£906,785)
From the collection of Mr Paul K. Von
Bergen and the late Caroline Von Bergen

Kakiemon model of a *bijin*
*c.*1680
15¼ in. (38.5 cm.) high
Sold 5 June 1990 in London for £77,000
($128,590)
Record auction price for a *bijin* figure

Opposite above:
SHIGEHIDE (calligrapher)
The History of Yuzu Nenbutsu Sect
Two volumes, manuscript, ink on paper
Each signed and dated 1528
Sold 13 November 1989 in London for
£154,000 ($249,480)

Opposite below:
HIROSHIGE
1797–1858
Complete set of *The Fifty-three Stations of the
Tokaido*
Each signed 'Hiroshige ga' and published by
Hoeido
Each approx. 9 × 13½ in. (22.6 × 34.4 cm.)
Sold 30 March 1990 in New York for
$440,000 (£267,960)
Record auction price for a work by the artist

FLOWERS OF FIRE: KAKIEMON PORCELAIN FROM THE ENGLISH COUNTRY HOUSE

Susan Moore

Daniel Defoe described the 'china-mania' that swept through late seventeenth-century England. In court circles, the craze prompted the 'piling' of predominantly Chinese blue and white 'upon the tops of Cabinets, Scrutores, and every Chymney-Piece, to the tops of the Ceilings…till it became a grievance in the expense of it and even injurous to…families and estates'. Nearly a thousand pieces of porcelain and Delft were displayed in William and Mary's apartments at Kensington Palace in 1697, some 193 in one bedchamber alone.

Of all the oriental porcelains, the most prized – and the most expensive – was Japanese Kakiemon. Imagine the impact of the first of these exquisite, brilliantly enamelled wares. How their elegant decoration, translucent jewel-like colour, and milky-white body must have dazzled our forebears, who knew only the limited palettes of Chinese blue and white, and crude maiolica.

Christie's exhibition *Flowers of Fire: Kakiemon Porcelain from the English Country House* gathered together Kakiemon from both familiar and little-known late seventeenth-century and early eighteenth-century country house collections, from Burghley House, Drayton House, Sherborne Castle, Blenheim, Arniston House, Welbeck Abbey, Audley End and Dunham Massey. George Carter's inspired sets of *trompe-l'oeil* tortoiseshell panelling suggested the kind of sombre, Dutch-style cabinets or rooms which the porcelains first embellished – and where they must have glowed and shimmered, aided by mirrored glass and candlelight. We may take porcelain for granted, but to our predecessors it was a material little short of miraculous. A vast Dutch still-life in the exhibition illustrated the formal, public display of Kakiemon, in which porcelain found a place alongside silver, fruit and flowers, piled up on the shelves of a stepped buffet. But the more beguiling image was provided by a 'reconstruction' of an intimate, essentially feminine, closet. Here rich Kakiemon pieces were arranged as a foil to blue and white in a pyramidal scheme above a corner chimneypiece, the type of arrangement devised by Daniel Marot for Queen Mary at Kensington and Hampton Court. Unlike the more formal, classical rooms of a country house or palace, such a private closet would be fanciful and exotic, hung with chintz and filled with flowers, oriental lacquer and porcelain, the 'fired' flowers of which had the allure of never fading.

The theatricality of the sets at Christie's, with their two-dimensional porcelains and lacquer chair and chest, and their painted tiger-lily tulips, gave the show a sense of fun. (The very valuable real Kakiemon was exhibited more securely alongside.) It also belied the

Kakiemon jar and cover
c.1680
10¼ in. (26 cm.) high
From Burghley House

underlying seriousness of the display. The judicious selection, by Mark Hinton of Christie's with Oliver Impey of the Ashmolean Museum in Oxford, encouraged us to review our opinion of what constitutes Kakiemon. The term itself is shrouded in mystery – does it refer to a family of potters, or enamellers, or is it the name of a kiln?

What normally springs to mind at the mention of Kakiemon is the magnificent hexagonal jars and covers at Hampton Court or the large oviform vases from Blenheim or Woburn, each panel decorated with a different, exquisitely balanced and asymmetrical design of ho-o birds, figures and foliage. At the exhibition we were also shown cruder provincial pieces and early experimental palettes, as well as blue and white from the Kakiemon kilns. Figures and animals also took a bow, including the splendid baggy-trousered elephant, whose appearance in the Burghley inventory of 1688 confirms that the Kakiemon palette was fully developed by that date. There were unexpected shapes, and those of a near-Eastern or European origin, such as a celadon double-gourd ewer, a salt, and a tankard with a biscuit-coloured ground, all from Burghley House.

Stylistic influence in Kakiemon ricochets between East and West – the Kakiemon style itself may even be Dutch-inspired Chinoiserie rather than a native Japanese invention. Certainly during the eighteenth century most of the Kakiemon designs were copied by the European porcelain houses, including Meissen, Chantilly and Chelsea. This cross-fertilization was more fully explored in the *Porcelain for Palaces* exhibition which opened at the British Museum in July 1990. Meanwhile, *Flowers of Fire* served to highlight the beauty of Kakiemon porcelain and the fact of its increasing rarity in Europe. These glorious wares, made specifically for export, are steadily being repatriated.

Below right:
The recontructed room-set used in the *Flowers of Fire* exhibition, based on the arrangement devised by Daniel Marot for Queen Mary at Kensington Palace and Hampton Court

Below:
Kakiemon elephant *c*.1680
11¼ in. (28.5 cm.) long
From Burghley House

Ivory netsuke
Signed 'Shugetsu'
18th century
5¾ in. (14.5 cm.) high
Sold 16 May 1990 in London for £51,700
(£84,219)

Opposite:
Oviform Kakiemon vase
c.1680
15½ in. (39 cm.) high
Sold 14 November 1989 in London for
£242,000 ($392,040)

Namban lacquer
Christian portable
shrine
Momoyama period,
*c.*1590
18 × 12¾ × 1¾ in.
(45.5 × 32 × 4.4 cm.)
Sold 5 June 1990 in
London for £209,000
($349,030)
Record auction price
for a Namban shrine

Lacquered palanquin
18th/19th century
The palanquin
41 × 53¾ × 35¾ in.
(104 × 136.6 × 91 cm.)
The pole 184 in.
(467 cm.) long
Sold 29 March 1990
in New York for
$220,000 (£133,980)

Copper red decorated
porcelain jar
Yi Dynasty
7 in. (17.8 cm.) high
Sold 29 March 1990
in New York for
$55,000 (£33,495)

Opposite:
Roman marine mosaic panel
c.1st century AD
26¾ × 26¼ in. (67.8 × 66.7 cm.) including
frame
Sold 12 December 1989 in London for
£363,000 ($580,800)

A magnificent Roman marine mosaic panel
(*emblema*), depicting a variety of fish, squid
and eel in lively naturalistic colour and detail.
It bears a dedication on the nineteenth-century
bronze gilt frame: 'Discovered in the ruins of
the Palace of Pope Leo the 12th at the Villa
Chichignola, presented by Pope Gregory the
16th to Sir Edward Thomason in the year
1832. This mosaic containing 20,000 silicious
pebbles is the work of Sosus Pergami, who
flourished 320 years before Christ and is
mentioned in the writings of the Elder Pliny.'
Reputed to be by the 'most celebrated'
mosaicist, Sosus (150–100 BC) of Pergamum
in Asia Minor (Turkey), who was
immortalized by Pliny the Elder in his *Natural
History*, it is almost certainly a Roman copy
of the 1st century AD, after a Hellenistic
original, and made for the prestigious owners
of a villa along the Via Ardeatina (parallel to
the Appian Way). It is the finest mosaic ever
to appear at auction and holds the world
record price for such an item.

Terracotta statuette of a mime theatrical actor
Western Asia Minor, *c*.2nd century BC
7½ in. (18.7 cm.) high
Sold 11 July 1990 in London for £5,500 ($9,900)

Marble portrait head
of the Emperor
Antoninus Pius
Reign of Antoninus
Pius, 138–161 AD
11¼ in. (28.5 cm.)
high
Sold 11 July 1990 in
London for £55,000
($99,000)

Roman marble head of a goddess or muse
1st–2nd century AD
13¼ in. (33.5 cm.) high
Sold 11 July 1990 in London for £28,600
($51,480)

Roman marble statue of Venus Euplaea, the
protectress of sea voyagers, standing with her
left arm resting on her attribute of a rudder
Early 2nd century AD
60 in. (152 cm.) high
Sold 11 July 1990 in London for £71,500
($128,700)

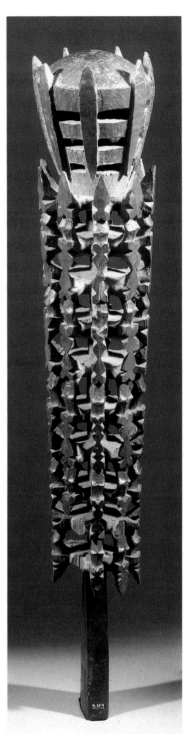

Right:
Mitiaro staff god made of toa wood
c.1800
22½ in. (57 cm.) high
Sold 3 July 1990 in London for £88,000
($154,880)

The human form has never been more
stylized than in the 'mace gods' of Mitiaro
and the 'slab gods' of neighbouring
Mangaia, Atiu and Aitutaki. Here the head
shape is reminiscent of a warrior's helmet,
while the shaft is surrounded by stylized
torsos.

Below:
Austral Islands necklace with whale ivory
pendants
Rurutu or Tupua'i
18th or early 19th century
15¾ in. (40 cm.) long
Sold 3 July 1990 in London for £99,000
($174,240)

Above:
Maori treasure box
c.1830
6¼ in. long
Sold 3 July 1990 in
London for £88,000
($154,880)

Opposite:
Batak wooden staff
Sumatra
68¾ in. (174 cm.)
high
Sold 6 March 1990 in
Amsterdam for
D.fl.32,200 (£9,968)

Attributed to
SAYYID MIRZA
*Portrait of Sultan
Muhammad Mirza*
Inscribed 'Sultan
Muhammad Mirza
Nawab Sayf
al-Dawla'
Persia, Qajar, *c.*1835
Oil on canvas
62¼ × 35⅛ in.
(158 × 89 cm.)
Sold 10 October 1989
in London for
£22,000 ($35,420)

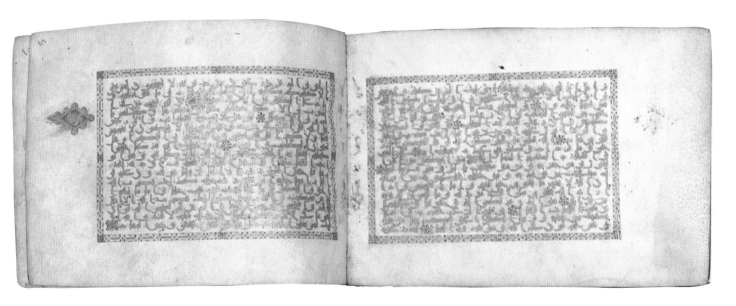

Above:
Qur'an section
Iraq or Persia, 9th century
Folio 7 × 9⅞ in. (17.8 × 25 cm.)
Sold 24 April 1990 in London for £176,000
($295,680)

Below:
Qur'an
Persia AH 943/AD 1536–7
Folio 6⅜ × 4¾ in. (16.2 × 11 cm.)
Sold 24 April 1990 in London for £24,200
($40,656)

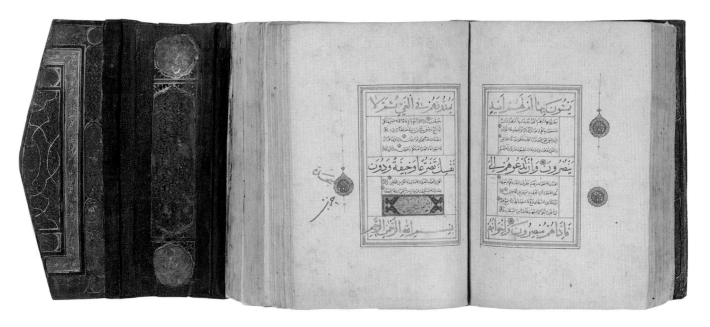

Patamanjari Ragini: Wife of Dipak Raga
Basohli, *c.*1690
8¼ × 8¼ in. (20.9 × 20.9 cm.)
Sold 10 October 1989 in London for £17,600
($27,808)

The Death of Ananias
Mughal, *c.*1650–80
7¾ × 12⅝ in.
(19.6 × 32 cm.)
Sold 10 October 1989
in London for £8,800
($14,168)

The subject of this miniature has been taken from a cartoon by Raphael, currently in the Victoria and Albert Museum, London. The work bears features which makes it seem likely that it was executed by a Mughal artist working at Bikaner. Christianity in India goes back further than in any place other than Palestine, and it is believed that Christ assigned the teaching of the Gospels in India to the Apostle Thomas. Tradition has it that Thomas reached India in AD 52, settling in Malabar, before expanding his mission as far as China. Missionaries began working in India soon after Vasco da Gama's arrival in 1498, and in 1580 Akbar invited a group of Jesuits to come to the court to explain Christianity and the Bible to him.

European influences are discernible in manuscripts of the 1560s and 1570s, and the European illustrations which travelled to India were then copied by the Mughal artists. The first European prints that were influential were German, by Albrecht Dürer and his circle. A second major group found in India included the work of the Antwerp printmakers of the sixteenth century. During the seventeenth century more European prints became available in India and the Far East, but in China and Japan the European traditions were too alien to be as influential as they were in India.

Mamluk gold ring
Inscribed 'my trust is
in him in every
affair'
Egypt, 14th century
1⅜ in. (3.4 cm.)
high
Sold 10 October 1989
in London for
£35,200 ($56,672)

Mon-Dvaravati
hardstone head of
Buddha
Thailand, 7th/8th
century
15 in. (38 cm.) high
Sold 5 December
1989 in Amsterdam
for D.fl.48,300
(£15,382)

Gandhara grey schist figure of the
Bodhisattva Siddhartha
North-west India, late 2nd century
60¼ in. (54 cm.) high
Sold 10 October 1989 in London for £88,000
($141,680)

Tibetan gilt-copper figure of Suvikranta, a
Buddha of Confession
*c.*15th century
10 in. (25 cm.) high
Sold 5 December 1989 in Amsterdam for
D.fl.34,500 (£10,987)

Mesopotamian silver
inlaid brass casket
Jazira, 13th century
7½ × 7¼ × 5½ in.
(19 × 18.5 × 14 cm.)
Sold 10 October 1989
in London for
£242,000 ($389,620)
Record auction price
for Islamic metalwork

MODERN
DECORATIVE ARTS

One of a pair of leaded glass windows
Made by Tiffany Studios for the Hill
Residence, Tarrytown, New York
Signed and dated 1920
62 × 28 in. (157.5 × 71 cm.)
The pair sold 9 december 1989 in New York
for $352,000 (£224,204)
Record auction price for a window

'Grand Vase Libellules', carved acid–etched and applied cameo vase
By the firm of Daum
Signed
23¾ in. (60.2 cm.) high
Sold 27 September 1989 in London for £60,500 ($98,615)

'Peony' double overlay lamp
By the firm of Emile Gallé
Signed
24¾ in. (63 cm.) high
Sold 13 May 1990 in Geneva for Sw.fr.682,000 (£291,453)

Pâte-de-verre lamp
By Gabriel Argy-Rousseau
Signed
15⅝ in. (39.7 cm.) high
Sold 11 April 1990 in London for $97,240

Right:
'Lampe au Hibou'
double overlay
carved and etched
table lamp
By the firm of Daum
c.1903
34½ in. (88.5 cm.)
high
Sold 8 June 1990 in
New York for
$880,000 (£517,647)
Record auction price
for a work solely by
Daum

Far right:
'Lotus' double
overlay mould blown
and carved glass and
bronze table lamp
By the firm of Daum
and Louis Majorelle
Signed
Sold 13 May 1990 in
Geneva for
Sw.fr.1,580,000
(£658,120)

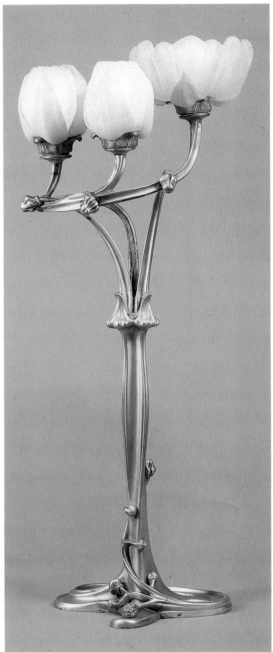

Left:
'Rosebush' leaded glass and bronze table lamp
By Tiffany Studios
29½ in. (74.9 cm.) high
Sold 9 December 1989 in New York for $363,000 (£231,210)
Record auction price for this Tiffany lamp model

'Pond Lily' leaded glass and bronze table lamp
By Tiffany Studios
26 in. (67.3 cm.) high
Sold 9 December 1989 in New York for $550,000 (£350,318)
Record auction price for an object made by Tiffany Studios

Right:
'Magnolia' leaded glass and bronze floor lamp
By Tiffany Studios
Stamped 'Tiffany Studios New York 1599'
378 in. (198.2 cm.) high
Sold 9 June 1990 in New York for $440,000 (£260,355)

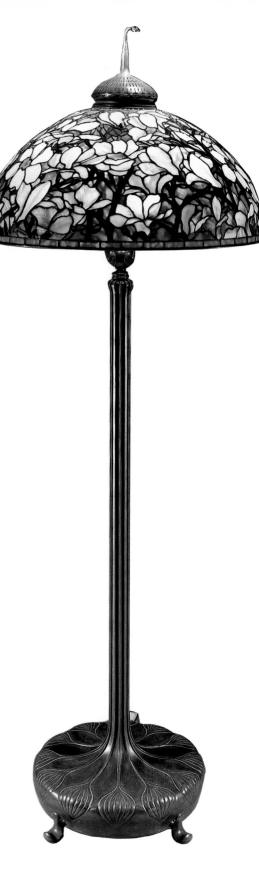

Below:
Acid-etched double overlay landscape vase
By the firm of Emile Gallé
Signed
32¾ in. (83 cm.) high
Sold 11 April 1990 for £88,000 ($149,600)

Three earthenware vases
By George Ohr
Signed
6⅞ in. (17.8 cm.), 13 in. (33 cm.) and
8¼ in.(21 cm.) high respectively (from left
to right)
Sold 9 June 1990 in New York for $11,000
(£6,509), $22,000 (£13,018) and $19,800
(£11,716) respectively
The centre vase achieved a record auction
price for a work by the artist

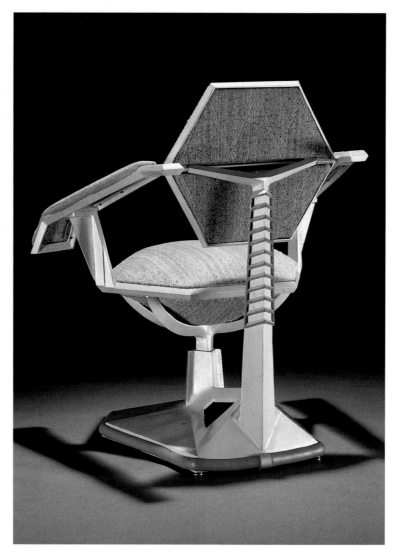

Tubular steel desk chair
Designed by Frank Lloyd Wright for the S.C.
Johnson Administration Building, Racine,
Wisconsin
*c.*1936
34¾ in. (88 cm.) high
Sold 9 December 1989 in New York for
$74,800 (£47,643)

Aluminium armchair
Designed by Frank Lloyd Wright for the
H.C. Price Company Tower, Bartlesville,
Oklahoma
*c.*1953–6
32⅝ in. (83 cm.) high
Sold 9 December 1989 in New York for
$46,200 (£29,427)

D.W. Hislop set of four silver
spoons and forks
Designed by Charles Rennie
Mackintosh
1902
Sold 31 January 1990 in London
for £22,000 ($35,200)

Hukin & Heath electroplated metal
and glass 'crow's foot' decanter
Designed by Dr Christopher Dresser
Stamped 'H & H', 1878
9½ in. (24 cm.) high
Sold 18 July 1990 in London for
£13,750 ($25,300)

A Morris & Company tapestry
Designed by Henry Dearle
c.1910
96¼ × 71⅛ in. (244 × 180.5 cm.)
Sold 18 July 1990 in London for
£38,500 ($70,840)

'Semiramis', cold-painted parcel-silvered gilt-bronze and ivory figure of a dancer
Cast and carved from a model by Demêtre Chiparus
Early 20th century
Signed 'Chiparus'
26⅛ in. (66.4 cm.) high
Sold 8 June 1990 in New York for $176,000 (£103,529)
Record auction price for a work by Chiparus

Carlo Bugatti ice bucket
Cast by
A.A. Hébrard
9¾ in. (25 cm.)
high
Sold 11 April 1990 in London for £93,500 ($158,950)

Loetz vase
Engraved 'Loetz Austria'
10¼ in. (26 cm.)
high
Sold 12 November 1989 in Geneva for Sw.fr.35,200 (£13,538)

Galuchat gondole chairs and
pietra dura bureau plat
By the shop of André Groult
*c.*1925
The bureau 30 in.(76 cm.)
high; the chairs 40 in.
(102 cm.) high
Sold 9 December 1989 in
New York for $231,000
(£146,202)
Record auction price for a
work by the artist

Palissandre and ivory desk
By the firm of Jacques-Emile
Ruhlmann
Signed 'Ruhlmann' in pencil
1927
37 in. (94 cm.) high
Sold 9 December 1989 in New
York for $165,000 (£104,430)

C.A. Lion Cachet fruitwood bookstand
44¼ in. (112 cm.) high
Sold 30 May 1990 in Amsterdam for
D.fl.46,000 (£14,433)

LUCIEN SCHELER
Lisières du devenir
Illustrations by
Raoul Ubac
Paris, 1963
Sold 12 November 1989 in Geneva for
Sw.fr.27,500 (£10,784)

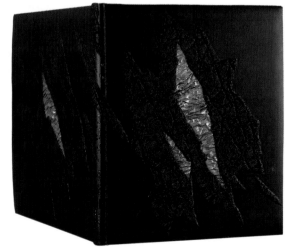

Wurlitzer 42 'Victory'
1943
65 in. (165 cm.) high
Sold 26 October 1989 in Amsterdam for
D.fl.34,500 (£10,207)

LOUIS ICART
Place de la Concorde
c.1940
Oil on canvas
21½ × 29 in. (54.6 × 73.7 cm.)
Sold 8 June 1990 in New York for $99,000
(£58,929)
Record auction price for a work by the artist

MARC CHAGALL
Russian 1887–1985
Cirque
One of 38 original lithographs
Paris, 1967
Sold 12 November 1989 in Geneva for
Sw.fr.495,000 (£194,117)

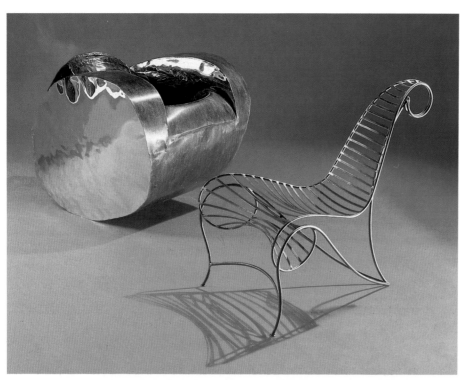

Far left:
'Rolling Volume' sheet steel armchair
By Ron Arad
Sold 31 January 1990 in London for £5,50
($8,800)

Left:
'Spine Chair' welded steel side chair
By André Dubreuil
Sold 31 January 1990 in London for £13,2
($21,120)

Below:
'Oisin' float glass and forged iron console table
By Danny Lane
Inscribed
37¼ in. (94.5 cm.) high
Sold 31 January 1990 in London for £6,05
($9,680)

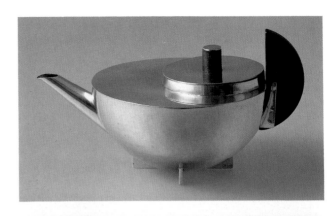

Right:
'Tee-extraktkännnchen' silver and ebony teapot
By Marianne Brandt
Executed at the Bauhaus metal workshop, 1924
3 in. (7.5 cm.) high
Sold 26 October 1989 in Amsterdam for D.fl.368,000 (£108,876)
Record auction price for a work by the artist

Below right:
'MT8' table lamp, *c*.1925
By Wilhelm Wagenfeld
14⅜ in. (36.5 cm.) high
Sold 26 October 1989 in Amsterdam for D.fl.247,250 (£73,151)

Below:
Venini vase
Designed by Fulvio Bianconi
Stamped 'Venini Murano Italia'
10¾ in. (27 cm.) high
Sold 13 May 1990 in Geneva for Sw.fr.176,000 (£75,214)
Record auction price for a piece of Italian post-war glass

Three stoneware
bottle vases
By Lucie Rie
Impressed 'LR' seal
c.1968, 1973 and 1959
respectively (from
left to right)
18⅞ in. (48 cm.),
13 in. (33.1 cm.) and
15 in. (38.1 cm.)
high
Sold 18 June 1990 in
London for
£6,380 ($10,910),
£7,700 ($13,167) and
£12,100 ($20,691)
respectively

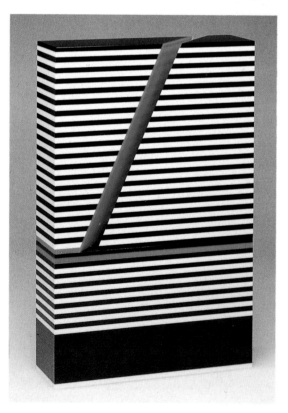

Far left:
'Sky scraper' glass
sculpture
By Ivo Rozsypal
Made at the Glass
Symposium in Novy
Bor, 1985
Engraved 'I.Rozsypal
85'
15½ in. (39.5 cm.)
high
Sold 13 May 1990 in
Geneva for
Sw.fr.12,100 (£5,171)

Left:
Stoneware cup
By Hans Coper
Impressed 'HC' seal
c.1972
6 in. (15.1 cm.) high
Sold 20 November
1989 in London for
£17,600 ($28,160)

ARMS AND ARMOUR AND MODERN SPORTING GUNS

Reinforcing pieces for the tilt from the
Rosenblatt (rose-leaf) garniture of Emperor
Maximilian II
By Franz Grosschedel of Landshut
1571
The grandguard 12 in. (30.5 cm.); the
pasguard 14¾ in. (37.5 cm.)
Sold 23 May 1990 in London at South
Kensington for £71,500 ($120,120)

Italian knightly sword, *c*.1400
32 in. (81.3 cm.) blade
Sold 20 September 1989 in London at South
Kensington for £11,000 ($17,182)

Right:
Left-hand dagger, late 16th century
17¾ in. (45.1 cm.) long
Sold 20 September 1989 in London at South
Kensington for £8,800 ($13,745)

Far right:
Saxon left-hand dagger, *c*.1570
14¾ in. (37.5 cm.) long
Sold 23 May 1990 in London at South
Kensington for £6,600 ($11,088)

Below, left to right:
Italian cup-hilt rapier, *c*.1660
40½ in. (102.9 cm.) blade
Sold 20 September 1989 in London at South
Kensington for £8,800 ($13,745)

Neapolitan cup-hilt rapier, *c*.1660
Signed 'Fecit Lavrentivs Palvmbo De Napoli'
44½ in. (112.4 cm.) blade
Sold 20 September 1989 in London at South
Kensington for £8,800 ($13,745)

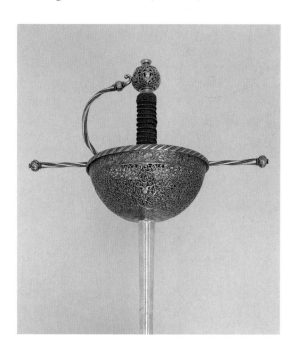

ectoral Guard comb
c.1580
May 1990 in London at
ensington for £12,100

fantry half-armour, *c*.1580
September 1989 in London
Kensington for £22,000

carved ivory powder-flask
century
4 cm.) high
September 1989 in London
Kensington for £11,000

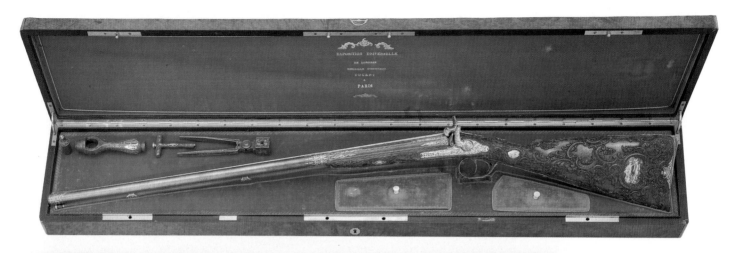

Cased pair of percussion duelling pistols, by Alden & Smith, London, *c.*1830
Numbered 441/2
14½ in. (36.8 cm.)
Sold 23 May 1990 in London at South Kensington for £6,820 ($11,458)

Above:
French exhibition d.b. percussion sporting gun
Signed by the gunmaker 'Tourey A Paris', by the engraver 'J.M. Cinlot-Collette, Herstal', and by the decorator 'J. Falloise, 1849'
30¼ in. (76.8 cm.) barrels
Sold 20 September 1989 in London at South Kensington for £33,000 ($51,546)
Record auction price for a double-barrelled percussion gun
The Reports of the Juries for the Great Exhibition of 1851 record the award of a Prize Medal to Tourey for 'An ornamental double gun, the master-piece of a gunmaker; guns and arms of excellent workmanship'.

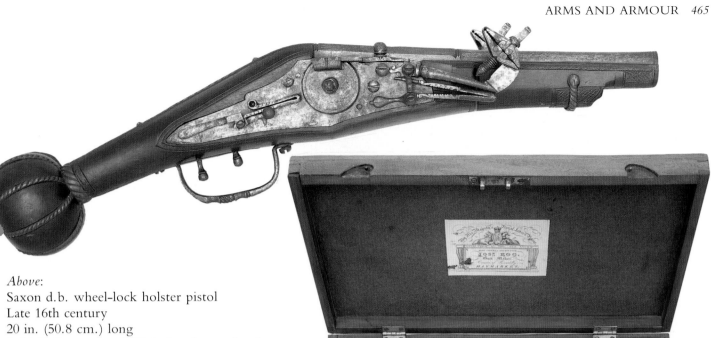

Above:
Saxon d.b. wheel-lock holster pistol
Late 16th century
20 in. (50.8 cm.) long
Sold 20 September 1989 in London at South
Kensington for £15,400 ($24,055)
This appears to be the earliest recorded
example of a double-barrelled side-by-side
firearm.

Cased set of two single-trigger
over-and-under flintlock pistols
By Joseph Egg
London silver hallmarks for 1815
12½ in. and 6¾ in. (31.3 and 17 cm.) long
Sold 28 February 1990 in London at South
Kensington for £15,400 ($26,103)

Pair of Silesian flintlock holster pistols
Late 17th century
19¾ in. (49.5 cm.) long
Sold 23 May 1990 in London at South
Kensington for £12,100 ($20,328)

Left:
Over-and-under sextuple-grip sidelock ejector 20-bore d.b. gun
By J. Purdey, London
Completed *c.*1927
Sold 13 June 1990 in London at South Kensington for £26,400 ($44,880)

Centre:
Under-and-over sidelock ejector 12-bore d.b. single-trigger pigeon-gun, with extra barrels
By J. Purdey, London
Engraved by K.C. Hunt in 1959, the extra barrels fitted in 1965
Sold 28 March 1990 in London at South Kensington for £29,700 ($49,005)

Pair of under-and-over sidelock ejector 20-bore d.b. single-trigger game-guns
By Abbiatico & Salvinelli, Italy
Completed *c.*1985
Sold 13 June 1990 in London at South Kensington for £18,700 ($31,790)

Over-and-under
sidelock ejector
20-bore d.b. selective
single-trigger
game-gun
By Boss, London
Completed *c.*1934
Sold 6 December
1989 in New York
for $38,500 (£24,679)

Over-and-under
sidelock ejector .410
d.b. single-trigger
game-gun
By Boss, London
Completed *c.*1938,
the first .410
over-and-under gun
built by this maker
Sold 6 December
1989 in New York
for $112,200
(£71,795)
Record auction price
for a single British
modern sporting gun

Over-and-under
sidelock ejector
20-bore d.b.
single-trigger
game-gun
By Boss, London
Completed *c.*1958
Sold 6 December
1989 in New York
for $35,200 (£22,564)

Pair of lightweight
self-opening sidelock
ejector 12-bore d.b.
'round-body' game-guns
By Boss, London
Completed *c*.1941
Sold 28 March 1990 in
London at South
Kensington for £24,200
($39,930)

Centre:
Pair of sidelock ejector
12-bore d.b.'Royal
Brevis Self-Opener'
game-guns
By Holland & Holland,
London
Completed *c*.1933 and
rebarrelled *c*.1979 by the
maker
Sold 28 March 1990 in
London at South
Kensington for £28,600
($47,190)

Below:
Self-opening sidelock
ejector 20-bore d.b.
single-trigger game-gun
By J. Purdey, London
Completed *c*.1959
Sold 6 December 1989
in New York for
$24,200 (£15,513)

Opposite:
Pair of self-opening
sidelock ejector 12-bore
d.b. game-guns
By J. Purdey, London
Completed *c*.1979
Sold 28 March 1990 in
London at South
Kensington for £38,500
($65,450)

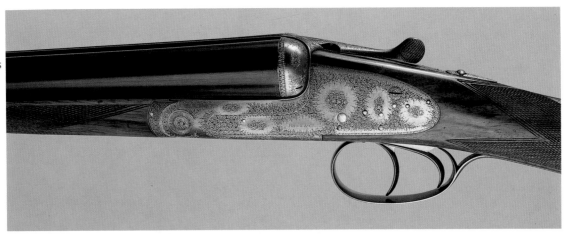

Pair of sidelock ejector 12-bore d.b.
single-trigger 'Royal Self-Opener' game-guns
By Holland & Holland, London
Completed c.1931
Recently re-engraved by K.E. Preater
Sold 28 March 1990 in London at South
Kensington for £19,800 ($32,670)

Centre:
Pair of self-opening sidelock ejector 12-bore
d.b. game-guns
By J. Purdey, London
Completed c.1976
Sold 28 March 1990 in London at South
Kensington for £28,600 ($47,190)

Below left:
Self-opening sidelock ejector 16-bore d.b.
game-gun
By J. Purdey, London
Completed c.1959
Sold 28 March 1990 in London at South
Kensington for £13,200 ($21,780)

Below:
Cased Borchardt 1893 Patent 7.65 mm.
self-loading pistol, No. 851
By Waffenfabrik Loewe, Berlin
With its original case and accessories
Sold 13 June 1990 in London at South
Kensington for £14,300 ($24,310)

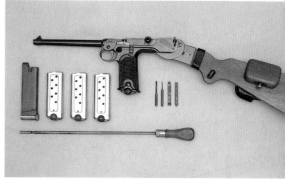

STAMPS

Top to bottom:
China 1897 small $1 Surcharge, mint
Formerly in the Ackerman, Scudder and
Johnson Collections
Sold 23 November 1989 in Zürich for
Sw.fr.315,000 (£124,309)

Canada 1857 12d., mint pair
From the Weill Brothers' stock, formerly in
the Hewitt, Ferrary and Foxbridge
Collections
Sold 22 November 1989 in Zürich for
Sw.fr.191,250 (£75,474)

China 1900–1 2m Tientsin Provisional,
hand-stamped
'China' during the Boxer Rebellion, originally
presented to General Saltzmann and formerly
in the Ferrary, Hind and King Carol
Collections
Sold (with an example of the 3m) 12 June
1990 in Zürich for Sw.fr.326,000 (£132,953)

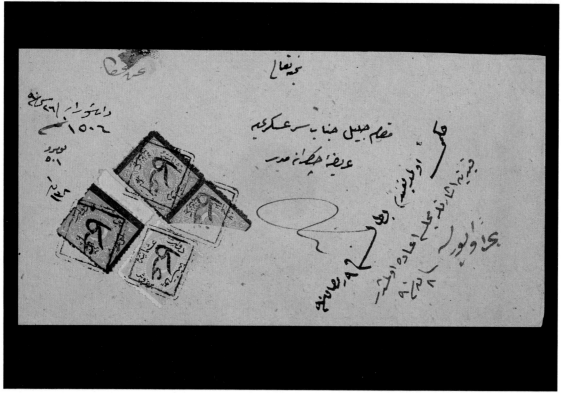

IMPORTANT COVERS
FROM THE BIANNUAL
AUCTIONS HELD BY
ROBSON LOWE IN
ZURICH

British Guiana 1850
2c. black on rose
'Cotton Reel',
vertical pair initialled
'E.D.W.' (E.D.
Wright) on entire
letter from Demerara
to Edward Gordon at
the Plantation Good
Hope
From the Weill
Brothers' stock,
formerly in the
Burrus, Ferrary and
Great Collections
Sold 22 November
1989 for
Sw.fr.585,000
(£230,860)

Holy Land 1873
cover from the
Turkish Post Office
at Acre to
the Ministry of War,
re-addressed to the
Assembly General,
Constantinople,
bearing Postage Due
20pa. vertical pair,
one bisected, 2pi. and
Postage 1pi.
From the Michael
Sacher Collection
Sold 22 November
1989 for Sw.fr.67,500
(£26,638)

IMPORTANT STAMPS AND
COVERS AUCTIONED BY
CHRISTIE'S LONDON

Top left:
Cyprus 1960 'Cyprus
Republic' 20m, variety
overprint double
Sold 9 May 1990 in
London for £6,600
($11,160)

Top right:
Nyasaland 1903–4
£10, mint corner
marginal pair
From the Dr Graeme
McFarlane Collection
Sold 12 September
1989 for £5,500
($8,575)

Centre left:
Great Britain 1864–79
1d. Plate 225, mint
block of four
Sold 9 May 1990 for
£3,850 ($6,510)

Centre right:
Great Britain
unissued 1½d.
rosy-mauve on blued
paper, mint block of
six
From the H.C.V.
Adams Collection
Sold 9 May 1990 for
£11,000 ($18,601)

Right:
Malaya Straits
Settlements 1868
cover to New York
From the Dr Wood
Collection
Sold 9 May 1990 for
£5,280 ($8,928)

Above:
United States 1918 24c.
'Curtis Jenny' Airmail Invert,
the unique Plate Number
block of four
Sold 12 October 1989 in
New York for $1,100,000
(£707,851)
Record auction price for an
item of US philately

Above left:
United States *c.*1846 5c.
Annapolis Maryland
Postmaster's Provisional
Sold 12 October 1989 in
New York for $286,000
(£184,041)
Record auction price for a
US cover and for any item of
postal stationery

Left:
United States 1846 5c.
Milbury Massachusetts
Postmaster's Provisional, the
finest of the seven recorded
covers
Sold 12 October 1989 in
New York for $231,000
(£148,648)

During 1989–90 Christie's international stamp department under Robson Lowe achieved a total turnover of £16,709,707 (approximately $28,239,404) at auction. The most important event of the season was the series of auctions for the dispersal of the stock formed by the famed brothers Raymond and Roger Weill from New Orleans which attracted world-wide attention. Sales were held in New York as well as in London and in Zürich.

In New York the highlight was the 1918 inverted Air Post block offered on the evening of 12 October 1989 and sold for $1,100,000 (£707,851), the world record price for a United States philatelic item. The most important offering of the United States Postmaster's Provisional issues ever to be presented at auction, also from the Weill Brothers' stock, was sold the same evening.

COINS
AND MEDALS

Gold and enamel Lesser George (enlarged)
Mid-17th century
Sold 21 November 1989 in London for
£55,000 ($88,000)
Record auction price for an English order

THE BEAUFORT GARTER JEWELS

Richard Bishop

The origins of the Order of the Garter, England's premier order of chivalry, have never been satisfactorily explained. The famous motto *Honi soit qui mal y pense* has been variously interpreted. The most popular version relates that Edward III uttered the words, almost as a threat, when he gallantly picked up the garter which a noble lady had accidentally let slip before the amused gaze of the assembled court. That such a trivial incident should have initiated one of the world's leading orders of knighthood is not utterly impossible, given the slightly rarefied atmosphere of Edward III's court, with its emphasis on chivalry, its love of histories and romances, and in particular the king's fanciful ambition to restore the society of Knights of the Round Table supposedly founded by King Arthur. More worldly considerations might have played a part at a time when England was at war with France, but no other story has won general acceptance. By Charles I's day the tale was widely believed, and when the king added rays – traditionally a symbol of divinity and sanctity – to the Garter, he caused a scandal among his puritan subjects. This royal ennobling of a frivolous piece of vanity was one more sign to the Puritans that the king was not God's representative on earth but rather an agent of the devil.

In 1644 Charles offered Edward Somerset, 2nd Marquis of Worcester, various rewards, including the Garter, in return for raising three armies, totalling 26,000 men. The armies were not raised, and the rewards were not given. However, Edward's son Henry, who became 3rd Marquis in 1667, received considerable benefits for his loyal support of the Stuart cause. He was installed as Knight of the Garter on 3 June 1672, and became 1st Duke of Beaufort in 1682.

Two mid-seventeenth-century Garter jewels which came to light early this century in a cabinet at the Beauforts' home at Badminton caused a minor sensation when first discovered. The Beaufort family had long maintained that one of the Lesser Georges in their collection of Garter jewels was once worn by Prince Rupert of the Rhine. However, since the earliest badge known in the collection was a late eighteenth-century example, this story had never carried much weight with historians. The discovery of not one but two mid-seventeenth-century pieces lent credence to the family tradition. Both badges show enamel work characteristic of the first half of the seventeenth century, and are likely to be by the same hand. The rubies and diamonds which once decorated the jewels had been removed, probably in the eighteenth century, but from the size of the settings the stones were clearly immensely valuable, which makes it more than likely that these two Lesser Georges were royal gifts.

Gold and enamel Lesser George with central onyx cameo Sash Badge Signed 'Santorelli' Early 19th century Sold 21 November 1989 in London for £22,000 ($35,200)

Far right:
Gold and enamel
Lesser George,
the centre after
Raphael
Sash badge
Early nineteenth
century
Sold 21 November
1989 in London for
£23,100 ($36,960)

Right:
Gold and enamel
Lesser George
Sash Badge
Mid-18th century
Sold 21 November
1989 in London for
£41,800 ($66,880)

The second duke succeeded his grandfather in 1699, and was installed Knight of the Garter on 4 August 1713. No doubt the Lesser Georges used by the first duke were still proudly worn. But then for two generations no Beauforts were installed at Windsor, and by the time the fifth duke was created a knight in 1786 it was felt a new badge was required. The fifth duke's Lesser George, while not set with precious stones, is a masterpiece. The enamelled equestrian figure is represented in its proper colours as before, but where possible the artist has added decoration of his own invention. The dragon's underwings are studded with peacocks' eyes, while the base is covered with delicate flowers, showing the French influence so typical of the eighteenth century. For the sixth duke, installed as a knight in 1805, it was again necessary to commission a new jewel. Tastes were rapidly changing, and the flamboyant style of the previous century had been replaced by a more austere classicism. The duke chose an onyx St. George, cut by the renowned Italian engraver Giovani Santorelli. Exquisite though this cameo is, it was possibly too large for practical regular use, and yet another badge was commissioned. This time the central figures were worked entirely in gold, finely chiselled in the round and set off wonderfully by the dark blue enamel of the surrounding Garter, thus successfully combining richness with restraint. An examination of these Lesser Georges shows clearly the changing tastes of the English nobility over the course of three centuries.

Right:
Mary, 1553 fine
sovereign of thirty
shillings
Sold 17 July 1990 in
London for £3,630
($6,534)

Far right:
Japan, Meiji 13 1880,
20-Yen
Sold 15 May 1990 in
London for £104,500
($169,290)
Record auction price
for a Japanese coin

Centre:
George II, 1746
five-guineas, Lima
below bust
Sold 10 October 1989
in London for £3,300
($5,313)

Right:
Hamburg, 1677 gold
portugaloser of
10-ducats
Sold 31 May 1990 in
Amsterdam for
D.fl.12,650 (£3,966)

Far right:
Archbishop of Trier,
Johann Hugo von
Orsbeck
Laudatory medal in
gold
Undated (1698)
One of only four
struck
Sold 15 May 1990 in
London for £12,100
($19,602)

*All the illustrations
on these two pages are
enlarged*

THE WICKLEWOOD HOARD

On 23 October 1989, 482 silver coins found on a farm near Wicklewood were declared Treasure Trove at an inquest held at Dereham, Norfolk. The coins were pennies, cut halfpennies and farthings of the mid-twelfth century. Found in sandy clay which at one time had formed a bank running alongside a road, the coins were probably buried some time after 1168. It is possible that they were the booty of one of the bands of mercenaries which campaigned in East Anglia during the rebellion of 1173. In that year Henry II's sons rose against him, taking advantage of the king's absence in France. The Earl of Norfolk also revolted, capturing Norwich with an army of Flemish mercenaries. In 1174 the rebellion collapsed, but many parts of East Anglia suffered considerable devastation.

The hoard is remarkable because of its inclusion of 325 coins struck during the anarchy under King Stephen (1135–54). These coins are generally scarce, and their discovery has enlarged our knowledge of this troubled period when, in the words of the *Anglo Saxon Chronicle*, 'God and his angels slept'. In particular it has confrmed the existence of a twelfth-century mint in Dunwich, once a thriving market town but now, due to coastal erosion, lost beneath the North Sea. The British Museum retained 158 of the coins, the remainder were sold on 15 May in London for £26,000 ($42,180).

King Stephen, type I penny, struck at London by the moneyer Baldewine

From left to right (obverse and reverse): Cut farthings and half pennies of Stephen, from unidentified East Anglian mints

King Stephen type II penny, struck at Ipswich by the previously unknown moneyer Alaien

King Stephen type II penny, struck at Norwich by the previously unknown moneyer Aliward

King Stephen type VI penny, struck at Norwich by the previously unknown moneyer Randulf

COLLECTORS' SALES

Beatles cotton dress
Signed by Brian Epstein, John Lennon, Paul
McCartney, George Harrison, Ringo Starr
and Cynthia Lennon, and inscribed 'To
Rosemary'
Worn by one of the usherettes at the 1964
world première of the film *A Hard Day's
Night* and signed while she was wearing the
dress
Sold 24 August 1989 in London at South
Kensington for £2,860 ($4,404)

Above left:
Pair of bowler hats probably worn by Laurel and Hardy in *Hats Off*, 1927
Stamped 'Hal Roach Studios Wardrobe Department'
Sold 20 December 1989 in London at South Kensington for £11,000 ($17,600)

Above:
JOHN LENNON
Fat Budgie
Pen and ink drawing
*c.*1965
8 × 9 in. (20.3 × 22.9 cm.)
Sold 24 August 1989 in London at South Kensington for £3,080 ($4,774)

Collection of clothes worn by Prince in *Purple Rain*, 1984
Each item accompanied by a letter of authentication from Apollonia Kotero
Sold 27 April 1990 in London at South Kensington for a total of £6,325 ($10,310)

Above:
Single-sided acetate
Good Rockin' Tonight,
an original recording
by Elvis Presley
Stamped 'W.H.B.Q.
Memphis'
Sold 27 April 1990 in
London at South
Kensington for
£3,300 ($5,379)

Right:
Gibson FJ-N acoustic
guitar
Owned and used by
Elvis Presley
Sold 27 April 1990 in
London at South
Kensington for
£6,600 ($10,578)

Gibson ES–345TDC
semi-acoustic guitar
Owned and used by
John Lee Hooker
Signed and inscribed
'John L. Hooker'
*c.*1960
Sold 27 April 1990 in
London at South
Kensington for
£4,400 ($7,172)

Far left:
Pressed
bisque-headed bébé
By Emile Jumeau
c.1880
16½ in. (41.9 cm.)
high
Sold 21 September
1989 in London at
South Kensington for
£4,950 ($7,772)

Left:
Plush-covered teddy
bear
Steiff button in ear
c.1907
23 in. (58.4 cm.)
high
Sold 17 May 1990 in
London at South
Kensington for
£4,180 ($6,813)

Far left:
Pressed
bisque-headed bébé
Impressed BRU. JNE 8
and BRU JNE PARIS
18½ in. (47 cm.)
high
Sold 17 May 1990 in
London at South
Kensington for
£14,300 ($23,309)

Left:
Carved and painted
wooden doll
c.1740
18 in. (45.7 cm.)
high
Sold 21 September
1989 in London at
South Kensington for
£10,450 ($16,407)

Above:
Tinplate clockwork Bing 'American Platform' fire truck
*c.*1904
Sold 17 May 1990 in London at South Kensington for £13,200
($21,516)

Right, top to bottom:
Wooden Noah's ark containing over 200 animals
Sonneberg, 19th century
Sold 17 May 1990 in London at South Kensington for £6,600
($10,758)

Märklin 20-volt three-rail electric LMS E800 Compound
locomotive and tender, with trucks
Imported into Great Britain solely in 1938
Sold 17 May 1990 in London at South Kensington for £24,200
($39,446)

Clockwork Märklin 'Draisine' or platelayer's trolley
No. 1100/11, *c.*1909
Sold 18 December 1989 in London at South Kensington for
£9,900 ($15,840)

Far left:
One of 110 photographs recording Amundsen and Ellsworth's 1925 flight from King's Bay, Spitzbergen, to 88 degrees North
Various sizes
Sold 8 February 1990 in London at South Kensington for £3,080 ($5,236)

Above:
One of a collection of 150 photographs recording the first crossing of the polar sea, 1926, by Roald Amundsen and Lincoln Ellsworth in the airship *Norge*
Various sizes
Sold 8 February 1990 in London at South Kensington for £4,180 ($7,106)

'Polar' board game for Amundsen and Ellsworth to play at the North Pole, in original box
The box stamped with the maker's details 'C.G. Hallberg Hof Juvelerare'
Signed 'A. Gustafsson', the game inscribed by him 'To be opened at the Northpol!'[sic]
10 × 14½ in. (25.4 × 36.8 cm.)
Sold 8 February 1990 in London at South Kensington for £5,500 ($9,350)

The explorers Roald Amundsen and Lincoln Ellsworth made the world's first transpolar flight in 1925. The game, 'Spelet Om Nordpolen', was to be played
'… on the occasion of an agreeable incident at the North Pole 1926', the aim of the game being for Amundsen and Ellsworth to capture the 'Polar Castle'.

Above:
Mahogany and brass Dubroni camera outfit, with accessories and instruction manual
Inscribed 'Appareil Dubroni, 236 Rue de Rivoli, Paris'
Sold 15 March 1990 in London at South Kensington for £12,100 ($19,360)

Platinum Leica R6 camera, No. 1750000, Lens No. 3500075
Inscribed '150 Jahre Photographie. 1989. 75 Leica Photographie. Leica'
Sold 9 November 1989 in London at South Kensington for £26,400 ($42,240), record auction price for a camera

Collection of material relating to the American photographer Oscar Jackson Martin, *c.* 1857
Sold 9 November 1989 in London at South Kensington for £16,500 ($26,400)

J. MICHAEL BROWN
British *fl.*1880–1916
A Rainy Day at
St. Andrews
Signed
Oil on canvas
24 × 36 in.
(60.5 × 91.1 cm.)
Sold 20 July 1990 at
St. Andrews, Fife,
for £71,500
($129,415)

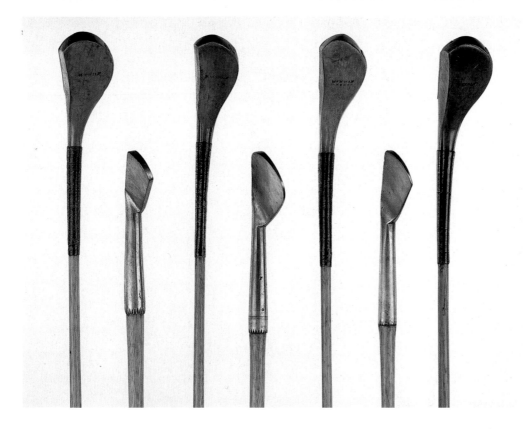

Selection of
scared-headed play
clubs by Jackson,
Philip, McDonald
and McEwan,
*c.*1830–70, and three
early iron clubs
Sold 20 July 1990 at
St. Andrews, Fife,
for a total of
£110,550 ($200,096)
From the property of
the Royal Perth
Golfing Society

RECORDS TUMBLE
AT THE 119TH OPEN CHAMPIONSHIP

Jacqueline Lacey

Records tumbled at St. Andrews in July 1990 as the 119th Open Championship got under way in high spirits and sizzling temperatures. Nick Faldo stayed cool to deliver a record-breaking 67, 65, 67, the lowest three-round score ever at a championship, eventually taking the title with an overall score of 270, a five-shot lead over his nearest rival.

Not far from the historic eighteenth green of the Old Course, Christie's Scotland was also busy setting new records. It was the first time an auction house had taken a sale of early golf equipment, memorabilia and pictures to an Open Championship venue, and as present-day golfing greats battled it out on the fairways nearby, a team of auctioneers put golfing history under the hammer, making a record £596,840 ($1,079,087).

A feather-filled golf ball was first to pitch into the record books at £14,850 ($26,879), nearly doubling the previous high for a golf ball set only a few days before. It was made in St. Andrews *c.*1840 by Allan Robertson, who was considered to be the supreme golfer of his era. His apprentice was Tom Morris, who went on to secure for himself the lofty title of 'Father of Golf'. This tiny ball had somehow escaped the disfiguring address of baffing spoons and track irons and was in the same condition as the day Robertson handed it to its first owner 150 years ago.

The very first time the game of golf was referred to in print was in 1566 when the Black Acts were published in Scotland. These included statutes which forbade golf as a pastime. Apparently it was felt that the safety of the realm was at stake as people abandoned the practice of archery to pursue a ball with a stick. A copy of the Black Acts with these famous statutes sold for £13,200 ($23,866).

As the sun beat down on St. Andrews, a painting was auctioned that struck a chord in every golfer's heart. The painting, by Scottish artist J. Michael Brown, showed what is believed to be the scene at the thirteenth hole of the Old Course during the final of the Amateur Championship in 1913. Silhouetted in the distance the spires of St. Andrews were clearly visible, while in the foreground a group of devoted supporters gathered round as the golfer addressed the ball. And the rain came down in sheets... *Golf Illustrated* of June 1913 records 'The rain came down in thick merciless torrents... The officials had to suspend play till the storm had spent itself...' As the 119th Open Championship at St. Andrews progressed under cloudless skies and Faldo eased toward the £85,000 ($153,680) prize money, Brown's recollection of another Championship went to a Japanese museum for £71,500 ($129,415).

Feather-filled golf ball
By Allan Robertson
Stamped 'Allan' and inscribed '29'
Unused
*c.*1840
Sold 20 July 1990 at St. Andrews, Fife, for £14,850 ($26,879)

Hand-coloured rebus valentine in the form of a heart opening to reveal 24 verses
Early 19th century
4⅜ × 4⅜ in. (11.3 × 11.3 cm.) folded; 13 × 13 in. (33 x 33 cm.) open
Sold 8 February 1990 in London at South Kensington for £385 ($655)

Far left:
ERNEST HOWARD SHEPARD
Tigger Comes to the Forest
Signed and inscribed
Pencil, pen and black ink
12½ × 10 in. (31.8 × 25.4 cm.)
Sold 18 July 1990 in London at South Kensington for £18,700 ($33,660)

Left:
MARK BOXER, 'MARC'
Prince Charles at the Cello
Pen, brush and black ink
16¼ × 11¼ in. (41.2 × 28.7 cm.)
Sold 18 July 1990 in London at South Kensington for £1,045 ($1,923)

CARS

1902 'Baby' Peugeot 5½ HP tourer
Engine No. 5133L
Sold 20 March 1990 at Beaulieu, Hampshire,
for £29,700 ($48,263)

1913 Sunbeam 12/16
HP four seater
Torpedo Tourer
Chassis No. 7038
Engine No. 6488
Sold 20 June 1990 in
Melbourne, Australia
for Aus$88,000
(£40,183)

1905 Milnes-Daimler
double-decker
omnibus
Chassis No. 922
Engine No. 852E
Sold 20 August 1990
at Pebble Beach,
California for
$253,000 (£131,964)
Record auction price
for a commercial
vehicle

Above:
1961 3-litre Ferrari 250 GT SWB Competizione Berlinetta
Chassis No. 2417
Engine No. 2417
Sold 20 August at Pebble Beach, California for
$2,200,000 (£1,147,520)

Below:
1977 2.8-litre Porsche 935
Chassis No. 9307700901
Engine No. 6772903
Sold 11 December 1989 at Beaulieu,
Hampshire, for £484,000 ($817,960)

Above:
1960 V6 Ferrari 196 S Dino
Chassis No. 0776
Engine No. 0776
Sold 22 May 1990 in Monaco for F.fr.24,420,000
(£2,574,591)

1965 Morris Mini Cooper '1275'S Ex-works
Rally Car
Chassis No. KA2S4/799887
Sold 28 July 1990 at the Silverstone Circuit,
Northamptonshire for £71,000 ($130,488)
Record auction price for a Mini Cooper

Photographed at the 1967 1000 Lakes Rally
during which T. Makinen achieved his third
successive victory in the *Rally in Finland*,
despite the bonnet flying open in the course
of a stage. The rubber safety straps failed to
hold it on one large jump, and Makinen had
to drive for some 10km. peering out of the
open door.
    The original paintwork and panels show
compression marks which are the result of
heavy landings and the bonnet still retains the
dents from the stage incident.

WINE

1825 Château d'Yquem
Sold 28 June 1990 in London for £14,300
($24,696) per bottle

INTERNATIONAL WINE SALES

Michael Broadbent, M.W.

Lacking the high drama of sales of Impressionist pictures or objects such as the extraordinary Badminton Cabinet, wine auctions present a rather humdrum scene, except to connoisseurs and to those engaged in the trade of one of the oldest civilized commodities. Moreover, the Wine Department at Christie's has to sell a very large number of bottles and process a great deal of paperwork in order to reach a level of sales from which a worthwhile contribution can be made to the company's coffers.

However, I am happy to report that we have achieved a record world-wide turnover – a total for the first time exceeding £10 million (approximately $18 million).

A new feature of the season, and one that seems to have been very well received, has been the introduction of catalogues of larger format and with full-colour covers. Several proprietors have been delighted with the world-wide publicity gained in return for the loan of transparencies of their châteaux.

All in all, we believe that the success of our wine sales is due to the regular, predictable, specialized sale dates, offering vendors a relatively speedy service and buyers an extremely wide range of wines on a frequent basis. Perhaps I should add the advantage of efficiency: speedy posting of results and invoices, prompt settlement of vendors' accounts, rapid and accurate provision of extended sale prices and valuations – all thanks to well-integrated computerization and, above all, to a long-serving, highly experienced and loyal staff.

KING STREET

This has always been the hub of our operation. Indeed, I think we can fairly claim that our very specialized activity is largely responsible for London's acknowledged leading position in the field of fine and rare wines.

In 1989/1990 we held twenty-two wine sales, one fewer than in the previous season, ten being devoted to the wines of Bordeaux, twelve loosely entitled Fine Wine, embracing all manner of other wines, older and rarer claret and sauternes, and vintage port.

THE AALHOLM CASTLE CELLAR

Wines come to Christie's from a wide variety of sources: large trade stocks of maturing wines are sold to raise capital to pay for younger vintages, smaller collections usually of older and rarer wines from private cellars, mainly in the United Kingdom but not infrequently from the continent of Europe.

Left to right:
Green Chartreuse
1930–41
Sold 5 April 1990 in
London for £286
($479) per bottle

Yellow Chartreuse
1930–41
Sold 5 April 1990 in
London for £264
($420) per bottle

Yellow Chartreuse
1920–50
Sold 5 April 1990 in
London for £116
($194) per half litre

Undoubtedly the largest, finest, best kept – in short, most notable – private cellar to have come up for sale in recent years belonged to Baron Johann Raben-Levetzau. The wines had been purchased by the present baron and his father, a Foreign Minister, and stored in the perfect, cool, dry cellar at the family's stately home, Aalholm Castle, in the south of Denmark.

Quite apart from the wide range, another attraction was the positive state of corks, labels and levels. Much of the fine claret, from the 1920s to the late 1940s, had been bottled in Copenhagen by the leading wine merchants of the day. It turned out to be uniformly excellent.

Over three hundred cases were packed by Christie's staff and shipped to London and sold for £101,000 ($161,499) on 28 September 1989.

OTHER SPECIALIZED SALES

At the request of the Hungarian Wine Board we organized a special promotional sale of old and rare vintages of Tokay on 23 November 1989. This was the third such sale that we have held at Christie's and we were only too pleased to re-introduce one of the lesser-known classic wines to English and overseas collectors.

A very successful specialized sale of straight malts and old and rare blends of Scotch whisky took place, appropriately, in Glasgow on 4 December 1989. The catalogue attracted world-wide interest and the 316 lots represented an immense variety of brands. High prices included the £3,300 ($5,138) paid by the Cheese and Wine Shop in Oban for a bottle of the Royal Gordon Perfection which was over 120 years old, £1,760 ($2,740) for a bottle of Glen Grant 1895, now residing in the Distillery Museum, and £1,320–£1,650 ($2,055–$2,569) per bottle for three bottles of The Macallan – over fifty years old – all now in Tokyo.

Presaging, as it were, the sale of the magnificent Badminton Cabinet, we sold on 7 December for His Grace the Duke of Beaufort a fascinating collection of very old wines. The bottles, in most instances, had been lying untouched in their original bins for up to one and a half centuries. The collection included rare sherry, madeira, burgundy, sauternes, even a rare early eighteenth-century liqueur, Crème de Thé, from Martinique, which was in perfect drinking condition. The highest price paid was £2,090 ($3,275) for a single bottle of unlabelled and uncapsuled 1866 Château d'Yquem with the original bin label.

OVERSEAS SALES

By far the most spectacular sales growth has been in America, with six wine auctions, in Chicago and in Los Angeles, totalling $3,878,457 (the equivalent of £2.4 million sterling), a seventy-five per cent increase over the previous season. Under the very capable management of Michael Davis, these now regular sales command wide respect and dominate the wine auction market in the United States.

Biannual sales in both Geneva and Amsterdam (organized and run by Paul Bowker from the London Wine Department) continue to meet firm demand and strong interest from principally private collectors in each location. Geneva has shown the greater strength, with a forty-two per cent increase in turnover, caused largely by the sale in May of selections from possibly the two most important private Swiss cellars, which instilled keen competition from bidders encouraged by the provenance. Highlights of the season were the sale in November of a single bottle of Château Lafite 1832 for Sw.fr.5,720 (£2,208), and a jeroboam of Château Latour 1961 which achieved Sw.fr.9,350 (£3,881), a record price for the wine.

1990 also saw the second auction to be held by the Wine Department in Tokyo (an event which almost came to a premature end with the occurrence of a Richter force 6 earthquake which shook the Imperial Hotel minutes before the auction started!). Achieving a total value double that of the inaugural sale in 1989, it reinforced the remarkable level of interest which fine wine holds in Japan, which is becoming an increasingly significant market. Four prices achieved are worth a special mention:

A complete collection of Château Mouton-Rothschild 1945–86 – Yen4,400,000 (£17,391)
One case Château Pétrus 1961 – Yen4,180,000 (£16,522)
One jeroboam Château Pétrus 1961 – Yen3,520,000 (£13,913)
One case Romanée-conti 1971 – Yen3,080,000 (£12,174)

King Street also plays host to a large number of overseas vendors each season. This year was no exception. Two Danish cellars featured in Fine Wine sales, coinciding fortunately with the arrival in the Wine Department of a young Danish staff member, Brian Ebbesen, who was able both to pack the cellars in Denmark and to liaise with the vendors in their native tongue.

The contents of the ancient vaulted cellars of Slot Aalholm, mentioned above, made up the first Danish sale on 28 September 1989. The second collection to be sold was the property of a noted Danish lawyer who had established over many years vertical collections of many vintages of each of the first growth châteaux of Bordeaux. One such collection, of forty-two vintages of Château Mouton-Rothschild, achieved £12,100 ($20,897). Also amongst the collection were a wide range of first growth and lesser clarets, vintages 1893–1970. Like the Aalholm cellar, this Danish cellar also raised a total in excess of £100,000 (approximately $180,000).

Right:
Vintages from the magnificent Aalholm Castle cellar
Sold 28 September 1989 in London
Left to right:
1927 and 1947 Château Cheval-Blanc
£902 ($1,442) per lot

1924 Château Mouton-Rothschild
£1,760 ($2,816) per magnum

1929 Château Mouton-Rothschild and 1929 Château Latour
£825 ($1,319) per lot

Above right:
A selection of wines sold 28 June 1990 in London
Left to right:
1808 Solera, Malmsey, Blandy
£209 ($361) per bottle

1814 Solera, Bual, Rutherford and Miles
£132 ($228 per bottle)

1792 Vintage, Bual, Blandy
£660 ($1,140) per bottle

1846 Campanario, Blandy
£198 ($342) per bottle

1862 Solera, Terrantez, Borges
£319 ($551) per bottle

HIGHLIGHTS OF THE 1989–90 SEASON
(prices include buyer's premium)

Claret

1865	Lafite	half bottle	£1,760	($2,923)
1865	Latour	bottle	£2,090	($3,469)
1929	Latour	dozen	£4,840	($8,034)
1945	Lafite	dozen	£4,400	($7,304)
1945	Mouton Rothschild	dozen	£11,550	($19,173)
1947	Mouton Rothschild	dozen	£5,500	($9,130)
1956	Mouton Rothschild	bottle	£825	($1,370)
1961	Latour	dozen	£5,500	($9,130)
1970	Pétrus	dozen	£3,190	($5,295)
1975	La Mission Haut Brion	dozen	£1,430	($2,374)
1982	Lafite	dozen	£968	($1,607)
1982	Latour	dozen	£990	($1,643)
1982	Mouton Rothschild	dozen	£1,045	($1,735)
1982	Pétrus	dozen	£3,080	($5,113)

Red Burgundy

1945	La Tâche	dozen	£6,050	($10,043)
1966	Romanée Conti	dozen	£4,070	($6,756)
1969	Romanée Conti	dozen	£6,820	($11,321)

White Burgundy

1982	Montrachet (DRC)	dozen	£2,200	($3,652)
1983	Montrachet (DRC)	dozen	£2,860	($4,748)

White Bordeaux

Year	Name	Unit	£	$
1825	Yquem	bottle	£14,300	($23,738)
1868	Yquem	bottle	£2,310	($3,835)
1893	Yquem	bottle	£1,265	($2,100)
1921	Yquem	bottle	£792	($1,315)
1929	Yquem	bottle	£484	($803)
1945	Yquem	bottle	£550	($913)
1949	Yquem	bottle	£506	($840)

Rhone

1976	Château Grillet	dozen	£484	($803)
1978	Hermitage, la Chapelle (Jaboulet)	dozen	£715	($1,187)
1978	Côte Rôtie, la Landonne (Guigal)	bottle	£149	($247)
1978	Côte Rôtie, la Mouline (Guigal)	bottle	£200	($332)

Champagne

1953	Krug	dozen	£1,100	($1,826)
1969	Dom Pérignon	dozen	£1,265	($2,100)
1971	Dom Pérignon	6 magnums	£1,705	($2,830)

Vintage Port

1927	Cockburn	dozen	£1,760	($2,921)
1945	Taylor	dozen	£3,190	($5,295)
1955	Taylor	dozen	£1,265	($2,100)

Brandy

Year	Name	Unit	£	$
1789	Meukow, Grande Champagne	half bottle	£1,375	($2,283)
1811	Napoleon, Grande Fine Champagne Reserve	bottle	£506	($840)

Collectors' Pieces

Windsor Castle Cellar Book	£4,400	($7,304)
French single-lever 'Le Rapide' corkscrew	£1,430	($2,374)
A pair of French 19th-century claret jugs	£4,840	($8,034)
Tristram Hillier (b.1905) *Hommage à André Simon*	£36,300	($60,258)

Christies International plc
Chairman: The Rt. Hon. The Lord Carrington, K.G.

SALEROOMS

UNITED KINGDOM

London
Christie, Manson
& Woods Ltd.
8 King Street, St. James's
London SW1Y 6QT
Tel: (071) 839 9060
Telex: 916429
Fax: (071) 839 1611/925 2330
Chairman:
The Hon. Charles Allsopp

Christie's South
Kensington Ltd.
85 Old Brompton Road
London SW7 3LD
Tel: (071) 581 7611
Telex: 922061
Fax: (071) 581 0431
Chairman: W.A. Coleridge,
FRICS

Bournemouth
39 Poole Hill
Bournemouth, Dorset
Tel: (0202) 292740

Scotland
Christie's Scotland Ltd.
164–166 Bath Street,
Glasgow G2 4TG
Tel: (041) 332 8134/7
Telex: 779901
Fax: (041) 332 5759
Chairman:
Sir Ilay Campbell, Bt.

AUSTRALIA

Melbourne
Christie's Australia Pty. Ltd.,
1 Darling Street, South Yarra
Melbourne, Victoria 3141
Tel: (613) 820 4311
Fax: (613) 820 4876
Chairman:
James B. Leslie, AO, MC

FAR EAST

Hong Kong
Christie's Swire (Hong Kong)
Limited
2804-6 Alexandra House
16–20 Chater Road,
Hong Kong
Tel: (852) 521 5396/7
Telex: 72014
Fax: (852) 845 2646
Chairman:
Baroness Lydia Dunn

ITALY

Rome
Christie's (Int.) S.A.
Palazzo Massimo Lancellotti
Piazza Navona 114
Rome 00186
Tel: (396) 687 2787
Telex: 611524
Fax: (396) 686 9902
Chairman: Maurizio Lodi-Fè

MONACO

Christie's Monaco S.A.M.
Park Palace, 98000
Monte-Carlo
Tel: (33) 93 25 1933
Telex: 489287
Fax: (33) 93 50 38 64

THE NETHERLANDS

Christie's Amsterdam B.V.
Cornelis Schuytstraat 57
1071 JG Amsterdam
Tel: (3120) 57 55 255
Telex: 15758
Fax: (3120) 664 08 99
Chairman:
Charles H. André de la Porte

SWITZERLAND

Geneva
Christie's (International) S.A.
8 Place de la Taconnerie
1204 Geneva
Tel: (4122) 28 25 44
Telex: 423634
Fax: (4122) 21 55 59
President: François Curiel

UNITED STATES OF AMERICA

Christie, Manson & Woods
International, Inc.
502 Park Avenue
New York
New York 10022
Tel: (212) 546 1000
Telex: 620721
Fax: (212) 980 8163
President: Christopher J. Burge
Executive Vice Presidents:
Stephen S. Lash
Doris P. Meister

CHRISTIE'S EAST

219 East 67th Street
New York
New York 10021
Tel: (212) 606 0400
Telex: 672 0346
Fax: (212) 737 6076
President: Kathleen Guzman

INTERNATIONAL OFFICES AND REPRESENTATIVES

ARGENTINA

Fernando Sánchez Zinny
Cesar Feldman (*Consultant*)
Libertad 1269, 1012 Buenos
Aires
Tel: (541) 814 0577
Fax: (541) 11 27 85

AUSTRALIA

Sydney
Sue Hewitt
298 New South Head Road
Double Bay, Sydney,
N.S.W. 2028
Tel: (612) 326 1422
Telex: 26343
Fax: (612) 327 8439

Adelaide
Ian Bruce
346 Carrington Street,
Adelaide, South Australia 5000
Tel: (618) 378 2837
Fax: (618) 223 1934

AUSTRIA

Dr Schönburg-Hartenstein
Kohlmarkt 4, 1010 Vienna
Tel: (43222) 63 88 12
Telex: 113265
Fax: (43222) 63 71 66

BELGIUM

Brussels
Bernard Steyaert
Christie's Belguim S.A.
33 Boulevard de Waterloo,
1000 Brussels
Tel: (322) 512 8830
Fax: (322) 513 3279

Antwerp
Annette Van Thillo-Gérard
Arenbergstraat 1, 2000
Antwerp
Tel: (323) 233 2471

BRAZIL

Rio de Janeiro
Maria-Thereza de Azevedo
Sodré
(*Consultant*)
Av. Rui Barbosa 582, 22250
Rio de Janeiro
Tel: (5521) 551 1467
Telex: 213 4285

Sao Paulo
Paulo Figueiredo
rua dr. Mello Alves, 717 c.l
01417 Sao Paulo
Tel: (5511) 881 3478
Fax: (5511) 280 3357

CANADA

Suzanna E. Davis
Christie, Manson & Woods
International Inc.
94 Cumberland Street,
Suite 416
Toronto, Ontario M5R 1A3
Tel: (416) 960 2063
Telex: 06–23907
Fax: (416) 960 8815

CHANNEL ISLANDS

Richard de la Hey
58 David Place, St. Helier,
Jersey
Tel: (0534) 77582

COLOMBIA

Harry M. Hanabergh
Aptdo. Aereo 250670,
Calle 71, no. 13–10,
Bogota, Colombia
Tel: (571) 2115049/255 1442
Fax: (571) 212 6538

DENMARK

Birgitta Ilillingsø
Dronningens Tvaergade 10
1302 Copenhagen K
Tel: (453) 332 70 75
Fax: (453) 313 0075

FINLAND

Barbro Schauman
Ulrikagatan 3 A, 00140
Helsinki
Tel: (3580) 60 82 12
Fax: (3580) 66 06 87

FRANCE

Paris
Emmanuel de Margerie
Chairman of Christie's Europe
François Curiel
Christie's France S.A.
6 rue Paul Baudry, 75008 Paris
Tel: (331) 42 56 17 66
Fax: (331) 42 56 26 01

Aix en Provence

Fabienne Albertini
2 rue Matheron,
13100 Aix en Provence
Tel: (33) 42 96 43 94
Fax: (33) 42 23 98 59

Bordeaux

Marie-Cécile Moueix
Tel: (33) 56 52 79 66

Lyon

Christiane de Meaux
Tel: (33) 78 43 72 44

GREECE

Mrs Elisavet Lyras-Logotheti
Christie's Hellas, Fine Arts
Ltd.,
27 Vassilisis Sophias Avenue
Athens 10674
Tel: (301) 721 9755

ISRAEL

Mary Gilben
Christie's (Israel) Limited
Asia House
4 Weizmann Street
Tel Aviv 61335
Tel: (9723) 250671/250695
Fax: (9723) 252751

ITALY

Milan
Giorgina Venosta
(*Consultant*)
Christie's (Int.) S.A.
9 via Borgogna, 20122 Milan
Tel: (392) 794 712
Fax: (392) 783 550

Turin
Sandro Perrone di San
Martino
Corso Matteotti, 33, 10121
Turin
Tel: (3911) 548 819

Naples
Angela Carola Perrotti
Via Fiorello 5, 80121 Naples
Tel: (3981) 764 2788

JAPAN

Sachiko Hibiya
Ichibankan Bldg., B1
3–12, Ginza 5–chome,
Chuo-ku, Tokyo 104
Tel: (813) 571 0668
Fax: (813) 571 5853

LUXEMBOURG

Countess Marina von
Kamarowsky
88, Avenue de la Faiencerie
L 1510 Luxembourg
Tel: (352) 47 24 86
Fax: (352) 47 52 44

MEXICO

P.O. Box 105–158, 11570
Mexico
Tel: (525) 531 1686/1806

NORWAY

Ulla Solitair Hjort
Colbjornsensgt.1 N-0256
Oslo 2
Tel: (472) 44 12 42
Fax: (472) 53 92 36

PORTUGAL

Antonio M.G. Santos
Mendonça
R. Conde de Almoster 44, 1° Esq.,
1500 Lisbon
Tel: (3511) 78 63 83
Telex: 12839
Fax: (3511) 60 95 10

SPAIN

Casilda Fz-Villaverde y Silva
Christie's Iberica S.L.
Valenzuela 7, Madrid 28014
Tel: (341) 532 66 26/7
Telex: 46681
Fax: (341) 523 12 40

SWEDEN

Stockholm
Lillemor Malmström
Sturegatan 26, 11436
Stockholm
Tel: (468) 662 0131
Fax: (468) 660 0725

South of Sweden
Baroness Irma Silfverschiold
23041 Klagerup
Tel: (4640) 44 03 60
Fax: (4640) 44 03 71

SWITZERLAND

Zürich
Maria Reinshagen
Christie's (Int.) A.G.
Steinwiesplatz, 8032 Zürich
Tel: (411) 262 05 05
Fax: (411) 251 04 71

UNITED KINGDOM

Argyll
Sir Ilay Campbell, Bt.
Cumlodden Estate Office,
Crarae
Inveraray, Argyll, PA32 8YA
Tel: (0546) 86633

Ayrshire
James Hunter Blair
Blairquhan, Maybole,
Ayrshire KA19 7LZ
Tel: (06557) 239

Borders
Gerald Trotter
The Wellnage, Duns
Berwickshire TD11 3EJ
Tel: (0361) 82550

Cheshire
Richard Roundell, FRICS
Dorfold Hall
Nantwich, Cheshire
CW5 8LD
Tel: (0270) 627024

Christie's in the City
Simon Birch (*Consultant*)
Brezetta du Buisson
56/60 Gresham Street
London EC2V 7BB
Tel: (071) 588 4424/
(071) 606 1848
Telex: 928637
Fax: (071) 600 1782

Cornwall
Christopher Petherick
Porthpean House
St. Austell, Cornwall
PL26 6AX
Tel: (0726) 64672

Cotswolds
Viscount Ebrington
Rupert de Zocte (*Consultant*)
111 The Promenade,
Cheltenham
Gloucestershire GL50 1PS
Tel: (0242) 518999
Fax: (0242) 576240

Devon
The Hon. George Lopes,
ARICS
Gnaton Estate Office,
Yealmpton
Plymouth, Devon PL8 2IIU
Tel: (0752) 880636

East Anglia
Charles Bingham-Newland
Sackville Place
44–48 Magdelen Street
Norwich NR3 1JU
Tel: (0603) 614546
Fax: (0603) 633740

Stuart Betts, MC, FGA.
(*Consultant*)
33 Constitution Hill,
Ipswich IPI 3RL
Tel: (0473) 252308

East Midlands
The Hon. Lady Hastings
Mrs. William Proby
The Stables, Milton Hall
Peterborough PE6 7AA
Tel: (0733) 380781

Bruce Clayton FSVA
Park House, Park Lane
Harpole
Northampton NN7 4BT
Tel: (0604) 831551)

Edinburgh
Michael Clayton
5 Wemyss Place,
Edinburgh EII3 6DII
Tel: (031) 225 4756/7
Fax: (031) 225 1723

Grampian
The Earl of Kintore
The Stables, Keith Hall
Inverurie
Aberdeenshire AB5 0LD
Tel: (0467) 24366

Hampshire & Berkshire
Richard Wills
Middleton Estate Office
Longparish, Andover
Hampshire SP11 6PL
Tel: (026472) 211
Fax: (026472) 271

Highland
John Douglas-Menzies
Mounteagle, Hill of Fearn
Ross-shire IV20 1RP
Tel: (086283) 2866

Kent
Christopher Proudfoot
The Old Rectory, Fawkham
Dartford, Kent DA3 8LX
Tel: (04747) 2854

Northumbria
Aidan Cuthbert
Eastfield House, Main Street,
Corbridge
Northumberland NE45 5LA
Tel: (0434) 633181

North-West
Victor Gubbins, FRICS
Eden Lacy, Lazonby, Penrith
Cumbria CA10 1BZ
Tel: (076883) 8800
Fax: (076883) 8020

South Dorset & Hampshire
Nigel Thimbleby
Wolfeton House, Dorchester
Dorset DT2 9QN
Tel: (03050) 268748
and at:
39 Poole Hill, Bournemouth,
Dorset
Tel: (0202) 292740

Sussex
Robin Loder
Leonardslee Gardens
Lower Beeding, Nr. Horsham
West Sussex RH13 6PP
Tel: (0403) 891 305

Tayside & Fife
Roy Miller, FRICS
3/5 Mill Street
Perth PH1 5JE
Tel: (0738) 43088

West Country & Wiltshire
Richard de Pelet
Monmouth Lodge, Yenston
Templecombe,
Somerset BA8 ON11
Tel: (0963) 70518
Fax: (0963) 70605

West Midlands
Michael Thompson
Stanley Hall, Bridgnorth
Shropshire WV16 4SP
Tel: (0746) 761891
Fax: (0746) 761831

Yorkshire
Sir Nicholas Brooksbank, Bt.
Miss Sallyanne Sime
192 Huntington Road,
York YO3 9BN
Tel: (0904) 630911
Fax: (0904) 644448

IRELAND

Desmond Fitz-Gerald,
Knight of Glin
Glin Castle, Glin, Co.
Limerick
Fax: (353) 68 34 364
Private Residence:
52 Waterloo Road, Dublin 4
Tel: (0001) 68 05 85
Fax: (0001) 68 02 71

NORTHERN IRELAND

Danny Kinahan
John Lewis-Crosby
(*Consultant*)
Castle Upton, Templepatrick,
Co. Antrim BT39 011A
Tel: (08494) 3348
Fax: (08494) 33410

**UNITED STATES OF
AMERICA**

Beverly Hills
Terry Stanfill, Susan Schneck,
Ursula Hermacinski,
Mary Hammid
342 North Rodeo Drive
Beverly Hills, California 90210
Tel: (213) 275 5534
Telex: 6711872
Fax: (213) 275 9748

Boston
Elizabeth M. Chapin
Lydia C. Fitler
Perry T. Rathbone
P.O. Box 2723
Cambridge Mass. 02238
Tel: (617) 576 0400
Fax: (617) 876 7725

Chicago
Frances Blair, Lisa Cavanaugh,
Susan Florence, Laura de Frise
200 West Superior Street
Chicago, Illinois 60610
Tel: (312) 787 2765
Fax: (312) 951 7449

Dallas
Carolyn Foxworth
7047 Elmridge Drive
Dallas, Texas 75240
Tel: (214) 239 0098
Fax: (214) 386 6102

Miami
Hannah Shore
P.O. Box 331364
Coconut Grove, Florida 33233
Tel: (305) 445 1487
Fax: (305) 441 6561

New Orleans
John Fowler
P.O. Box 15529
New Orleans, Louisiana 70175
Tel: (504) 899 2380
Fax: (504) 899 9531

Newport
Betsy D. Ray
228 Spring Street
Newport
Rhode Island 02840
Tel: (401) 849 9222

Palm Beach
Helen Cluett, Lucy Ullman
251 Royal Palm Way
Palm Beach, Florida 33480
Tel: (407) 833 6952
Fax: (407) 833 0007

Philadelphia
Paul Ingersoll
Molly Wood
P.O. Box 1112
Bryn Mawr, Pennsylvania
19010
Tel: (215) 525 5493
Fax: (215) 525 0967

San Francisco
Ellanor Notides,
Elizabeth Allyn
3516 Sacramento Street
San Francisco, California
94118
Tel: (415) 346 6633
Fax: (415) 346 8084

Washington
Marya Oja
Hamilton Court
1234 31st Street N.W,
Washington, D.C. 20007
Tel: (202) 333 7459
Fax: (202) 342 0537

VENEZUELA

Alain Jathiére
5 Avenida Cachimbo 11,
Los Chorros, Caracas
Tel: (582) 238 0503
Telex 24950
Fax: (582) 357613

WEST GERMANY

Düsseldorf
Jörg-Michael Bertz
Inselstrasse 15
D-4000 Düsseldorf 30
Tel: (49211) 498 2986
Fax: (49211) 492339

Hamburg
Christianc Gräfin zu Rantzau
Wentzelstrasse 21, D-2000
Hamburg 60
Tel: (4940) 279 4073
Fax: (4940) 270 4497

Munich
Fürstin zu
Hohenlohe-Langenburg
Residenzstrasse 27, D-8000
Munich 2
Tel: (4989) 22 95 39
Fax: (4989) 29 63 02

Index